Praise for *The Totally Unscientific Study of the Search for Human Happiness*

"*The Totally Unscientific Study of the Search for Human Happiness* is so much the universal daily plot for human beings that any reader will feel just as plugged in to her hilarious commentary as they have felt listening to her engage with the nice couple from Des Moines in the fourth row during her second show on a Thursday night."

—*PopMatters*

"Reading Paula Poundstone's *The Totally Unscientific Study of the Search for Human Happiness*, I laughed until I got fit, wired, earthy, organized, you-name-it. I'm happy now. I've discovered that the secret to happiness is to let Paula do all these things while I read her hilarious book about it."

—P.J. O'Rourke

"Bringing the same dry wit and casual observation style of her stand-up to the page is impressive in and of itself, but to do so with such honesty and heart, particularly when sharing the dizzying peaks and emotional valleys that come with parenting, is doubly impressive. Her scientific process may need some work, but her writing is top-notch. This was a lot of fun."

—*San Francisco Book Review*

"It's hard not to root for Poundstone. She's funny, observant, and sentimental as she spends seven years conducting a variety of experiments to find a small amount of happiness."

—*Washington Independent Review of Books*

"Paula Poundstone is the funniest human being I have ever known. Everything she does, thinks, or says is hilarious. She is made of funny. If you chopped her into bits, each piece would be hilarious. (But don't.) Air becomes funny having been breathed by her. So, thus and naturally, this book is hilarious. Even the punctuation is a scream. Buy it."

—Peter Sagal, host of *Wait Wait . . . Don't Tell Me!*
and author of *The Book of Vice*

"A pure romp . . . A deeply revealing memoir in which the pathos doesn't kill the humor—delivers more than it promises."

—*Kirkus Reviews*

"*The Totally Unscientific Study of the Search for Human Happiness* is a remarkable journey. I laughed. I cried. I got another cat."

—Lily Tomlin

"Did someone finally do it? Did Paula Poundstone discover the secret to human happiness? I don't want to give away the ending, but she did make me laugh a *lot*, and even shed some tears. Read this book!"

—Pete Docter, screenwriter and director,
Inside Out, *Up*, and *Monsters, Inc.*

"If you haven't met Paula Poundstone, I highly recommend that you get to know her now. I flew through her book and laughed at every page."

—Dick Van Dyke

"For readers who want a break from the current madness in the world and a good dose of Poundstone humor, this book will certainly provide."

—*New York Journal of Books*

"Paula Poundstone deserves to be happy. Nobody deserves to be this funny."

—Roy Blount Jr.

"Paula Poundstone never disappoints with her stand-up, and now she has written an informative and highly entertaining book which deserves to be read and discussed . . . and I highly recommend that it is."

—Carl Reiner

"My God, this is a funny book! Bright shafts of the incomparable Poundstone wit come at you from every page."

—Dick Cavett, author of *Brief Encounters*

"Paula Poundstone is hilarious. She says that deep-rooted happiness requires a sense of purpose. I started reading this book because I knew it would make me laugh, and it did. I finished this book with hope, my own sense of purpose, and a renewed faith in people."

—Trisha Yearwood

"Smart, sweet, and laugh-out-loud funny balm for exceedingly stressful times."

—*Booklist*

THE TOTALLY UNSCIENTIFIC STUDY OF THE SEARCH FOR HUMAN HAPPINESS

ALSO BY PAULA POUNDSTONE

There's Nothing in This Book That I Meant to Say

THE TOTALLY UNSCIENTIFIC STUDY OF THE SEARCH FOR HUMAN HAPPINESS

PAULA POUNDSTONE

ALGONQUIN BOOKS OF CHAPEL HILL 2018

Published by
ALGONQUIN BOOKS OF CHAPEL HILL
Post Office Box 2225
Chapel Hill, North Carolina 27515-2225

a division of
WORKMAN PUBLISHING
225 Varick Street
New York, New York 10014

First paperback edition, Algonquin Books of Chapel Hill, May 2018.
Originally published in hardcover by Algonquin Books of
Chapel Hill in May 2017.
Printed in the United States of America.
Published simultaneously in Canada by Thomas Allen & Son Limited.
Design by Steve Godwin.

Library of Congress Cataloging-in-Publication Data
Names: Poundstone, Paula, author.
Title: The totally unscientific study of the search for
human happiness / Paula Poundstone.
Description: First edition. | Chapel Hill, North Carolina :
Algonquin Books of Chapel Hill, 2017. | "Published simultaneously
in Canada by Thomas Allen & Son Limited."
Identifiers: LCCN 2016042921 | ISBN 9781616204167 (HC)
Subjects: LCSH: Poundstone, Paula. | Comedians—United States—
Biography. | Happiness—Humor. | American wit and humor.
Classification: LCC PN2287.P573 A3 2017 | DDC
792.7602/8092—dc23
LC record available at https://lccn.loc.gov/2016042921

ISBN 978-1-61620-806-6 (PB)

10 9 8 7 6 5 4 3 2 1
First Paperback Edition

Thank you, Robin

The experiments in this book
were conducted over a period of seven years.

No dolphins were harmed in the process.

CONTENTS

INTRODUCTION

IS THERE A secret to happiness? I don't know how or why anyone
would keep it a secret. It seems rather cruel, really. If I knew
it, I couldn't go to Target without stopping at customer service
just inside the door, grabbing the microphone and shouting it,
to release everyone in the entire place from their misery, and
that's without even getting as far as the housewares section or
women's lingerie, not to mention Haiti. Have you been to a bank
lately? How could anyone holding the secret to happiness be so
steely cold as to not give it away after seeing the faces of people
in a bank?

They say ignorance is bliss. I'm living proof that this is not
true. Some people think money is the key. I used to have more
money than I have now, though, and in fact, I was much less
happy. Still, that only tells us that I might not have had enough.

We often wish one another happiness but only for brief periods of time: Happy Birthday or Happy New Year. I think most
of us view happiness as an occasional lucky break from some
form of drudgery that we've come to expect. So we would not
presume to send along a Happy Birthweek card. That would
seem like greedy overreach. Even the question "Are you happy
now?" is only asked sarcastically.

Happiness is the trickiest of all of the emotions. It is elusive. If you crack an egg into a bowl and a small bit of eggshell gets in there, it slips away at every approach of your finger, but if you don't bother looking for it and just cook it up, you're likely to chomp down on it without even trying. Happiness is like a rogue piece of eggshell, I'll bet. I just don't know. If I did, I'd run up to the snooty street north of where I live and yell, "Put the yoga mat down; it's not the answer," to all of the people getting out of their BMWs. It could be yoga, though. I hope not. I've never enjoyed putting my foot in my ear.

Unfortunately, not only is happiness the most elusive of the emotions, it also has the shortest shelf life. It vaporizes. Most of us have found momentary happiness here and there, but no one that I know of has figured out how to make it last. No one has discovered the Viagra for happiness.

When I was young, I don't know how many times I sang that song with the words "If you're happy and you know it, clap your hands" and clapped as loudly as I could, never really reflecting on whether or not I was actually happy. I simply enjoyed the clapping and the subsequent foot stomping, jumping, and the fill-in-your-own-action-here that the song calls for. Maybe happiness can be achieved just by proclaiming it. Or by clapping. I don't know. It's a secret.

Where could it be? Is it deceptively simple? Is it on a bumper sticker? Did *The Thinker* go stiff just before he could explain it? Does it melt at a certain temperature? Can you buy it? Must you suffer for it before or after? It had better not be one of those rip-off answers as in *The Wizard of Oz*: "You always had the power." If Glinda knew that, she should have said so earlier. The Good Witch of the North had a cruel streak.

We Americans are given constitutional permission to pursue happiness, but I can't say that I've ever done so consciously. Don't get me wrong. I've certainly done things that I have enjoyed in the moment—I have a Ping-Pong table—but I never planned on maintaining some level of happiness as a goal. I have often feared that if I were ever really happy I wouldn't get a parking space for a long time. I've come to a place in my life, though, where I think it's time to risk parking far away and walking.

I live in Santa Monica, California. I am an American. I am a single working mother with three children, twelve cats, a German shepherd mix dog, a bearded dragon lizard, a lop-eared bunny, and one ant left from my ant farm. I have been a stand-up comic for over thirty years. Based on current life expectancy, I am middle aged.

Now, I, Paula Poundstone, being of soundish mind, pledge to devote myself to the totally unscientific study of the search for human happiness and to record my findings here in this book for the benefit of mankind, naturally, but mostly for you, the reader. I know I'm not the first to document such an endeavor. People have tried to unlock the secrets of happiness both before and after the advent of the Happy Meal. I can't help hoping, though, that it is through these particular pages that you find a bit of yours.

THE
GET FIT
EXPERIMENT

CONDITIONS

I am not the sort who worries a lot about my looks. I notice, I just don't worry a lot about it. I color my hair only because HBO wanted me to, and that was just to get the service. I am about five feet seven inches tall, and I have played with gaining and losing the same several pounds for most of my adult life. I certainly wouldn't mind being beautiful, but if it takes more than a few minutes a day, forget it.

HYPOTHESIS

I'd often heard that being physically fit, however, could be a key to happiness and so it is where I began my study.

VARIABLE

There is a little storefront studio down the street from my house in Santa Monica with a sign in the window advertising self-defense and taekwondo. One day, after getting my kids off to school, I walked down and signed up for some classes.

FIELD NOTES

My back started to hurt about an hour before my first-ever professional physical activity training. I kind of hobbled in. There were two women just wrapping up their taekwondo lesson. They were taking high twisting leaps and yelling, "Hyah!" before teaching a big padded cylinder what for.

Mr. Victor King was the instructor. He did a rapid pretend assault on these women, and they successfully deflected his blows, following up with a series of elbows to an inch before his nose, and knees to an inch before his groin. They looked pretty advanced; they must have been learning to almost hit someone for quite a while. As a driver, I'm a natural at that. I was really intimidated watching them do it with hands and feet, though.

I harbor a fantasy that since I don't like sex and therefore never seek it, perform it, look for it, dream about it, dress for it, hint about it, or purchase products that are sold by suggesting that if you own this thing you'll get more of it, there must be some other unknown, untapped skill in life for which I have a gift. Deep down I was hoping that, especially because I'd be an unlikely candidate, I'd do a kick or two and this Mr. King guy would say, "Whoa, I thought you said you had no prior training."

"That's right," I'd reply.

"Well, Ms. Poundstone, is it? Normally I start my students off at a beginner level, but I'm going to ask if you'll teach with me. I simply can't believe that you haven't kicked the stuffing out of a padded thing before."

Instead, he got me started with some calisthenics, and Kleenex kept dropping out of my sweatshirt pocket as I staggered around the floor mats. I have terrible allergies. I can't go anywhere without Kleenex. If I were defending myself from an attacker, I'd need Kleenex. My allergies are so bad I can't watch *The Bee Movie*.

Mr. King told me to do ten wind sprints across the small gym. This was a private lesson so when my breasts began to make a flappy noise, it was tough to pretend that I was not the source. I tried wrapping my biceps around them as I ran, which made me run like a really slow *T. Rex* with flapping breasts and a lung condition.

After doing ten wind sprints across his small workout space, my breathing was labored enough to begin with the actual training. I executed the side kick that Mr. King showed me. My fantasy was instantly dashed. If his face registered impressed at all, the expression was quickly erased by the time I finished picking up my Kleenex, which fell with every kick.

Although I was practically incapacitated after the wind sprints and side kicks, I jumped rope. I did squats and crunches. I punched a large padded cylinder. I leaned on a wall and lifted my right leg a bunch of times. I leaned on a wall and lifted my left leg a bunch of times. I leaned on a wall while Mr. King lifted my legs at angles that hips weren't designed for.

QUALITATIVE OBSERVATION #1
Happiness may be overrated.

PROCEDURE

After I was done, I dragged myself to a chair and filled in my calendar with as many classes as I could. I paid for two packages of twenty-one sessions each, for science.

QUALITATIVE OBSERVATION #2

The door to the taekwondo studio seemed much heavier on the way out.

PROCEDURE

I walked the few blocks home, past the bars where the sidewalk becomes increasingly gum strewn, past the knitting store, the inexplicable breast-feeding store where they must actually sell Lord knows what, and turned the corner at the Jack in the Box, where I instinctively look down to avoid the minefield of to-go ketchups that litter the way. I was achy and tired but feeling pretty satisfied with myself. The real test was, of course, back in my regular life.

CONSTANTS

I keep a brisk pace at home. I sift litter boxes about three times a day. Imagine needing something else to be happy? The litter boxes alone are the envy of all who see them.

Because I am a stand-up comic, I travel hither and yon to tell my little jokes. I kill in yon but generally have a hard time selling tickets in hither. I have stacks and stacks of notebooks and loose papers on which I've quickly jotted down "inklings," which is the infant stage—developmentally even before "ideas"—of a piece of material I think might be funny onstage. Not surprisingly, that's some of what I do. I love that part. If I could do that most of the time, it would be the perfect job. Unfortunately, it is not enough to just tell jokes. You have to have an audience to tell them to. That's the hard part. Much of my job is self-promotion, which I loathe.

I am a road dog. Not every weekend, but many, I am away performing in theaters around the country. During the rest of the week, I do interviews for radio, local television, and periodicals that cover those theaters, in order to let potential ticket buyers know where I'll be. I've been doing this for years and I still just suck at it. Because I often work on the East Coast but live on the West Coast, and morning drive-time radio has the most listeners, my radio interviews usually occur over the phone at 5:00 a.m. on morning shows like *The Lawn Mower and the Monster in the Madhouse*.

Maybe one in ten of these interviews goes well. The whole idea is to give the listening audience a little blast of humor that will hopefully be fun but also might encourage them to come out to see me. I try to say something funny. It rarely happens. I don't have a clue how long the interview is going to be, and I almost never have any chemistry with the hosts. They never seem to know when I've hit the punch line.

"Thanks for joining The Lawn Mower and the Monster here in the Madhouse this morning. We've got a special treat for you now. We have comedienne Paula Poundstone on the line with us. Paula, thanks for getting up so early."

"No problem. I was up already."

"What time is it in California?"

"It's five a.m."

"What are you doing up at five a.m.?"

"I have three kids, and this year I—"

"That's great! Paula's gonna be at the Plaza Theater this Saturday night. You should go down and check her out. Thanks for being with us, Paula."

Surely such exchanges work like a magnet on those audience members who spend their entertainment dollars exclusively on early risers.

The radio station usually calls me. So after a couple of these experiences, I've learned my lesson. I take control of the interview right away. The phone rings, and I jump right in.

"Hi, Paula, this is the Camel and the Cowboy calling from FM 108.6."

"Hi, guys, I was just working on a school project for my kid. I have three school-aged kids, and this year I have a new system. I just do their homework. We fight less. They get more sleep. My printer is almost never broken, and their grades are better. My daughter Toshia had to read *Of Mice and Men* and do a project. I made a mobile for her, using real rabbit fur and scented condoms. It's museum quality."

"Oh, wow, that's great. Stand by, we're gonna be on the air here in just a second."

The most important work I do all day is, of course, taking care of my kids. Parenting is often like a jigsaw puzzle to me. Sometimes the pieces go together with ease and other times I'm trying to bang together a piece of sky with what is clearly the top part of the olive picker's feet. I'm not always as good at it as I would like to be, but I get up every day and give it everything I've got.

UNCONTROLLED VARIABLES

Although I did gain some weight while each of my children developed in the womb, all three of them are adopted. Toshia, my oldest, was four when she came to me. She has a great sense of humor, loves to laugh, and has become a voracious reader. She is the strongest person I have ever known, and when she decides to lead with that, she'll be hell on wheels. Toshia has cerebral palsy. It mostly affects her legs and balance. At the time when we were lucky enough for her to become my daughter—and my daughter Alley's sister—Toshia used a walker to get around. As a result of weekly appointments with a physical therapist, daily exercise sessions on the plus side of an hour, twice-a-day stretching, and a ton of walking practice on top of that, she learned to walk with crutches. Then, by the fifth grade, Toshia did away with crutches altogether. I did the insisting, the coaching, and the hammer dropping, but Toshia did the work. She still wears plastic braces that go from her feet to her calves, and walks with a funky gait, but she is a powerhouse.

The hardest thing about raising Toshia has been fighting for the rest of the world to have high expectations of her. When she is older, I am pretty certain she will wish she had more often tried to convince people that she *could* instead of allowing people to assume that she *couldn't*. So far, however, how do I say it nicely? She fakes a lot.

For whatever "Toshia reason," she doesn't often let people know what she is capable of. She allows only brief, rare glimpses of her true abilities. I've often thought I should have her filmed by the crew from *National Geographic* or those Discovery Channel guys who got the footage of penguins stealing. I wish I had had them with me one morning during the summer after her third-grade year when she went to Tumbleweed Day Camp. We arrived late on her first day. The kids in her group were already at the ropes course, so I walked her over there. They were only doing the section of the ropes course on which the climber, in a harness and on belay, ascends a very tall telephone pole, using the traditional spikes hammered into the sides, then at maybe twenty feet up, walks across a single rope stretched from that pole to another, while holding on to a parallel rope mounted about five or six feet above.

Toshia and I took a seat below to watch a camper already up on the pole. Some of the kids had been there the week before and already knew one another. They watched and shouted encouragement to the climber, who stood, terrified, about to step from the pole to the rope. The young girl inched along, looking kind of pale, as various "You can do its" made their way to her ears. It took several minutes and a few dead stops before she shakily came to the end of the rope and was lowered down to scattered laconic applause.

I wanted to see how Toshia would handle this, so I asked the counselor if she could go next, and I'm so glad I did. The other kids had yet to even be introduced to Toshia, and it was hot and dusty there so they weren't paying much attention by the time she teetered over to be harnessed up. After the safety ropes were drawn through the correct carabiners, Toshia grabbed shoulder-level spikes on each side of the climbing pole and, looking down, slowly raised one knee, at the end of which a foot dangled about, near the first spike she might step on. Her sneakered foot bounced, slipped, and skittered around the step.

It was like watching someone try to pick up a plush toy with the hanging claw in an arcade game. She lowered her foot back to the ground and tried the other the same way. Then I could swear I saw a switch flip on in her head. She looked up, grabbed a higher spike with her one hand, and pulled herself up the pole, one spike at a time, without stepping with her feet at all, until she got to the top. One young boy camper below, who had been quite disinterested, sat up, flicked his friend with the back of his hand to get his attention, and said, "You've gotta see this." And it was a sight to see.

Once she was at the top, Toshia grabbed the overhead rope and stepped out onto the lower one, with no fear and not a moment's hesitation, just like it was our living-room floor and not a rope twenty feet in the air. She sidestepped across in a matter of seconds. This remains the single greatest athletic feat I've ever seen, and I've seen Roger Federer's backward shot, every one of Michael Phelps's Olympic-winning swims, and several Cirque du Soleil shows. I regret that I have no film nor any proof of my daughter's achievement, but I would recommend that you look up "penguin stealing" on YouTube.

My son, Thomas E, was a newborn when I got to pick him up at the hospital, pop him into a plastic baby carrier, and bring him into our family. He was in the fourth grade when I first tried taekwondo.

Thomas E's curly head houses quite a brain. He is smart, impulsive, and wild. Though, even with a top-notch vocabulary, he probably says far less of what he's really thinking than is healthy for either of us. That may be, in part, because I rarely shut up. He is funny and has bursts of empathy well beyond his years.

He worked his way up the gymnastics ladder of levels for several years and can do some amazing moves, but he gravitates to art, which for a guy who is such a live wire always astonishes me.

Thomas E has always saved most of his unholy terror behavior for me. With most everyone else, he generally aims to please. I suppose, really, it's admirable. He does his best not to bother the outside world with that which bothers him. He just stores it up for me. There are days when I pull up to the school, open the door to the van, call out, "Hi, honey," and the Tasmanian devil hurls in a backpack. I could swear sometimes I hear a fight bell.

My middle child, Alley, was the first of the three kids to come to me. She was three weeks old when I first took her in my arms. When I began the Get Fit experiment, she was in the eighth grade. She mostly does what she is supposed to do. She is the least like me of any of my children. The rest of us are in awe of her. She does her homework. We can't really figure her out. Once, in an effort to reach out to her, Thomas E explained to her that the reason I always know she has homework is that she writes it down. I thought it was quite moving in a screwed-up Poundstone sort of a way.

Alley started playing the violin in the fourth grade. The Santa Monica school district has a kick-ass music program. She has been in all of her school's orchestras; she is a crack violin player with a highly trained ear for music. Often when I sing a song, she'll say, "Mom, that's not how it goes." I quickly respond, "I'm singing a different song."

She successfully juggles a full schedule of many interests. Like Thomas E, she has painstakingly mastered spectacular gymnastics maneuvers in every event to work her way up many levels. In addition to being an excellent student, she's an animal lover and volunteers at the animal shelter. She's also the unofficial "family keeper." Alley is the first to ask if we'll all play a game, watch our home movies, or listen to the radio plays we made when they were little (complete with improvised commercials).

FIELD NOTES

The morning of my second taekwondo class was upon me and I was looking forward to it. So when I woke up, found a little brown thing on my blanket, picked it up, and realized it was cat feces, I didn't overreact, although I don't know that one can under those circumstances. I just took solace in the fact that if I could figure out which cat it was, my mourning period at its eventual passing had now been shortened by at least a day. Perhaps it was the famed endorphin boost from yesterday's arduous workout that buoyed me through the trauma of holding cat poop between my fingers at 7:05 a.m. If so, no amount of muscle strain was too much to endure.

After getting my kids off to school with as few repetitions of "When we're late, it's helpful to move our hands and feet quickly" as I could keep myself from shouting, I loaded up my calendar and soda bag and headed to taekwondo and self-defense class in search of happiness.

VARIABLES

Mr. King is a short, energetic, muscular black man from an island country. I forget which one. He speaks with a strong accent, in short, clipped bursts.

ENVIRONMENT

His studio is a clean, open space, with a fresh paint job on the wall behind a row of folding chairs. One walks into the storefront business along a four-foot-wide strip of wood laminate flooring. Most of the rest of the large room is covered in enormous blue mats. The tenets of taekwondo (respect, strength, integrity, fashion sense) are painted on the wall in large letters.

FIELD NOTES

On the first day, Mr. King explained to me that one traditionally bows before stepping out onto the mat. It's part of the taekwondo ritual and I tried to abide by it, but I have a terrible memory. Plus, I drink a lot of soda and had to keep running on and off the mat to use the bathroom. I never knew whether if I had already run onto the mat I was supposed to go back and bow, and if so, was I one bow behind? Did I now need to bow twice? I didn't want to be disrespectful, but I'm not much of a bower. Ask anybody. Anyway, eventually I gave up on bowing altogether and Mr. King never said anything. He even stopped bowing while I was there, but it may be that he made up for it by bobbing up and down like a wind-up toy to catch up as soon as I was out of the room.

Again, the workout was grueling. Honestly, I could turn in after the jumping jacks and wind sprints, but Mr. King said that was just the warm-up.

We worked a lot on the side kick, in which you lean your upper body to the right while bending your left knee toward your chest until, when you kick it out, you look like a *T* with a long top. I often fell over in the delivery of my side kick, which he said was wrong. I think maybe my head is unusually heavy, providing the wrong counterbalance, but I deferred to him because he is the expert, and because, remember, during my stretch, I face the wall, holding a bar, and he holds my leg up, forcing it beyond its capacity. So it's not a good idea to piss him off.

ANALYSIS
After the hour, I implored my unwilling legs to carry me home to chop the apple and lettuce that Daisy, my bearded dragon, would topple from his dish into his sand instead of eating. I hoped my dog Cal would sense that I was incapable of any more walking.

QUALITATIVE OBSERVATION #3
There was no part of me that didn't hurt.

ANALYSIS
They say it's important for the family to eat together to keep kids off drugs. I'm not sure what "they" are basing that on, though. Our family eats together, and although I don't succumb to it, I for one almost always feel like doing drugs after we dine.

Tonight over dinner, I made the mistake of asking, "Who put the Frosted Flakes box with only three flakes that appear to have had the frosting licked off back in the cabinet? I picked up the box, and Tony the Tiger said, "They're go-o-o-ne!"

Thomas E: I didn't.
Toshia: Not me.
Alley: Not me.

Me: Come on, you guys. What's the big deal? Why would you lie about this? It's not like you've ever suffered some cruel punishment for anything, let alone for mishandling the Frosted Flakes box.

(*Silence*)

Me: Well, it didn't put itself in there. One of you must have done it.

Thomas E: No, someone else could have brought it over.

Me: Thomas, could you please put the remaining disfigured flakes in the mulch container, put the liner bag in the trash, and put the box in the recycle?

Thomas E: Why me? Someone else could have brought it in.

Me: Thomas, this is a much longer conversation than I meant to have about a cereal box. *Just do it!*

QUALITATIVE OBSERVATION #4

You have to be able to execute a good side kick to remain calm while conducting a Frosted Flakes interrogation.

FIELD NOTES

Today I did sixty crunches in two sets of thirty, and thirty-six push-ups in three sets of twelve, the kind with the twisty handles "as seen on TV," but not on my toes—I did them on my knees, the wussy kind. Mr. King said that on Monday he was going to have me do one push-up not on my knees but the toe kind. I did assume the push-up position on my toes, without the twisty things, for one minute, and my entire body trembled like a just-bathed kitten. I think Mr. King is in for a disappointing Monday. I hope he has some plans of his own to lift his spirits.

QUANTITATIVE OBSERVATION #1

I did 150 rope jumps today. I ran out of rhymes after the first 50.

ANALYSIS

Thomas E wanted to play on the computer after school, and when I told him he couldn't, his reaction measured 5.0 on the Richter scale. Yet I felt pretty good all day.

Last night, just as I was stepping out of the shower to towel off, Alley came into the bathroom with paper and pen and asked me to sign a letter telling the teacher that our internet wasn't working so she could not complete her science homework. I said, "Can't I sign it when I'm not naked?"

And she said, "Why?"

I think her point was that her teacher wouldn't know that I had signed the paper naked, but that was not my point.

Sometimes when I talk to my kids, I feel like their brains are little safes and my words are hundreds of unmarked keys hanging from a giant key ring in my head. I just have to find the right key at the right moment to unlock their safes and make sense to them.

I spend a lot of time turning that imaginary key ring around and around trying to find how to inspire Toshia. I talk to her about reaching for her dreams and taking the risk to try things in life that will help her find out what fills her up and makes time seem precious. I tell her how capable she is, that she is an important member of our family and has much to offer the world.

Either my lectures aren't as eloquent as I imagine them to be or she's not an auditory learner, because my eldest doesn't exactly have the fire in the belly. I gave a real rouser a couple of days ago, and then I asked, "What do you want for yourself?"

She said, "A big house."

I said, "You realize Mom can't afford a big house, right?"

"Right."

"Okay, well, that's an okay goal. Nothing wrong with that." I plodded forward, slowly taking that key out, wishing I could find a way to mark it to remind myself not to try that one again, and then rotating the key ring, continuing the search for the perfect fit. "What else? What do you think would fill you up? What would make you happy?" I continued, straining to uncover the virtue of her innermost desire.

"A Van Gogh," she said.

Jingle, jingle went the keys. This one won't even fit partway into the keyhole, let alone turn in the lock. I began to crack. "Do you know a Van Gogh would cost millions?"

She said, "Uh-huh," but left her jaw somewhat slack, not with awe but rather to show me that she just wasn't going to put out the energy it takes to close her mouth.

"Toshia, you don't even write down your assignments," I said, throwing the whole key ring down in frustration and grabbing a crowbar. "You refuse to learn to spell the name of your street, and sometimes I have to remind you to swallow your food. You know what? You're not going to get a Van Gogh, and by the way, the big house isn't looking likely either."

QUANTITATIVE OBSERVATION #2

I meant to measure myself before starting my taekwondo classes to get fit. I realize it is basic science to have a baseline before you change the variable, but I just didn't get around to it before. Now that I am exercising, I've got more energy for that kind of thing. Once I'd taken eight killer one-hour classes over a period of fourteen days, I bought a tape measure, which I think certainly showed initiative, but it's the retractable kind and I hurt myself when the metal end struck me, zipping back in. I took a week to recover and I'm still a little skittish around the thing.

Anyway, my waist is 30½ inches, my hips are 38 inches, and my thighs, well, I only measured my right thigh. I'm assuming its girth is commensurate with my left. My right thigh, and I assume, my left, is 57 centimeters. I used metric because it's more European, and my thighs hope to travel for pleasure someday.

FIELD NOTES

There's a lot of left and right in this taekwondo stuff. There's this exercise called a form, where you do a right punch, a double step, a left punch, a right front kick, a right low block, a left punch, a right muscle block, a right side kick, and a whole bunch of other stuff, but after jumping rope two hundred times, I can't tell right from left without pretending to eat. I'm counting on slow attackers, so I can use my imaginary fork before each move.

Mr. King has lost confidence in the toe push-ups, by the way. There's been nary a word about it for days. I think he realized he couldn't take the disappointment. I did some more knee push-ups with the Ronco twisty hand things. He said to do thirteen, and by eight my arms were quaking, my face was about to pop, I was grunting with each push, and only my left arm, I think, could go straight. "You're supposed to come up straight," he corrected.

I'm not Jack LaLanne, but I know what a push-up looks like. I'm weak, not stupid.

ANALYSIS

I still can't detect a consistent measurable increase in my happiness necessarily, but I'm exhausted. I went to Volunteer Appreciation Day Breakfast at Thomas E's elementary school before I went to my class today. That could have wiped me out. It was in the auditorium, which was festooned in an island theme. Attendees (community members and parents of students from every grade) each received a plastic bottle containing a message written by members of the third-grade class pretending to be pirates.

A third-grade teacher addressed us over a microphone, which she had to keep checking by saying "test, test," something they do way too much of in the schools now, to tell us about the writing project. She explained that the first batch of letters her class had written had to be thrown out because they were "inappropriate." On their first pass, the third graders had written violent and sexual messages. The ones we would find in our plastic bottles now were a sanitized version. "Hi, I'm a pirate. There's nothing more I can say."

I don't know who decided that pirates were charming characters. They are lawless thieves with funny hats and boats that used to belong to someone else. Next year's theme may be big banks, and the third graders will write notes as if they were white-collar criminals. "Hi, I'm still trading derivatives. Thanks for the bailout!"

The truth is, I was pretty drained before I even arrived at the pirate fest. There's an Apple advertisement on a billboard along our drive to school. Thomas E. never misses it, and today, as always, it prompted him to ask if he could have a laptop. I always say no. And he'll say, "Why?" And I'll say, "Because I'm not

Thurston Howell and you're not Lovey." It's often a downhill slide after that.

By the way, I don't allow my children to watch television, so he doesn't know exactly who Thurston Howell and Lovey are, but they're such great names, you can kind of figure it out without ever having seen them. Because Thomas E has never watched television, I have often plagiarized from that rich source for stories while walking. Many are the times I delighted him with the tale of the man who was walking down the street, concentrating on the peanut butter he was eating, only to smack straight into the similarly distracted bloke coming in the other direction, eating chocolate. I allowed him to believe I made up that story myself and I know he sometimes searches my room for my Pulitzer Prize.

FIELD NOTES

My last two taekwondo classes started early. I couldn't follow the simplest of verbal instructions. I barely crawled from task to task. In class #10 I jumped rope two hundred times, twice. In class #11 I jumped rope three hundred times, and that, by the way, was in a row. I lost my rhythm and whacked my toes with the rope so many times I destroyed my dream of foot modeling. Mr. King's gym has a big window facing Santa Monica's main street. People often glance in while strolling by, but today they averted their eyes as though they saw someone taking a beating they were powerless to prevent.

QUANTITATIVE OBSERVATION #3

I'm down to 142 pounds. No one else seems to be able to tell, though, and I'd feel silly carrying the scale around with me. Besides, I hardly talk to anyone except the kids' teachers, and I don't know how to casually work my weigh-in into a parent-teacher conference without appearing self-centered.

"Thomas E is failing math. He's bright, but he works carelessly."

"Really? What do you say we measure my thighs."

ANALYSIS

It's tough to tell if my happiness has increased. I will say that while doing push-ups I don't worry about the state of the world so much. It's hard to be concerned about war in the Middle East while you can't breathe. I might enjoy asthma.

So, am I happier? Part of the problem is that we as a species have never come up with a standard form of measure for happiness: teaspoons, volume, decibels, maybe something akin to a blood alcohol level. Maybe a small amount of happiness could be a "hep," after my old cat Hepcat. I like that: a hep of happiness, and if you're lucky enough to amass four of those, you've got yourself a whole "balou" of happiness. That's a lot. And, yes, I did have a cat named Balou.

I had to rush home after my class to check on my dog. I'm spending a lot of time with my big cat-eating dog, because he is sick. I got him years ago, when I drank. Yes, to my undying shame, I had a drinking problem. In my defense: cats are enablers. In fact, I was drunk when I got my dog, Cal. He was a crazy cat chaser early on. Eventually the cats schooled him, but he still gets a craving for one now and then. Otherwise he is a great dog. He is energetic and excitable, but sweet. He even sings when I play the harmonica. We've had a symbiotic relationship. I used to walk him, because he needed to be walked, when I felt like never going out of the house again. It always made me feel better.

Cal hasn't cared about food for a while. I figured he had just eaten an infected cat, but the vet showed me his x-ray and there it was, a tumor the size of a football. It's crushing his stomach. He hasn't done one crunch and he lost ten pounds.

I go to the vet a fair amount because I have so many pets, but I don't generally return with the same pet over and over again. When an animal gets sick in my house, it means they might die. I take great care of them. I love them. I clean their waste, feed them, pet them, throw balls, and drag strings for them, but there is a beginning, a middle, and an end to a life. Americans don't do well with that.

There is a protocol in the vet waiting room. It is socially proper to look into the plastic pet carrier of the other waiting pet owners and, no matter what you see, exclaim, "Isn't that beautiful." It's just what you do. I've got to tell you, though, I've now seen the same people waiting in the waiting room at the vet, with the same animals over and over again. I looked into one cat carrier. Fluffy was not doing well. I'm not even certain Fluffy was still alive. His rear legs had been replaced with wheels. They must have run out of money because they used a bent coat hanger for one of the front legs. They had replaced Fluffy's fur with carpet scraps, and Fluffy's owner sprayed Fluffy with a plant mister every few minutes to keep his nose moist. Death is sad, but life does not go on forever. You've got to chase the string while you can.

FIELD NOTES

I'm pretty sure I heard a tearing sound in my knee during a stretch today, but Mr. King didn't seem troubled by it at all.

I must be getting stronger and faster in my punching. The big padded cylinder seemed to fear me today. I'd be frozen in my tracks if a person came at me on the street, but I pity the couch that attacks me.

UNCONTROLLED VARIABLES

The last few days have called into question the meaning of life. I visited Walter Reed Army Hospital on Saturday. I talked to five soldiers and their emotionally ravaged wives, parents, siblings, and children. I had no idea what to say, but I said it for about twenty minutes with each soldier. I maintained my composure by dipping into at least a small supply of the heps of happiness I had earned from "getting fit," like borrowing from the tens column when there are not enough in the ones in a subtraction problem. Missing legs. Missing eyes. Missing buttocks. "Thank you for your service" seems inadequate when speaking to a bedridden soldier with a missing buttocks and a morphine drip. It was as if an earthquake knocked all my priorities off their shelf, where they shattered at my feet. I didn't feel sorry for them. I just felt sorry.

What do you say? What I felt like saying was, "My God, you've had your ass blown off!" When someone has their ass blown off in Iraq in the service of their country, it really drains a lot of conversational topic choices from their hospital room. But we did talk and laugh. I marveled at their courage and strength, felt very small, and wished, silently, that the world was an entirely different kind of place.

It was an odd warm-up for the show I performed at the Birchmere in Alexandria, Virginia, but that's where I went straight from the bedside of the wounded warriors. The Birchmere is one of my favorite rooms to work, and it was a great crowd that night. There were lots of laughs. I talked about politics, education, and raising my children, plus I talked from the stage to an audience member who had met her husband on a blind date at a family event. The husband, it turned out, had a toothpick collection. I wondered aloud what kind of a family participates in setting up their daughter with a man whose dating profile prominently features "toothpick collector" and if he spent a lot of time at the family function hovering near the tea sandwiches.

After the show, I got a couple hours of sleep in a hotel bed, then slept soundly enough on the first flight out for other passengers to hang their coats on my neck. I arrived home to celebrate my son's birthday. We went to brunch and a show at Hollywood's famous Magic Castle. It's a brunch buffet. The trick is that children could never eat enough to make a brunch buffet cost effective. That's the only trick that I could figure out at the Magic Castle.

We drove home so that Thomas E could open presents and break them, and I found Cal dead in the backyard.

It's hard to know what's important sometimes.

ANALYSIS

I have to admit that although I feel the weight of all that is difficult and sad, same as I ever have, I don't feel as lost to it as I once might have. I would, cautiously, say that I am happier as a result of the Get Fit experiment. I think I am more resilient.

CONSTANT

I spend a lot of time at the gymnastics gym for Thomas E's and Alley's practices. We go there immediately after school five days a week. I toil an hour each day preparing the snack bag and loading the car with books, uniforms, and skill-building activities. It's like we go camping every day. I mostly sit with Toshia while she disassociates herself from grammar while writing and skips steps in math. I also look for Thomas E when his practice is over and Alley's is still in session, to try to get him to do his homework. His hiding has really improved. He once disguised himself as a balance beam for the entire girls' team's practice.

FIELD NOTES

I finally bought a sports bra, but as I was taking my sports bra off over my head after a lesson, the elastic thwacked me really hard on the nose. It hurt a lot. Taekwondo class #17 focused on side kicks and defending against knife attacks, which seemed like a moot point if I couldn't withstand the impact of the sports bra.

As I dragged myself through the last few minutes of my workout, a big Black Belt guy named Tony, a longtime student of Mr. King's, came to begin his session, as he often does. Tony frequently mentions how strong I am and how good I am getting. He says he has seen lots of people take classes and that I am really developing better than the others. I know that this could not possibly be true, but this does not stop me from smacking my lips with pleasure after swallowing the hook, the line, and the sinker. I would hope, however, that I would show at least some improvement. I'm taking three, four, and sometimes five classes a week. My son takes drum lessons one day a week, whines for an hour a day over practicing for twenty minutes, occasionally even flails about with the sticks, and yet he is a really terrific drummer. I don't think I'm exactly shooting for the stars to expect some muscle development from all of these hours of ass-kicking workouts. I'm fairly certain that Mr. King and Tony strengthen their stomach muscles by laughing about me after I barely squeeze my way past the heavy door.

QUANTITATIVE OBSERVATION #4

My size 8 pants still leave an imprint of the fabric on my pudgy waistline, so I've obviously underestimated how long it would take me to get fit, as well as how many Kit-Kat bars could be offset by exercise.

FIELD NOTES

I wore ankle weights while I jumped rope 250 times today. I almost threw up.

ANALYSIS

If physical fitness makes me feel happier, it begs the question, why don't I save the money and work out at home?

I don't think I could do that on my own. I believe I am qualified to work the equipment, but I don't think I would push myself hard enough. We have had ankle weights and jump ropes at our house for years and it has never occurred to me to use either one to the brink of vomiting. Also, I don't have shock-absorbing mats, and we only rent this house. If I knock the house off the foundation, I'll have to pay for the repairs.

I do like Mr. King's mats. We have terrible living-room carpet. It is shredded and filthy, but having it cleaned seems to nauseate my cats.

Mr. King has expertise, too. I like that. He can look at my body and know what exercises to prescribe. In truth, though, without any specialized training, I can tell that my butt looks like a bag of white raisins and that even rolling over occasionally could whittle it down a bit. Still, I think I need the professional.

In sculpting terms, we're still using a chisel and a mallet. It's not yet time for the fine detail work.

I try hard to share my happiness now. I often describe my workouts to my children over dinner. Our kitchen table is too small for all four of us, so I almost never sit at the table to eat if we're all together. If I sit, I sit on a red plastic step stool, facing the table, with my back on a cabinet and my plate on my knees. I don't usually sit, though, since our table is also too small to hold serving dishes. I generally wait on the table, refilling the milks, noodles, and occasionally confiscating the shredded Parmesan cheese after Thomas E has, once again, accidentally poured out too much.

I do some of my best shows in the kitchen. I used to pretend to be Edna, a former Olympic runner, who after her retirement had been forced to serve these ungrateful children. The clanging of the silverware would often remind her, bitterly, of her silver medals and she would sing the National Anthem while slamming the ketchup down on the table.

More recently, I dance, lip sync, and hand gesture to the lyrics of various CDs playing while I prepare dinner. I have made dinner and set the table to *The Barber of Seville*, landing the last glass of milk on the very last note. I even give an occasional rap performance as a character named Piece O' Me:

> You need your strength, Mr. Thomas E
> I know there's shit you want to throw at me,
> So then you gots to, gotta eat yo broccoli.

My kitchen is a goddamned performing-arts center, that's what it is. Stories from my taekwondo classes have quickly become the most requested. Just the thought of me kicking and swinging about in spandexy athletic wear has made for hours of family entertainment. A few times I've regaled my kids with details of the agonies of my struggles and grunts just in time to derail a squabble. I don't know if this is a desirable dynamic, but hearing that my body made involuntary sounds during my front kick has broken Toshia's lifeless stare and rebooted her any number of times. In this way, my taekwondo has been an invaluable contribution to family life.

FIELD NOTES

I broke boards today. It's a bit of a hoax. You feel very powerful when you do it, but they're not strong boards. They're not Wheat Thins, but they're not sturdy pieces of lumber either. The third little pig would not build with them. Still, I hurt my hand.

ANALYSIS

One of my best friends is dying of cancer. Martha was a staff member at the therapeutic residential program I was in when I was a fucked-up teenager. We've remained friends throughout my fucked-up adulthood. She's the kind of friend with whom there is nothing that isn't funny. I could be falling off a roof and my last fleeting thought would be, *Martha and I are gonna laugh ourselves silly over this.*

It seems rude to be happy under the circumstances. Life keeps happening, of course. Happiness has no bearing on most of what happens next—cyclones, earthquakes, cancer, and so on. Happiness doesn't even fit in sometimes. I think there's more to this happiness idea than meets the eye. Happiness needs to be like a soaking rain, an aquifer, a tucked-away capacity to store enough so that when your friend Martha gets sick, you don't fade away forever.

FIELD NOTES

I dread the day I don't have Mr. King telling me the next thing to do and the next thing to do. He told me to run ten "suicides" today, which is where you touch the floor on one end of the gym, run to the other end, touch the floor, run back, and on and on. We're not even counting a back-and-forth as one. A back is one, and a forth is another. Still, I employed my best effort, and when I was done, my chest was searing with some chance of exploding. I was leaning over, attempting unsuccessfully to gulp in enough air to satisfy the needs of a functional brain, and Mr. King said, "Bring your knee up twenty times." That was the part I didn't think I could do. It was not that I couldn't bring my knee up twenty times while gasping for breath. I could and I did. It's just not something I would think on my own. In fact, at the time I was thinking something more along the lines of an oxygen tent or dormant period. His idea really took me by surprise. After I did five hundred rope jumps, which he thought were way too slow, I flopped onto the mat and he said, "Get up."

See? I wouldn't have thought of that in a million years. It was the furthest thing from my mind.

CONSTANT

Sometimes I notice Mr. King's eyes drifting to my potbelly. It's kind of the elephant in the room. Here I am wearing these tight black pants and tight middrift sports bra, and despite having done a few thousand crunches in the last couple of months, my fish-belly-white torso bulges relentlessly from just above my naval on down. It won't go away. It's like trying to get a red wine stain out of a white linen dress.

ANALYSIS

I was carrying two big trash bags full of kitty litter down the alley to the trash today, and I noticed that I felt great. It gave me pause. It was an odd time to feel great. It has to be the physical fitness. I've carried twenty or thirty pounds of kitty litter down the alley to the trash thousands of times. It is generally not a mood enhancer.

FIELD NOTES

I did five hundred rope jumps again today. It's amusing child's play turned evil. Next he'll have the London Bridge actually fall on me.

I also sparred with my taekwondo instructor for two three-minute rounds today. I wore padded shoes, padded gloves, and a padded vest. Mr. King said I was supposed to move around the floor and strike him with combinations of punches and kicks, which he would try to block. He would do the same. He said it was good for cardio. He didn't say it was good for *my* cardio. I think it was like a celebrity episode of a game show. I was sparring for the benefit of someone else's cardio. It was some couch potato in St. Louis.

Mr. King began our bout with a fierce "Hyah!" which nearly startled me out of my padded shoes. This guy is so fast that there is not a padded appendage I could swing at him that he couldn't block. Besides, I had what seemed like long periods where I forgot to do anything at all, mesmerized by the dull thuds of his kicks and punches on my padded vest. He began shouting out what I should do: "Use your front kick! Punch! Use your side kick! Higher!" I suspected that if he had to shout instructions at me, I might have been losing the element of surprise, but it did seem to be tiring him out. As with most sports, it's not just brawn, it's strategy. I didn't so much "float like a butterfly, sting like a bee" as I was more "bump into things like a light drunk moth, curl up like a roly-poly."

When it was over, I lowered myself to the mat in my padding and lay there like an expired Michelin Man.

ANALYSIS

My manager, Bonnie, says that these taekwondo lessons are good for me because they are something I am doing for myself and that I don't usually do things just for myself. That's not exactly true—she doesn't know about the malted milk balls in my glove compartment, and she obviously thinks I'm kidding about the *Perry Mason* videos I watch over and over again when I'm on the road. Years of therapy and drinking may fall into the self-indulgent category as well. Not exactly a legacy of selflessness.

The time is nearing to end my sessions of taekwondo. I've

really enjoyed Mr. King. I'm going to miss him shouting "Use power!" when I just did.

QUANTITATIVE OBSERVATION #5

I have lost twelve pounds, but I have a bad feeling that my fat has a highly developed homing instinct. When I stop killing myself exercising, I'll bet it comes back faster than the old dog in *The Incredible Journey*.

ANALYSIS

Currently, there is a world food crisis and prices are soaring. Our country is in a number of very sad and terrible wars, which seem to have devalued human life like a Beanie Baby. I am broke. I don't have enough work this month to pay my rent, let alone to pay the rat catcher we've recently found need of. The high school isn't teaching my daughter. My dog died. Martha died. And you know what? I feel good.

I'm not sure that weight loss per se is the secret to happiness, because in the last few days I've been up a couple of pounds, and my back hurts almost all of the time because I'm not in quite the right position on the two sets of twenty to twenty-five push-ups I do each session, but I definitely feel stronger, more durable. I have this sense that I'm ready for whatever happens next. Sometimes when I breathe in, I feel as though I'm filling with possibility. Sometimes when I breathe in, I also cough for a really long time. People often move away from me.

FIELD NOTES

Mr. King showed me that he had been trying to repair the sink in his studio and accidentally Super Glued his fingers together.

It looked quite painful. Right away I suggested we spar, figuring it would give me an advantage. Instead, he showed me how to grab someone's oncoming fist and flip them. I'm not very good at it. I did it once, though. I threw him right onto his back, and from his prostrate position, he said, "Not like that."

I said, "What are you talking about, Mister Four-Time Taekwondo World Champion? You're on the floor. How much better could I do it?"

When it comes to self-defense, I'm results oriented.

I think he was looking for controversy to make our parting easier. Teenagers do that. Toshia started it when she was four.

CONCLUSION

On my final taekwondo lesson, I brought my kids. They laughed and laughed as they watched me work out. There is no question that my efforts to become physically fit have given them a hep or two of happiness. And I have definitely gained a balou and a half (six heps) of happiness myself.

I suppose I could stop the whole happiness quest right here were it not for my devotion to science. It's going to be very hard to give this up, but I have many more happiness experiments to conduct.

I can now jump a rope five hundred times in a little over three minutes, plus complete a few sets of twenty push-ups each during a workout. I can disarm an attacker bearing a knife, if he comes at me from the left and when I'm ready. I can block, front kick, side kick, flip a man, push him down, and wear tight black pants under the delusion that I have no worries from the back.

THE
GET WIRED
EXPERIMENT

CONDITIONS

We own a big desktop computer, but I never touch it. I'm kind of Amish, without the religious beliefs or the bonnet. I have a website, paulapoundstone.com. I take all of the pictures and write all the text, but my manager, my friend Wendell, or my assistant posts everything. I don't even know how to turn on the machine. My assistant has always printed out my emails, I hand-write a response, and she types it in. This is why I have at times been years behind on email.

I wrote a book called There Is Nothing in This Book That I Meant to Say. I also coauthored a series of three math workbooks, with Faye Ruopp, my former high school math teacher, called Math with a Laugh (*Venn Can We Be Friends?*, *The Sticky Problem of Parallelogram Pancakes*, and *You Can't Keep Slope*

Down). I wrote them all by hand, and throughout the entire process, I heard a chorus of "Writing is so much easier on a computer" from just about everyone.

HYPOTHESIS

I would like writing to be easier. I would also enjoy being able to write and perform comedy online circumventing the gatekeepers of television so as to hook up with my audience directly, unfettered by the opinions of the powers that be—the modern-day equivalent of putting up a stage and a curtain in my barn. The entire world seems to believe that "being connected" is the key to happiness; I wish to no longer stand on the outside looking in. Happiness experiment #2 is the Get Wired experiment. I will become computer literate.

EQUIPMENT

I decided to start with the purchase of a laptop because you can carry it door to door and beg for help, whereas to get tech support for the big computer, you have to lure people into your house, and let's face it, Jeffrey Dahmer ruined that for everyone.

So off I went to the horrible Best Buy store. It's so poorly staffed that customers have to stalk the employees like birds of prey. I sprang out at one from behind a big-screen television and held him captive long enough to purchase a shiny white MacBook. I drove home all tingly with excitement. Now it was just a matter of figuring out where I was going to stack all of the happiness that was surely on its way.

VARIABLES

My manager, Bonnie, booked an appointment for me with a computer guy she felt sure could teach me how to use my brand-new Apple laptop. I was champing at the bit. I was like Jude from *Jude the Obscure* waiting for the Latin books.

On the day the tech instructor was to arrive, I got the kids to school, cleaned the kitchen, hung the laundry, sifted the litter boxes, plugged in the computer, and waited expectantly for the world to open up to me. Bring on the happiness. About fifteen minutes before his scheduled arrival, the computer expert called to say he was running late. I've come to find out that this is part and parcel of the IT experience. The geeks who know how to work computers can pretty much call the shots. They have what the rest of us want. They don't have to be on time, and they know it. They are the big man on campus and we are the self-conscious, flat-chested, acne-ridden girl with a lisp, waiting by the phone.

FIELD NOTES

Bonnie was kind enough to come for my first appointment with this guy, just in case I was too technically illiterate to communicate with him at all.

"'Plug?' What is this 'plug' you speak of?"

She said she didn't want him to teach me a bunch of stuff that would overwhelm me. I dare someone to try.

I had heard gut-wrenching stories from haunted souls with gaunt, almost lifeless faces about how they pushed the wrong button on their computer and "lost everything." I was terrified of losing everything and I didn't even have anything on my computer yet. Much later, when the computer guy showed up, I quickly forgave his tardiness. Not aloud, because he didn't even say a word about it. He knew he didn't need to. I forgave him in my own head, anxious as I was for him to give me what he had in his.

As soon as we had made our introductions, I brought him into the kitchen, shoved a cat off the table, and deputized him to do the same whenever he felt the need. Then I did what I always do when I'm nervous. I talked. Not only do I talk, I reveal and then immediately regret revealing the most personal of information. I've always been like that. I tell myself not to, but I just can't stop. I don't remember the whole conversation with the tech guy because I was in an agitated state, but as always, there were some exchanges I thought better of later.

"See this little arrow? It's called a 'cursor.'"

"A therapist once said I had vaginismus."

He asked me what I wanted to learn, which is hard to answer when you don't know anything about it. This emailing thing seemed important to others, though, so I asked him to show me that. I emailed Bonnie, who was on her computer in the other room. I wrote, "This is my first email." I could have just leaned my head out the door and told her, but this was so much faster.

FACTOR

During my first month of laptop ownership, I made more appointments with the computer expert, but he only showed up once. When I complained to him about standing me up repeatedly, he explained that he also taught Ben Stiller. He seemed to think that was a good excuse for blowing me off, and Ben, apparently, was just pounding on the computer keys all willy-nilly, requiring unavoidable emergency technical support after unavoidable emergency technical support. The guy couldn't pick a font without calling in tech support for an hour emergency tutorial.

FIELD NOTES

I struggled along with the few computer skills I learned. I could type, delete, email, and Google. I could cut and paste, but the way I did it in kindergarten was faster. I didn't think there was so much as a fraction of a hep of happiness anywhere in this machine. I mastered use of the pen a long time ago and never had to call anyone for help with it.

QUALITATIVE OBSERVATION #1

Computers are frustrating.

QUALITATIVE OBSERVATION #2

The delete key should be off by itself on the keyboard. Instead of eliminating a typo, I often type \\\\ just beside it.

QUALITATIVE OBSERVATION #3

I hate auto-correct. I don't need a machine correcting me. I have two teenage daughters.

FIELD NOTES

I made a couple of funny little films with my digital camera. I wasn't so good with a camera, though, so I kept accidentally turning it on before I was ready and off when I began. I made lots of four-second films of me looking for the camera controls at an unflattering angle in different places around the country.

ANALYSIS

My hope was that I would make rough, quirky little films that would compare something daunting, scary, and important—like politics, or man's inhumanity to man—with something ordinary, simple, and familiar—like an ant farm or plastic figurines or a chat with my son—and it would be funny, clever, and insightful, and some of the fear in the world would fall away, and in its place would be a kindness and understanding that would uplift.

I don't know how I allowed myself to get away with thinking I could do something like that and that there would be a groundswell of interest—not overnight but in a grassroots, one-person-told-another-who-told-another kind of a way—but that's what I thought. It's not as though I wanted to be flocked by such large crowds that I'd require security to get me from place to place or need to have Sears closed to the public while I shopped in order to avoid an incident, but I did picture a fairly steady stream of people approaching me in public places.

"Paula I saw your little film on YouTube last night. Oh my God, that was . . . man, I never laughed so hard. My wife and I both. And I want to thank you. We're staying together now. Could I just hug you?"

"Paula, my abductor saw your film on YouTube last night. He let me go. Thanks."

"Miss Pauoola, I have been a ruthless dictator for many years. I am not proud of that. I recently, however, saw your funny film on the YouTube, and in the laughter there was healing and a change in my heart. We will now have free elections. High five. How funny do I bump into you here at the Sears. Do that you shop here often? You can't beat the prices, huh?"

QUANTITATIVE OBSERVATION #1

I think I have, in fact, reached my fan base. There are about two hundred of them. Bonnie sends out occasional eblasts so that the four people who love me in each state will know when I'm coming to a theater near them, and they can carpool.

FACTOR

Bonnie also set up a Facebook account for me, which is great because I hadn't counted my friends since I was in the fifth grade. It's good to get back to it. Leave it to computers to destroy the meaning of one of the most valuable words in the human language. Although politicians may have had a hand in that as well.

FIELD NOTES

I spent hours trying to post a film of me at the baggage claim in the Chicago airport on Facebook and it only appeared on the Delta check-in kiosk screen in Juneau, Alaska.

ANALYSIS

I checked Facebook constantly. I was sleep deprived. I'd only been sleeping a couple of hours in hotels or at home, and a couple of hours on the airplane, because I've been up monitoring Facebook. There was no legitimate reason to do this. It was just that I had this feeling as though something might happen. When I was exercising in the Get Fit experiment, I had the feeling that

I could do anything. With the internet, I had the feeling that if I did anything it might be on YouTube. So I needed to stay up and check if I did.

Deep down inside I know that I am often wasting my time using this inane machine, and I can't help feeling guilty about it, but the worst part is that I can also see how much time everyone else wastes on it. It's a dirty little secret.

QUALITATIVE OBSERVATION #4
Computers are addictive.

FIELD NOTES
Hey! Kathy Jo Wisniki found me on Facebook. That is so cool! I haven't seen her since we shared a phonics textbook in the second grade. She was challenged by the *ph* concept. She didn't get that it made an *f* sound. She pronounced the *p* and the *h* when she read a *ph* word. So, for example, she would sound out *phony* as *Pahony*. She was fun, though, and a natural at duck, duck, goose.

Her profile picture looks fantastic.

QUALITATIVE OBSERVATION #5
My "status updates" on Facebook are, so far, my strength. I actually enjoy coming up with them, but as with everything about the computer, I've become compulsive about it. I limit myself to those activities that can be relayed in short, pithy bursts of text.

ANALYSIS
This happiness thing has a lot to do with balance and profit/loss margins. I don't just mean money, of course. It's about what I put in, what I get out, and what I give up to do so.

There is an outside chance that my work posting films, jokes, and information about my shows, which has caused many weeks of sleep deprivation and strain, has also slightly increased ticket sales for some of my theater appearances. But I'm a wreck. I've lost touch with my children's activities, we eat Subway every night, and I haven't dangled a toy from a stick with an elastic string for my cats to bat since this experiment began.

FACTOR

Although I was understandably wowed by my first email experience (by the way, my manager had still not gotten back to me), the thrill was gone in a few days. It was really just more clutter.

I made the mistake of giving my email address to CVS. I was not a loyal CVS customer. I was just too new to email to know any better when I went to the store to buy some rechargeable batteries and they asked me for it. They emailed me every day. There wasn't a day on the calendar that they couldn't somehow tie to the necessity of stopping by CVS for another purchase. "It's National Punctuation Day! Come celebrate it at CVS!" Gee, I'd love to, CVS, but we're spending it with relatives.

QUALITATIVE OBSERVATION #6

Email is vastly overrated.

FIELD NOTES

I started to hate email. At Toshia's school the other day, I stood right in front of a teacher and asked her a question.

She said, "Email me."

I said, "I'm not so good at that. Couldn't we just—"

"Uh-uh, no, email me."

"But that could take hours. We could just talk quickly now."

She put her finger to her lips in the traditional shushing gesture and mouthed, "Email."

Someday science will prove that a phone call is about a hundred times more efficient for a back-and-forth exchange than email. For now, however, Toshia's teachers are committed to email.

There are some exceptions to the rule. There's an elderly design engineering teacher who still uses a CB radio.

"Hey there, good buddy, this is Flunkin' Mama giving you a shout. Just wondering how my little hub cap is turning there in your class."

CONSTANT

It is important that I stay in touch with Toshia's teachers. She benefits from parent-teacher cohesion because she sometimes strays from the truth. If I don't stay in close contact with her teachers, she'll have them believing that she is being home-schooled and that she is only visiting the school to give some pointers to those students less fortunate than she is, but that the teacher shouldn't call me because I'm traveling with the Russian circus right now, and if my cell phone rings, I could lose my balance on the high wire and it wouldn't be good to disturb me while I'm recovering from brain surgery anyway.

FIELD NOTES

Along with all of these other blessings, being "wired" allowed me to check my high school students' grades online, which I now also couldn't stop doing. I could find out how many points they received for each assignment, for tests, for class participation, and for long-term projects. One class even had a category for "cooperation." That was for the students who clung to the doorjamb and had to be forced into their seats with sticks. "Eddie was quite uncooperative today."

In the first few weeks of school, Toshia's grades were stellar, but when I looked closely online at what the grades were for, they were for returning the teacher's "Welcome back to school!" letter with her parent's signature. You could receive an A+ for that. If you coupled a returned, signed paper with a day of good cooperation, you could be college bound from some of these classes. Sharpen your pencil before class started and it was scholarship time.

By now some of her classes had a few quizzes and tests. One or two even had some homework that required something more than my signature. Toshia's math tests were all Fs, but she refused to study or go in for extra help. She turned in math homework, but she never checked it, so most of it was wrong. Nonetheless, she got As in the homework category, just for the act of turning it in.

I noticed that in English she got "effort points" instead of an education. I'm not sure how this "effort" was measured. Did they look for a throbbing vein in the temple? Was there a grunting sound?

Whereas Toshia has had some really crackerjack educators, cerebral palsy made many teachers find it easier to feel sorry for her than to teach her. Her education was often crippled by the handicap of lowered expectations.

My preferred method of communication with those of her teachers who employed that philosophy would have been a note, tied to a rock, and thrown through their windows, but instead,

I emailed them and asked for a meeting, during which, I imagined, we would sit across the room from one another and email back and forth.

QUALITATIVE OBSERVATION #7

Often when I use the cursor to grab the gray thing on the side to scroll, I accidentally move the whole page.

FIELD NOTES

I heard from Kathy Jo Wisniki again on Facebook today. She homeschools all four of her kids. Boy, it's good to reconnect with Kathy Jo Wisniki! She used to love mustard. Sometimes she still had a bit on her face after lunch.

VARIABLE

For ninety dollars plus tax you could take a year of computer classes called One to One which were taught at the Apple Store. They were hour-long private lessons that you signed up for each week. Unfortunately, you had to sign up online, which put me at a disadvantage. It took me forever. My face was still stained with tears of frustration when I walked through the door to my first lesson. It's wasn't just me. Every student I saw at the Apple Store had been through a similar ordeal. I'll bet the teachers there talked more people out of suicide than the counselors at the suicide hotline.

QUALITATIVE OBSERVATION #8

Sometimes when I scroll, I stop at what I'm trying to read, and I accidentally move my thumb as I lift it from the scrolling rectangle, and I'm lost again. It's worse than losing a bookmark in a book, because without the weight of the pages, I have no sense of where I left off.

FIELD NOTES

I like the Apple Store. It's bright and uncluttered, and everything looks so easy. I had a sense that if I could just remember anything they said to me, it would be really helpful information. It took me four classes just to remember where the Apple Store was located.

QUALITATIVE OBSERVATION #9

My memory isn't good enough to keep track of all of the secret codes for every account. I got a new kitten, just to have another password I could remember.

ANALYSIS

I've had this laptop now for several months, and the mere sight of it sends my son into fits. Every day we have agonizing conversations about when and if Thomas E can use the computer. My hope is always that if he wants to play on the computer, he will quickly finish his homework, his cello practice, his drum practice, and his reading. It seems so simple. It works at Sea World. The dolphin never says, "Can I just have a little fish first, and then I'll stand on my tail and swim backward?"

"How about if I balance the ball twice tomorrow?"

"You said, if I went through the hoop yesterday, I could just eat fish and float today. Don't you remember?"

"I think I'm sick."

"I can't flap."

"I'm not coming up on the cement. It hurts my belly."

I may die of negotiation exhaustion.

It's still hard to believe that Thomas E chose the cello as his instrument in the fourth grade. I would never have thought it would suit him. He broke the neck off of the thing twice and snapped the bow once. He plays well, though. We're hoping it will get him into a good gang.

I don't force him to play the cello. He says he wants to, but he whines and complains over the idea of practicing for twenty minutes. He says it's too long. The interesting phenomenon of the computer, however, is that if I offer him twenty minutes of computer use, he howls that it is too short.

QUANTITATIVE OBSERVATION #2

Computer minutes are shorter than cello minutes.

CONSTANT

I believe Thomas E is addicted to computer screens. I began to seek help with this problem from therapists only to be told, "Video games are important for boys," "It helps them socially," and "If you take away video games, he'll feel hopeless." Something is seriously wrong here, and none of the therapists I've talked to get it at all.

This machine calls to me all day long and I can't imagine how crazy making it must feel to a kid. In this regard, it has certainly not brought me happiness.

ANALYSIS

I am showing signs of erratic behavior. I bought a puppy at the animal shelter. We had gone there to get a kitten. I was so bleary eyed that this three-month-old German shepherd mix looked just like a kitten at the time. I made the whole transaction in a daze. Now I'm up all night checking email and Facebook and cleaning puppy waste.

The good news is that the puppy is a much faster learner than I am. We named her Ramona. She knows "sit," "down," "walk," "stay," and "Microsoft Word."

Every day I shove her in between the uniforms, the snacks, the books, and the drama in our van and she rides with us to the Broadway Gymnastics gym, where I train her while waiting for Alley and Thomas E.

CONSTANT

I wrestle with whether or not spending so much time at gymnastics is a good thing for my children. It's a demanding sport. I don't mean for the participants. I mean for the parent. A good cartwheel will cost you a few thousand bucks. It takes hours and hours of training for the young athletes to learn even the most basic trick. I never much cared about gymnastics before, but about five years ago Alley said she was interested and joined up. I assumed Thomas E was too young to take a class at that time, but it turns out there is no such thing as too young. They have a Mommy and Fetus class.

FIELD NOTES

I wasted half the day today trying to post on Facebook a film of me testing the endurance of Ramona's "stay" by reading to her from *There Is Nothing in This Book That I Meant to Say*, but I couldn't do it.

QUALITATIVE OBSERVATION #10

I have struggled to overcome loneliness, depression, obsessive compulsive disorder, alcohol, terrible loss, and both public and private failure, but the feelings of hopelessness and helplessness from not being able to put a film up on Facebook may be insurmountable.

FIELD NOTES

Last week my manager called to tell me that tickets weren't selling well to my show in Vancouver, British Columbia. Bonnie said that the problem seemed to be that no one in Vancouver knew me except the guy who booked me there. I worked there about twenty years ago. I didn't remember the show specifically, but I thought if I had played to empty seats, it would have stuck out in my mind. There must have been an audience there at that time, but apparently they've moved.

Anyway, Bonnie said that she and some of my agents at William Morris thought that if I made a film about my Canada job and put it up on YouTube, it would help. It was a mystery to me, even if her fantasy world could come to life, how this could help, but Bonnie said that it was better than doing nothing. My thought at the time was, *What if we each stamp our left foot three times, and say "hoo-ha, hoo-ha" while waving our hands over our heads? That's not nothing.* I didn't say it, though. It was, of course, another chance to use technology to bring happiness to my life.

I put my mind to the problem that very evening, and over the next two days I grabbed props, did my own hair and makeup, filmed several segments, and edited, using skills I didn't even have.

Once I had the shot of myself in my son's hockey uniform, highlighting the main canned foods in my pantry, my excitement began to grow. I had a vision. I was frustrated when I looked at the clock and it was time to pick up the kids. Since I started the technology portion of the happiness experiment, I had begun to cut corners on preparing the snack bag that I take to the gym for the children. Occasionally I'd be so involved with something on the computer, I'd decide to just run to the store and get something on the way to pick them up. This time I thought, *We're in an agriculture state. I'll hack something off a tree on the way to the gym.*

ANALYSIS

Although my children were complimentary and encouraging, they were burdens, dead weights. It was all about my Canada film now.

FIELD NOTES

I worked on it late into each night, and when it was completed, I even figured out how to send it to Bonnie.

As soon as I sent it, I was filled with anxiety about her reaction. I called to let her know I had sent it, and then I waited. The minutes were long. They were cello minutes, not computer minutes. Then she called.

"It's great," she said. "Really, really, funny. I can't wait to send it to William Morris."

My heart soared. *This could be the beginning,* I thought. *I just never had the tools to express myself before. Now they'll see.*

I had put in the baseball field, and now they would come. Hollywood would finally appreciate me, and Canada would discover me. We might, now, even have an overcrowding problem at my date in Canada. Out of the frying pan into the fire, huh? Where to get good security guys at the last minute? Would it cause an international incident if we couldn't accommodate all of my Canadian fans? God, I loved the computer.

ANALYSIS
Happy? You betcha. By the balou.

FIELD NOTES
A few minutes later the phone rang and it was Bonnie again, this time with news of William Morris's reaction. It was a school night, and dinnertime, though I hadn't yet prepared it. As I picked up the phone, the children looked at me. I pointed to the refrigerator and the pantry, and mouthed, "Eat!" Honestly, must I do everything? This could be big, and after all, it wasn't just for me. The tide that lifted my ship would certainly buoy their little tugboats. I wouldn't go to the Academy Awards alone. I know the invitations usually only include the star plus one, but I figure when I threaten to boycott the whole shootin' match, they'll find a way to sneak two more tickets into my envelope. I wasn't going to forget about my kids, and by the way, I wasn't sure that film editing of the caliber I now had in mind could be done adequately on the small screen anymore.

"They love it!" Bonnie effused. "They said it's 'brilliant.' Really, Paula, and it's amazing that you did it all yourself. I mean you're new to this whole process. Really. They used the word *genius*, so many times it was almost annoying."

"Yeah, that can be a drag," I said.

"This is going to be great. Brad's going to put it up on You-Tube for us right away, but they want to know if you can cut it down to one minute thirty seconds."

There was a pause.

"Bonnie, it's three minutes."

"Well, they say things do better when they are one minute and thirty seconds."

Apparently this was a full two times more genius than the viewing public could tolerate. I tried to be professional and not take it personally. Still, I couldn't help wondering why if some people knew that there was a particular amount of minutes that a film had to be to be successful, they wouldn't just pass along that little tidbit of information when they made the original request for the film. But I didn't want to be difficult.

The next morning I got up at 5:00 a.m. in order to shoot a shorter introduction before I had to get to the airport, but the lighting sucked because the sun wasn't up, and my eyes looked sunken and haunted, as if I had spent the night at the diner on the Boulevard of Broken Dreams.

I was on my way to a job in San Francisco, and I was thrilled to be taking my daughter Alley with me, but before I could give her my full attention, I had to cut one and a half minutes out of my Canada film. I just gritted my teeth and did it. But then I wasn't able to send it on to Bonnie. I don't know why. I did exactly what I did before only this time the computer kept telling me that the film was too big, which made no sense since I had just brutally cut it in half.

QUALITATIVE OBSERVATION #11

Computer frustration is in a category all its own.

FIELD NOTES

Finally, so stressed out I was ready to cut *myself* in half, I called Bonnie to tell her I couldn't send it. She said, "Why don't you just tell me what you cut and I'll do it on my end."

So I told her, "I cut 'Beans in my pantry,' 'Look how many years we've supported William Shatner,' and 'Even with our most sophisticated cartography, on many maps, Canada doesn't exist.'"

And she said, "Oooh, I wouldn't have cut those."

Later in the afternoon, while Alley watched *Twilight* in the hotel room, I spent hours on the phone with Wendell, who was kindly trying to figure out why the computer wouldn't send the shortened version of my Canada film. Meanwhile, Bonnie had this tech savvy guy, Brad, from William Morris edit my film and put it up on YouTube, with a tag offering a 20 percent discount on tickets to my show in Vancouver. Brad knew how to link to other sites to get the little film viewed.

Over the next couple of days Bonnie called me with updates about how many views there had been. Brad said it would "go viral." Within days, it was up to ten thousand, which was certainly more views than my film about my son becoming Barry White had received, but something about the math began to trouble me. Isn't this the *World* Wide Web? Those ten thousand viewers were probably not even in Canada. Most likely, they were on a remote Indonesian island.

Perhaps you've guessed by now that the video didn't "go

viral." It made it to about twelve thousand views—more than my Great Paulini circus video and more than my video of Theodore Pie, host of the late-night talk show *It's Past Your Bedtime*, who raved about my book and interviewed Joan of Arc. Not really viral, though.

QUANTITATIVE OBSERVATION #3

I believe, when all the ticket counts were in, it was estimated that my Canada video sold eight tickets.

QUALITATIVE OBSERVATION #12

Hoo-ha, hoo-ha, hoo-ha.

ANALYSIS

As soon as I returned from my triumphant Canadian tour, I had a meeting at Toshia's school. I get to go to these meetings because Toshia's cerebral palsy qualifies her for special ed. They host lots of meetings.

I sat at a table with a team of teachers and the school psychologist, all of our eyes turned, like silent film stars, imploringly, toward Toshia, begging her to go in for help in algebra. This meeting was for the purpose of creating an IEP, which stands for individual education plan. It is a legally mandated process for special education. We had one last year, too. The house principal attended that one. She wore sneakers with her skirt and was very enthusiastic about encouraging our youth. She didn't come back this year because the thing about encouraging youth is that it wears you out without proper arch support.

Today's meeting, which was potluck in terms of snacks,

featured my concerns about Toshia not receiving homework. Her perky young English teacher sat across the table from me.

She handed me a folder full of Toshia's papers to fly in the face of my argument that there had been no writing assignments the entire year. "It's class work," she explained. I had asked Toshia many times if she did any writing in class and she said yes, but that she couldn't show me because the teacher kept it in a folder. Frankly, I had doubted her. Now here it was—the folder. It contained a handful of page-long essays, which my daughter had written in class before they were mysteriously secreted away by the teacher. There were no rough drafts. If there had been any corrections, the students had not been asked to address them, no rewrites, no "not like this, like that," no purpose in doing the assignments. It was just a bizarre private collection. She probably had china dolls from around the world and a big ball of string somewhere, too.

I asked that Toshia not be allowed to read manga books for academic credit. The special education history teacher queried what manga books are. I explained that they are Japanese comic books, and he turned to the English teacher and asked, "So, the pictures support the text?"

Gee, I don't think even Stan Lee has ever described comic books that way.

Instead of saying that she would encourage Toshia to enjoy manga books during her leisure time but ask her to read a novel or two for school, Perky told me that studies showed that when students were allowed to choose their own reading material, they became lifelong readers.

I'd love to know how a study of lifelong readership was

conducted. I mean, to know that someone was a lifelong reader, you'd have to check in with her throughout her long life.

"Hello, Bessie, I'm calling from the Lifelong Reader Study. I was wondering if you're still reading?"

"Not now, I'm on the phone."

"Of course. I meant before you answered the phone."

"What?"

"Were you reading before you answered the phone?"

"I was in the shower. Who is this?"

"Bessie, my name is Dr. Susan Carrington, and I'm calling from the Lifelong Reader Study. You remember me. We met at the library several years ago and you told us that you had been allowed to choose your own reading material in school?"

"I did? That's right. I chose my own books in school. We had two books. We could read the Bible or a Latin primer. I'm ninety-two."

"So now you're a lifelong reader?"

"I still know how."

"Isn't that wonderful."

"Who is this?"

I didn't communicate well with these teachers. Lewis Carroll could have written most of our dialogue. They would say absolutely wacky stuff, and no one batted an eye. Last year, Toshia's history teacher told me that they don't give their students homework because it "sets them up for failure when they don't do it," and the other faculty members around the table nodded their heads like vacant bobbleheads.

The "Teacher of Record" was at this meeting. He follows the student's progress and is in charge of all the paperwork. He has a lot of paperwork to fill out, so he spent most of the meeting just trying to keep up with that. Every few seconds he'd hand me another piece of paper to sign.

"I am concerned that Toshia has no homework."

"Sign this to say that you were here."

"Sure, um . . . Since she has been in high school, she hasn't had a rough draft corrected by a teacher so that she could learn what she is supposed to do."

"Sign this to say that I was here."

"Oh, okay, I was saying, that two-fifths of the language-arts portion of the Exit Exam required to graduate is writing, and no one seems to be teaching it to Toshia."

"Sign this to say that you asked for the meeting."

"Sure. There you are. I asked for the meeting because—"

"Sign this to say that I responded promptly. Could you also put a heart after my name. I get extra points if you say I gave good service and you put a heart beside my name. Oh, and sign this to say you approve of her class schedule."

"But I don't. I've asked why she is in special ed history at the last three meetings and I can't get an answer. Just because she has balance problems doesn't mean she needs the Revolutionary War explained more slowly."

"Sign this to say you received the goldenrod copy of the IEP and that you were not served any snacks containing peanuts at today's meeting."

"She's failing every test in Japanese. I don't even know how she got Japanese on her schedule. She supposedly needs to color the thirteen colonies again this year in special ed history, but she is taking the most challenging language that the school has to offer. What is the purpose of her taking Japanese? Who helps her make her schedule?"

"Sign this to say you have a student in this school."

"Why don't I just give you power of attorney?" I asked.

He didn't even look up.

I complained that in five out of six of these meetings the principal wasn't in attendance, and someone told me that the "adviser" was there as the representative of the principal. I was blown away. I had no idea what her role was. The adviser never said a word. Not a word. I didn't even know she was the "adviser." I thought she was there to hold the pencils for the Teacher of Record, who goes through writing implements like Oprah goes through dog masseuses. She must give advice like, "Kids, keep your head low, and try to blend in with the furniture."

The sixth meeting was very much like the other five, although it was less well attended.

The school psychologist was there again. That was helpful in case the Teacher of Record had a breakthrough or any dreams he needed to go over: "There was this long, dark corridor that emptied out into a room with a huge mountain of forms that needed to be filled out, but they were all in Japanese, and Toshia Poundstone was the only one there to translate."

"Thank you for sharing that. We are really making some progress."

INFERENCE

I'm guessing that the school psychologist will be retiring soon to spend whole days listening to the sounds of her bangle bracelets on different surfaces.

FIELD NOTES

Cello minutes of this crap dragged on until eventually, having made no progress at all, I crawled dispiritedly from the meeting.

It was reassuring to know that every one of the meeting attendees was always available by email, and I could likely find the school psychologist at the Bakelite booth when the jewelry show came to the convention center.

I checked Facebook when I got home. Kathy Jo Wisniki posted a picture of her oldest daughter, Serena, receiving a creative-writing award from the *Philadelphia Inquirer.* Serena's teeth were really straight, too. Isn't that wonderful! Serena must be quite a pahenomenon. I mean, the *Pahiladelpahia Inquirer,* that's really something.

I made my most important discovery in the entire Get Wired experiment on a day when, with my van's tantrum-ravaged interior once again brimming with uniforms, backpacks, soda cans, trash, and snack bags, I got lost driving to Thomas E's gymnastics meet in Bakersfield, California.

CONSTANT

I love long car rides, although I don't know why. I have restless leg syndrome and an annoyingly small bladder. I easily get highway hypnosis and I almost always get lost. I like having our family together in one place, though, even if it takes door locks, seating restraints, and no safe exits to achieve it. We talk, we sing, and we argue. We've also listened to lots of great audiobooks over the years, and that's a wonderful way to take in literature. I have always loved reading aloud to my kids, as well, but when I'm driving, I think an audiobook is safer.

FACTOR

Finding Bakersfield from Los Angeles is not, for most people, particularly challenging. It was for me. First of all, there were no bakers anywhere to be found, but their fields, one identical to the other, were everywhere.

Second, I am notoriously bad with directions. I've been lost so many times, in so many places, that everything looks vaguely familiar. I have pulled over and gotten directions from Lilliputians.

ANALYSIS

Bakersfield from LA is pretty much one freeway. Still, I got viciously turned around and confused. And, before you say it, I did use a GPS. It didn't help. Perhaps the Harry Potter CD distracted me. I remember saying, "Why does everyone make such a fuss over Harry? He couldn't even do a summoning charm without Hermione," while pulling a U-ie. The rest is a blur. All I know is I went back and forth over a good deal of territory.

Being lost is worse when I have my kids with me, because I hate for them to lose confidence in me. I hate the tone in their voices when I've done it again.

> **Alley:** Mom, are you lost?
> **Me:** Nooo, nooo, I'm taking a special way.
> **Alley:** You guys, Mom's lost.
> **Me:** I'm not lost. I just have to turn around at this next exit, which is perfect because I have to use the bathroom and get gas.
> **Toshia:** You just used the bathroom and got gas.
> **Me:** Yes, but we're about to go up a big hill.

Thomas E: Will you guys shut up? I can't hear.

Me: You know what? That's not okay to ask like that. The Sorting Hat is going to put you in Slytherin if you're not careful. We can always back up on the CD, if you missed a part, but I can already tell you that it's Hermione who really saves the day.

Alley: Mom, you passed the exit.

There are places on the 5 Freeway where you can't get off to turn around for many miles. I found those places, in both directions, several times. Mercifully, even though we were hours late we still made it. The session of gymnasts before us had run over its allotted time.

FIELD NOTES

I was full of tension, ready to snap, but—and I'm embarrassed to say this—I knew I would feel better after posting a status update on Facebook. Having endured hours of trauma, I was especially anxious to synopsize the experience and throw it up for my thousand or so nutty cat people "friends" to see.

We walked into a lovely, new gym. I kissed my little gymnast and watched him skitter off to join his team for their warm-up, as if we'd pulled up in a timely fashion and it had all gone smooth as silk. I said yes to some snacks for Alley and Toshia, who were really good sisters to not only go to every one of Thomas E's meets but to genuinely cheer him on, regardless of what little brother torment he put them through, and therefore they deserved a Kit-Kat here and there. I then quickly found a bleacher space and opened up my laptop. My heart was pounding with anxiety that could soon be soothed with a finger sashay across the keys, and a satisfying press on the old Post button.

I clicked on Safari, and in a few seconds that heartbreaking "none of your preferred networks are available" message came up. Of course, I know that people have suffered worse things. I saw the people on the rooftops during Katrina. I read *What Is the What*, about one of the Lost Boys of the Sudan. I know that there are people stranded in airports who can't turn the TV off when Nancy Grace is on. However, in that moment, not being able to check my email and my Facebook was almost too much for me.

I happened to see another parent using her iPhone's internet capabilities right there in the gym. The gym was a no-go for me and my laptop, but there she was, pushing buttons and getting responses. I asked her about it, and she told me that a smart-phone connects to the internet in lots of places that a laptop can't. Then she showed me Twitter. She showed me a couple of posts from people she followed. She followed Shaquille O'Neal and some others. She got a big kick out of it. Although I can't imagine what Shaquille O'Neal can say that's different from one day to the next? "I'm up here again."

QUALITATIVE OBSERVATION #13
Twitter grabbed me.

FIELD NOTES
As soon as we made it home from the Bakersfield meet, I got a Twitter account and an iPhone. Twitter has to be one of the stupidest, most narcissistic activities humans have ever come up with, and I was enjoying it very much.

ANALYSIS

I was easy prey for the Twitter jones, like an orphaned caribou with a limp.

I've been in hotels and airports for countless hours over many years. I'd like to thank the hospitality industry, by the way, for the recent occasional added amenity of the artfully folded towel. Holiday Inns sometimes fold their towels in an elephant shape, and I believe I enjoyed a bunny-shaped towel at a Kimpton hotel. Sometimes I drip-dry just so I don't wreck the towel origami. These are among the many things that I would like to draw a traveling companion's attention to with an elbow and a whispered, "Can you believe this?" As I generally have no such traveling companion, I have been an avid postcard writer for much of my life. Just a few lines of observation or jokes, or an "I am here," give me that deep, satisfying feeling of connection, even if unbeknownst to me on the receiving end my postcards are used as coasters on which to set condensation-dripping beverage glasses.

"I don't want to leave a ring on your beautiful coffee table. You got something to put under this glass?"

"Yeah, here."

"Oh, look at that, someone named Paula is in Shirlee, Massachusetts. She thinks she might go to Bettee next."

With just a pocket device, Twitter allows me to instantly send the postcard messages that rattle around in my head. From the moment I was introduced to it, I knew we were made for each other. It was life changing. It was like when Davy Jones kissed Marcia Brady. And I am always delighted when "followers" tweet back that I somehow lifted their spirits.

Of course, soon after I jumped on it, Twitter became a huge

part of the relentless and loathsome self-promotion required in my profession. So instead of just putting up jokes and making observations, I'm sometimes stuck tweeting, "Get your tickets before it's too late," as though I were some kind of apocalyptic used-car salesman, which takes some of the fun out of it.

Still, I get in the occasional "I'm taking a quick Twitter break from writing, and I'm only writing because banging my head against a wall chips the paint" sort of line, and that does give me a momentary hep or two of happiness.

QUALITATIVE OBSERVATION #14

Boy, if you accidentally close a laptop on your nipple, you don't use it while propped up in bed for at least a couple of weeks.

CONCLUSION

I now have a laptop, a desktop, an iPhone, a Facebook account, a Twitter account, two Gmail accounts, a YouTube account, plus a website. In the interest of my devotion to the study of the search for human happiness, I think it's time to complete and move on from the Get Wired experiment. It's hard to get away from technology now that I've started. I wish I could say the same for the Get Fit experiment. As I predicted, my twelve pounds have come flying back, and they brought their friends this time.

My Thanksgiving video, "Gee, Thanks" is up to 3,542 views, and although my *Cooking with Rhonda* videos are less than an internet sensation, people who see them say they enjoy my Rhonda Puckett character's cooking classes for the beginning cook, which tosses some heps of happiness my way. On the other hand, the frustration caused by a failure of the computer or of my computer skills is only slightly less dramatic than nature's fury, and the surprising dark magic of having thousands of "friends" is that it can be quite lonely.

Undoubtedly, deleting and cutting and pasting have a certain lure of convenience, and jokes and funny videos used sparingly are lovely diversions. Still, I am certain I will never carry an email close to my heart. Getting wired comes with too much compulsion to be the key to happiness and you miss too much real life while messing around with tech stuff. If Sir Isaac Newton had employed a computer, he would never have noticed apples falling, and we'd still be wondering why we can't jump higher. For every hep of happiness one can garner from computer use, the machine sucks it back up again with interest, sometimes moments later, like a powerful shop-vac.

THE

GET EARTHY

EXPERIMENT

WITH SCREENS TAKING such a huge chunk out of our lives, nature calls to me. Backpacking was one of the big offerings at my high school, and I went on every trip I could. I even chaperoned a hiking group a few years after my departure from the school.

CONDITION

I got it in my head that such a trip would do Toshia and me a world of good. I became obsessed with the idea of going backpacking with Toshia. Although everyone I talked to about it thought I was nuts, I knew Toshia had a good deal of endurance and suspected that secretly her sleeves were bulging with tricks, even if her legs didn't lift high or straight. I chose a schedule of four days and three nights, which seemed about right.

HYPOTHESIS

None of our pencils have erasers on them anymore, so once I penciled in the trip on my calendar, we had to go. Outdoor survival skills or no, happiness could lie waiting at the top of a mountain or along the trail. With Toshia by my side, I was going to embark on the Get Earthy experiment.

EQUIPMENT

I explained our limits to a lovely woman at the Adventure 16 store, and she recommended we go to the Angeles National Forest. I bought a beautiful waterproof map, which I would learn during the first day of our trip that I did not know how to read.

PROCEDURE

The REI store in Santa Monica can actually be along the route from the high school to home if you miss the turn onto the freeway. I told myself that I wouldn't go there. To keep costs down, I would use the equipment we already had for our trip and fill in with what I could borrow from others.

QUALITATIVE OBSERVATION #1

My life is a series of self-delusions.

EQUIPMENT

The first thing I bought at REI was long underwear made of a material that claimed to wick the sweat away from your body, which the saleswoman assured me was practically the sole key to any successful outdoor adventure. I beat a path to REI many times, and eventually just being in there made all of its contents seem so necessary. I bought a book of poems to read to squirrels. At the time it made all sorts of sense. A friend told me we could borrow a backpack she had bought for a recent trip, and I had planned on using it until she brought it over and I saw it was a small daypack. My friend has a bit of the Amelia Bedelia in her. When I told her I thought we needed something a little bigger, she said, "Oh, yeah, on our trip the food, tents, and sleeping bags were carried in a truck."

"Well," I said, "I'm sure the wet bar and the perfume were a load in themselves."

I did borrow my former high school math teacher's son's backpack, which was metal framed with two main pouches, similar to what we used on high school trips, and I'm sure it would have been okay, but I happened to go into the backpack section at REI, the very section I had sworn in the name of all that was good and credit worthy that I would not go into. There were so many different colors. Some were two toned. They had padded belts, pockets upon pockets, padded pockets, belts with pockets. They were stuffed and hung neatly on display. It was more than I could bear.

I told myself the things that you tell yourself when you are spending money you don't have. I told myself that I was helping the economy, and that now that I had wicking underwear, it wouldn't be right to just shove it into my math teacher's son's two-pocketed antiquity, and that if I did go flat broke, it'd be good to have a nice backpack with which to live on the street. I bought a beautiful blue-and-black one. I don't remember the price. I tried to forget that part. Once I had made that purchase, it was clear that budgeting was just not the path I had chosen. Falling off a cliff became the key to my revised financial plan.

We have sleeping bags at home, but what they had at REI was

irresistible. They were so light we'd have to tether ourselves to a tent stake while we slept. They were stitched with freeze-dried cloud. I got two of those babies, which happened to be right beside the tent section. I got a tent.

QUALITATIVE OBSERVATION #2
Backpacking involves a tremendous amount of preparation. Collecting the equipment and supplies alone requires a keen, organizational mind, or one can run out of nutritious snack foods along the trail.

ANALYSIS
The center of my bedroom/office floor was stacked high with what would, inconceivably, eventually be carried on my back. Although Toshia, being a Poundstone, seemed to enjoy seeing me shovel money toward purchases for her, overall, she grew less enthusiastic—some would say morose—as the trip loomed closer. I pointed out that although it would take some good old-fashioned effort, in the end she would, at the very least, have a nice pair of sweat wicking long underwear to show for it. Some would say she grew moroser.

EQUIPMENT
I saved purchasing the dehydrated bill of fare until last. I bought enough freeze-dried casseroles, omelets, and soufflés to run an outdoor restaurant. I always say, you never know when the after-bar rush might hit. My favorite part was selecting the high-energy treats. They are high in calories. I eat lots of foods that are high in calories, but these high-calorie treats are sanctioned by the extremely fit hiking community.

Normally I eat a lot because I'm a pig. Really, I think I would have to hike for years to get to a weight where I couldn't just live off my own fat for months, but in this setting I could convince myself that this kind of eating was necessary for my survival. I have come close to convincing myself of that in regard to Reese's Pieces on airplanes, but there is a small part of me, soon to be the only small part of me, that knows this to be a dubious claim. Now, however, I could purchase a tasty caffeine-and-calorie-filled thing called GU Energy Gel, in mint, chocolate, strawberry, and blueberry flavors, which would potentially power my otherwise weak, broken frame through the wilderness. Sweet.

While I stood making my selections in the cooking section of REI, I heard another customer asking a knowledgeable staff member about their bearproof food containers. This is the first I had thought of that, and I saw *Jeremiah Johnson* in the theater in 1972. Naturally, I waited my turn to ask the knowledgeable staff member whether I, too, needed that nifty bearproof food container that he was counseling my fellow customer to purchase. I told him I was investing a king's ransom in life-giving, high-calorie hiking food that I was taking on a backpacking trip to the Angeles National Forest. He assured me that that area was clear of bears. I felt so relieved I ate a Boston-cream-pie-flavored energy bar right there in the store. Surely I would burn it off carrying that huge bag of food to the car.

Just before my final purchase had been rung up, a particularly helpful and, of course, knowledgeable REI staff member approached, telling me in a low voice that there was one more product in which I might be interested. I thought it was drugs. *Now,* I said to myself, *we're going to find out how the real hikers do it. Look out, Mount Everest!* This woman was beautiful, by the way, and in fantastic shape. She sure didn't look ravaged by chemistry. Apparently, if you hike enough, the benefits of drugs cancel out any of the drawbacks. Here was a sport I could devote my life to.

The salesperson looked both ways to see that the coast was clear, then withdrew from behind her back a gizmo that made it possible for a woman to pee like a man while on the trail. I swear it. It looked like the lid through which you pour gas from a gas can. It had a clear, thick, plastic tube attached to a cupped plastic piece. A woman could press it to her crotch and spout pee through the tube. The salesperson insisted that it would enhance the quality of the trip manyfold. I still thought drugs had a better shot at it, but I bought the pee-like-a-man thing anyway.

FIELD NOTES

After months of planning, the night before arrived. I began to wonder if I had bitten off more than I could reconstitute with water and chew. On further reflection I realized that although I did some backpacking thirty years ago, I never actually led nor organized a trip. I just brought the supplies that were on the list and followed the person in front of me. I knew I could pick my feet up and put them down again millions of times without bathing, but that was the limit of my expertise. As for the trip I chaperoned, when I thought about it now I could see that *chaperone* was more of an honorary title.

The packing was excruciating. My obsessive-compulsive disorder flares up during times of stress, and by now it was clear that I was going to be carrying sixty pounds on my back while dragging along a miserable teenager who occasionally used faking or actually causing injuries to herself to get out of doing stuff. Challenging? Yes, but I saw *Follow Me, Boys!* with Fred MacMurray in the theater, and now I have it on videotape. Fred plays a musician who spontaneously gives up the road and becomes a scout leader who hikes with an at-risk boy (played by Kurt Russell) who goes on to become a doctor and eventually joins in a moving tribute to the elderly Fred MacMurray character— and I'm not getting any younger myself.

PROCEDURE

Packing is always hard, but for hiking you want easy access to everything. Mosquitoes specifically target people that they know don't carry repellant in an outer pocket. What about the Kleenex? The damp cloth? The water? The trash? The map? The whistle? The camera? The snack food? The first-aid kit? What about the extra underwear? If you need your extra underwear quick, it's bad enough to have need of it, without having to dig to the bottom of your pack to find it.

I had Toshia carry her own clothes and some toilet paper in a day pack, and I took the lion's share of the equipment in my own. I swear, I could barely make it to the car, the thing was so damned heavy. I could hold the straps, hoist it up to just above the knee, and then use a yelling technique I've seen weight lifters use in the Olympics to kind of toss it around and onto my shoulder. I comforted myself with the thought that the weight of the pack would decrease as we ate the dehydrated foods and energy snacks. We stopped for a quick bite on our porch, and then it was on to conquer the thirty feet between us and the car.

CONSTANT

I drink over sixteen diet sodas a day. I sleep with a soda beside my bed, which I sip throughout the night. Safe to say, I am addicted to caffeine.

PROCEDURE

When I talked to anyone who knew me before this trip, they asked how I was going to carry all of those sodas. Trust me, I tried to think of a way. It just wasn't going to be possible. If I had carried so much as a stick of gum more, my knees would have given out.

I settled for bringing one can to drink on our drive to the forest and one to drink as a reward for a job well done on the first night. I didn't pack the reward soda right away. I kept it chilled in the car, waiting for the last possible minute for it to begin the warming cycle in my backpack.

FIELD NOTES

After completing a trouble-free motor trip to our destination, as we disembarked from the car, my cool, fresh soda fell from my hand and rolled under the car beside us in the lot, springing a leak along the way. Hsssss. I bent down only to find it beyond my reach no matter what side of the car I tried. Jeremiah Johnson, you may recall, lost his wife and son to the hatchets of some angry Crow Indians. I resolved to press on.

I must say that perhaps buoyed by the strength of my example, Toshia kicked herself into gear and was a goddamned machine of a hiker. In the beginning, I let her use two walking sticks but she kept using them like crutches, so I took one away.

She was a thing of beauty. Really, she was. She wore khaki cargo pants, a bright blue nylon, sweat-wicking shirt, and sneakers, as always, because they are the only footwear that fit over her plastic braces. We started around midday and did five and one-tenth miles the first day. Not too shabby. We could have gone faster, but I worry about Toshia's health, so I made us stop every fifteen minutes or so to have some water, and besides, by evening I had an almost unsupportable GU jones.

QUANTITATIVE OBSERVATION #1

This trip was in the spring. The beauty of the surroundings was almost unimaginable. We counted over a hundred lizard sightings and even more butterflies. Unfortunately, our mosquito, fly, and other little annoying fucking bug counts were in the millions.

QUALITATIVE OBSERVATION #3

Bugs do, and always have, loved my hair, but boy, they loved every part of Toshia.

FIELD NOTES

The bugs hovered maddeningly over us, but mostly around Toshia, for at least the last two miles on the first day. I wanted this to be a mother-daughter adventure not an ordeal, so I did my best to defend her. I rolled up the map and kind of used the force. I swung, fanned, and struck hard and long enough to get us to our first campsite.

Our first campsite was right on a gorgeous little stream. As we neared it, the bug population grew worse. Poor Toshia was pretty frustrated with having to constantly wave, slap, and thwack. I used it as a teachable moment. I said, "Frustration sucks, huh? I feel frustrated when you lie to me and I have to be Nancy Drew, piecing together what did and didn't happen. I hate it. Every one of your lies is like a hundred of these bugs to me."

QUALITATIVE OBSERVATION #4
I think, sometimes, I'm annoying to Toshia.

VARIABLES
We never saw a single soul along the way, but there was some evidence of civilization at our campsite, including a paper sign tacked to a bulletin board showing the silhouette of a bear and the words YOU ARE IN BEAR COUNTRY.

ANALYSIS
Oops.

FIELD NOTES
Fortunately, there were careful instructions on how to thwart the bears. The sign suggested hanging your food from a tree. No problem there, except I didn't have a rope, I'm not Will Rogers, and a bear could easily reach any branch I could reach with a bag of my food. There was, however, a good chance that the sight of me trying to hang my food from a branch would double over a bear with laughter just long enough for us to get away. I

did have some bungee cords, though, and a certain savvy about how to use them.

Using lots of teamwork and some limited use of the phrase "I don't think it's supposed to look like that," we set up the tent and prepared a meal, which included freeze-dried potatoes au gratin and blueberry crumble dessert.

QUALITATIVE OBSERVATION #5

Comfort achieved while backpacking is of infinitely higher quality than what can be provided in any four-star hotel, no matter what shape they fold the towels into.

ANALYSIS

We were absolutely glowing with our success. Happy? I'd say a balou's worth of increase. I missed my other kids, but it really felt great to be with my older daughter, whose strength and capabilities I have never doubted for a moment.

FIELD NOTES

Having finished with our dinner and being mindful of the ways of bear country, I tossed the rest of the food into a netted bag and looked for an eligible tree. Hooking one bungee cord to another, I crafted a double bungee a full four feet or so long. I threaded the hook through a hole in the netting, and hurled it over the highest branch I could. When I got it tethered securely, it came to about my navel if I were flat footed. That's about snout level on a brown bear, I would imagine. It had the added attraction of bobbing at the end of the bungee cord, like a cat toy.

QUALITATIVE OBSERVATION #6

Knowing that you can make do in the wild gives a person a certain sense of security. I can tell you that.

FIELD NOTES

With the help of these really cool headlamps I bought at REI, I read *Silas Marner* to Toshia in our tent until I couldn't keep my eyes open another second. It must have been about seven o'clock at night.

Sometime in the wee hours of the night, we woke to some sort of loud noise. I told Toshia I thought it was a bear eating our food and that in the morning we'd have to clean up the mess and head back to the car, because we couldn't continue our trip without food. I pictured myself weak from trekking out with no nutrients, crawling on my belly to the few warm sips of diet soda in the can under the car in the parking lot.

In fact, when we got up in the morning, I found our bag of food still hanging from the tree, untouched, not even bobbing up and down. I felt triumphant. As quickly as we could, we added hot water to something that became a ham-and-cheese omelet, toast with butter and grape jelly, assorted fruit, and orange juice. We ate it out of the bag it came in. I can kind of see why the bears rejected it.

QUALITATIVE OBSERVATION #7

Food doesn't taste that good out of a bag.

FIELD NOTES

We packed up. I fired up the pee-like-a man gadget, and off we hiked.

I'm not quite sure where we hiked. It was all uphill for a couple of hours. We counted lizards and ascended. Many of the lizards were winded. We stopped for water and peed like men at least every twenty minutes. It was a wide trail, and clearly we were on it, but it didn't seem to be headed where I thought we were going. It was hard to tell. I'm no more successful as a navigator without a car than with, as it turns out, but also part of the map had been rubbed away when I used it to thwack bugs off Toshia.

We did pass a Boy Scout troop that morning, and I should have asked them.

QUALITATIVE OBSERVATION #8
After you pee like a man, you don't ask for directions.

FIELD NOTES
Eventually we settled on a path that seemed clearer, but Toshia's spirits had dampened from the uphill climb. I sang all of the trail songs by myself. The view from up there was stupendous. I kept telling her that only the people who make this effort get this view. I tried to use it as another teachable moment. Toshia did that teenagery thing where she faced the view—her eyes pointed toward it—but made it clear that she wasn't seeing it.

CONSTANT
They make movies out of everything now. Disney defied logic by making a movie out of a ride. When they make a movie out of the expression "You can lead a horse to water but you can't make it drink," Toshia will play the horse.

ENVIRONMENT

The woman who had originally recommended this forest trail did so, in part, because the map showed a blue line alongside the trail, which indicated a river. That, of course, was good; you'd have access to water, without which you'd die. Whereas I think it's true that something that could have at one time been a river ran parallel to the trail, on this warm spring day in California, it often ran to only a slimy sort of trickle and, more often than not, could be found way down the side of a steep incline beside us. In fairness to the cartographer, the map may have indicated such, but I didn't know what those blobby circles that show depth were.

FIELD NOTES

Eventually we ran out of water. I was forced to break the very wise national park rule about not going off the trail. I saw a spot where, with a bit of a hike, I could get down to the river with my water pump and filter, but I continued past it, hoping farther along the trail the river would come up closer. When I saw that the river actually moved farther away as we continued down the trail, I asked Toshia if she wanted to wait for me where we were or come back a little way to the spot where I thought I could get water. She plopped down on the ground, choosing to wait.

I grabbed my water contraptions, walked back, and climbed down the hill. I'm sure that there are hikers who can do this with one hand tied behind their back, but for me the water pump and filter required great concentration and three hands. I was trying hard to keep the weighted end of the tube, from which you draw the water in, out of the scuzzy part of the water while pumping the handle on the bottle itself when I heard Toshia yelling, "Mom! Mom! A snake!" It was yet another opportunity for a teachable moment. The story of the boy who cried wolf would have been a perfect fit, but instead I dropped my water pump and scrambled up the hill, leaving thin strips of my skin on the tips of prickly bushes, trampling the flora and the fauna. Future generations be damned—ask me, I'll tell you what fauna looked like—my daughter was in danger. How would I live without her? Maybe I would never forgive myself for pushing her so hard. When I crested the edge of the trail, she was still sitting exactly where I had left her. The snake wasn't even coming toward her. It was just slithering across the trail. I said, "Toshia, the snake isn't after you personally. It doesn't know you. I think you could get up and get away from it."

Still, it was nice to be needed.

ANALYSIS

I was massively relieved, but I don't know if I'd call that happy. Which is probably good. If that made me happy, then the answer to how to be happy would simply be: snakes.

PROCEDURE

I think you're supposed to make noise on the trail to ward off bears, but if you actually see one you're supposed to talk, preferably on a subject of no interest to a bear. I recommend leveraged buyouts. Stay still or gradually ease away, and make yourself look tall. Bears don't like tall people. Has Kobe Bryant ever been attacked by a bear? I rest my case. Did you see the news story on the wedding of the tallest man in the world a couple of years ago? There wasn't a bear in sight.

I don't know what you're supposed to do if you actually come face-to-face with a snake. I think you ask it to manage your campaign.

FIELD NOTES

I returned to my water-pumping equipment, clawed my way back up the embankment, reunited with Toshia, and was off again, not like a rocket but like an out-of-shape person with a Winnebago on her back.

CONSTANT

I talk a lot. Poor Toshia has had to put up with it her whole life. The problem is that everything that gets said reminds me of something else that I feel compelled to say, which means I say one more thing, which reminds me of another. Live with that in a two-man tent. I dare you.

FIELD NOTES

Sometimes I'd walk up ahead of Toshia just to give her a break. I never stopped talking, mind you, I just did it where she couldn't hear me. Several lizards found me scintillating.

After seeing almost no one for days, we arrived at a campsite that was teeming with outdoor recreaters. We fit ourselves into the outermost area. There was a campsite or two between us and the river. A couple at one of these sites had a little black Toto-looking dog on a leash, but it wasn't tied to anything. It just ran around with the leash dangling from its collar, waiting for the thrill of an abrupt stop from snagging on a protruding root. Dogs love that.

As Toshia and I strolled to the river, the little black dog started barking and running toward me. It was running pretty fast, but I thought that as it got closer it would see that I was clearly a dog person. So I just stood there while the dog ran all the way up my body to my waist and bit my hand. I guess I don't look like a dog person. In fact, I must look like I deserve to be bitten because the woman who owned the dog barely said a word other than that the dog was a rescue and they didn't know it that well. One might think that that would be a good reason to hold on to the end of the dog's leash when in a public place. I didn't say anything like that, though, because I never do.

What I did say to my daughter, who waited up on the riverbank for me while I once again pumped water for us, was, "If that little dog runs toward you, take this walking stick and whack it." The little dog did not come toward Toshia, by the way, but if it had and if Toshia had whacked it, I would have explained that I didn't really know my daughter that well and that I was just bringing her to a public place to see if she would hurt anyone. For the first time in my life, I sympathized with Almira Gulch.

Later that day, we left our packs at the campsite to hike about with fewer burdens. I didn't worry about anyone stealing mine. They couldn't lift it. We came to a pastoral setting by a creek and took off our shoes. Toshia undid her braces and we dangled our feet in the water. Toshia's feet are long and not too worn on the bottoms, because she doesn't walk stably without her braces. Her hair, like mine, is like a museum field trip of second graders who won't be asked back. It just doesn't follow directions. On her, it somehow has the effect of making her smile more beautiful. The yellows of the afternoon light looked fantastic on her brown skin. The water was so cold it made us laugh, after it caused shortness of breath. I put my head back on the grass and mud to relish this balou and a half. *Someday,* I thought, *she'll tell her kids that when she was a kid, I made her go backpacking and get her feet really cold.*

QUALITATIVE OBSERVATION #9
We had become experts at setting up our camp, breaking it down, and peeing like men.

FIELD NOTES
We were beginning to feel a titch homesick. The following morning we were just going to pack up and head to the car. There were no bear signs at this campsite, but there were a lot of squirrels about and I didn't want them rummaging through my things in the night, so I took our backpacks into the tent with us.

I read *Silas Marner* aloud as long as I could and fell off to sleep. It must have been about 1:00 a.m. when I awoke to snuffling just on the other side of the ridiculously thin nylon tent wall.

VARIABLE
It was loud snuffling. I woke Toshia, and we both flicked on our headlamps, instantly blinding each other. We popped up from our sleeping bags and clung to each other like Laverne and fucking Shirley. I had no idea what to do. We couldn't be sure what it was, but I can tell you its snuffle was loud, plenty loud enough to be a bear.

FIELD NOTES

Toshia kept saying, "Unzip the tent and put your head out to see what it is."

I could picture my head emerging from the flap and right into a bear's mouth. I said, "You've never loved me," then unzipped the tent at the bottom, just enough to wrap my fingers around the walking stick that lay on the ground against the tent. I guess I thought I'd smack the bear with the stick if I had to. There was also the chance that this could rile the otherwise peaceful bear who had only come to our tent seeking Pop-Tarts. "Don't you hit me with that walking stick," he'd say, wrenching it from my trembling hands.

The loud snuffling continued unabated until I had the bright idea for us to sing songs from Jimmy Cliff's *The Harder They Come* as loud as we could. The snuffling slowly moved off at about "Gonna get my share now of what's mine . . ." Contrary to what some may believe, bears do not like songs about the struggle for social justice.

We did a second show, to much the same response, when the snuffling returned at about 3:00 a.m. This time we added a percussion section, with loud claps. I am relieved, and perhaps alive, to tell you that that ended our engagement in the Angeles National Forest. I'm thrilled to say that we were not held over.

I don't know how long we sat, stiff with fear, after we were pretty certain the bear had left us this time. Eventually we felt safe enough to fall back to sleep.

When we woke up, not eaten, I think we both appreciated it.

QUALITATIVE OBSERVATION #10

It's good to not be eaten.

FIELD NOTES

We packed up for our final time, laughing that reggae was just the right thing and agreeing that had we rapped to the bear, we might be dead.

I didn't bring my laptop or iPhone, and I could already feel the benefits of being away from them. But I did film and photo-document our trip for the purposes of posting them on my website upon our return.

CONCLUSION

I now have a film of Toshia Poundstone backpacking in the Angeles National Forest on my iMovie, and it is a spectacular view.

Toshia and I have told our story a hundred times already. She likes to say I almost killed her. Not everyone will be able to backpack in the Angeles forest with my daughter Toshia, which is unfortunate, because I can tell you it's good for a couple balous and a few heps of happiness. By the way, we laugh whenever we tell the tale, which gives us a residual hep or two as well.

THE

GET ORGANIZED

EXPERIMENT: PART ONE

CONDITIONS

I lost my beautiful house years ago. I went broke before it was cool. We moved to a smaller house, which I rent. I got rid of lots of stuff, but I was still putting a bigger-house amount of stuff into a smaller house. I was at that time several years behind on finishing my first book, *There Is Nothing in This Book That I Meant to Say*. I decided that in order to complete the book, I would have to put blinders on, so to speak, and write despite the boxes. I ignored cleaning my room and let papers pile up. Christmas gift boxes accumulated. I didn't pay much attention to the bins of toys that my children were outgrowing.

Our ballroom—so named because it's the room the jukebox occupied before I had to sell that, too—became lined with boxes of books, topped by a Sit 'n Spin that we found in the alley when we were moving in, and now there was barely room for the foosball table in the middle of the ballroom, let alone a decent ball. One waltz and I'd be liable for injuries.

I generally knew where things were, but my desk was stacked so high it was at severe avalanche risk, and my closet had become rolling hills of sweatshirts, sweaters, khaki shorts, high top sneakers, and ball gowns. Sometimes when I walked past a Hold Everything store, I made a mournful keening wail. By the time I completed my first book, I was so overwhelmed by the chaotic residue left behind, I didn't know where to begin. So I didn't. Then I didn't some more.

HYPOTHESIS

I am sure that getting organized will make me happy. I just know it will.

PROCEDURE

Originally, I thought I'd start in my bedroom/office and work my way through that disaster before anywhere else, but then, while walking through the kitchen puzzling over what about my parenting makes the simplest of requests result in mind-numbing arguments, it occurred to me that the New Year's Party Kit for 10 People, which contains:

5 glitter foil hats

5 tiaras

5 9-inch foil horns

5 squawkers

10 leis

and says right on the front that it's "a celebration in a box . . . ready to party" and which I have kept on the bench beside the kitchen table for years, just in case, might be agitating my children. I would have to start there.

After that, I was cleaning the Milk Bones off the top of the refrigerator. They'd been up there for ages, because they gave my dog diarrhea. I used to give her one to take with her when I put her in the backyard when I went out. Of course, I didn't know they were making her sick. It's no wonder she didn't like to be left. I used to give them to her as good-behavior treats, too. That could explain the biting.

I hate to waste, and I'd never been sure what to do with the Milk Bones—I couldn't in good conscience give them to any other dog—so they decorated my kitchen for years. This is the sort of conundrum that stymies me.

ENVIRONMENT: THE TOP OF THE FRIDGE

FIELD NOTES

I jumped in with both feet today. I put the Milk Bones in the disposal, threw out the contents of the New Year's Party Kit for 10 People, and recycled both boxes, which meant, that if I ever had a New Year's Eve party, five people wouldn't have squawkers. From high atop the step stool, while cleaning the top of the refrigerator, I could see that the little desk by the phone, where the mail gets stacked, had to be dealt with.

ENVIRONMENT:
THE LITTLE DESK BY THE PHONE IN THE KITCHEN

FIELD NOTES

I was dwarfed by the tower of mail that had collected on the little desk. I misinterpreted the forever stamp. I thought if you received mail posted with one, you had to keep it forever. The huge pile of envelopes mostly contained solicitations, what I call give-us-money mail. A lot of times I don't throw those out because although I'm not flush when they arrive, I always have fantasies that my ship will come in and I'll become a big philanthropist. I dream like Ralph Kramden: when I get it, I'm gonna spread it around. Occasionally, I grab one of those envelopes, shove a twenty-five-dollar check in there, and send it off. Not often enough for the pile to dwindle, though. Some of that mail had been there for a long time. I kicked myself when I cleared down to the envelope asking for financial support for the Mondale-Ferraro campaign.

I spent tedious hours bent over the little desk sorting through save-the-date announcements for dates long past, Bed Bath & Beyond coupons that I never have with me when I go there, and to-do lists that I to didn't. I found new places all over the house for what I didn't put in the recycle bin. I especially enjoyed the bone-deep satisfaction of slipping the report cards into each respective child's three-ring binder, where I store their important papers, for which I received what I guesstimate to have been one hep of happiness. Then, as the desk was still covered, I went back for more.

CONSTANT

I am an amazing procrastinator. Part of the problem is that everything becomes for me a little stroll down memory lane. For example, I keep a green notebook full of plastic sheet protectors on this little desk by the phone in the kitchen to hold the rules, course synopses, and schedules from the kids' schools. Instead of just discarding the outdated pages, I find myself rereading them, getting sentimental over the rules from past years ("Oh, I remember when he broke section IV, article B"), and making new discoveries in the course synopses and schedules ("So they *did* have school on Mondays, and she *was* supposed to bring a pencil").

FIELD NOTES

I had been at this for hours and hours and I now beheld a clean surface. I was dusty, and the closer to the surface of the desk I got, the more the mail smelled like cat pee. There must have been something wrong with the post office back then. I wouldn't have been surprised to come across a gift card for Frontier Frank's Buffalo Shack that expired in the mid-1800s. It seemed too early to get discouraged, but there were piles like this in every room. The dozens of magazines I'd bought because their covers screamed GET ORGANIZED! always made it look so easy. Of course, I hadn't actually read the articles, but still.

EQUIPMENT

I decided to read the thick, glossy magazine for airy-fairy-rich-people-who-buy-soy-products-and-do-yoga, which I'd been lugging around in my carry-on bag for months because the cover promised GET ORGANIZED. STAY ORGANIZED: HOW TO CONTROL

THE CLUTTER FOR GOOD. It suggested your batteries be rubber-banded together and stored in a dry place instead of in the refrigerator. Who puts their batteries in the refrigerator? What the hell is the matter with rich people? We barely had room for the leftover pizza. Batteries? Surely this has brought waves of relief to multitudes. The article didn't have a word of advice about how to dispose of the oscillating Santa, which my son ripped the head off of, without crowding the landfill. It had not even a blurb about where to put all of the various plastic pieces that you find on the floor and that look like important parts of things and that crowd in among the pencils with no erasers and pens that only write with every other use in the junk drawer of the little desk beside the phone in the kitchen.

QUALITATIVE OBSERVATION #1

If I throw away a screw I find in the junk drawer today, I guarantee the refrigerator door will fall off tomorrow.

EQUIPMENT

I sought further counsel from a copy of O magazine, because it had a cover story about Oprah getting organized. Organizing has replaced orgasm as the "Big O" of women's magazines, and Oprah knows it. There was a quote in the magazine from a professional organizer. He said a study found that if people regularly tidied their homes and offices, most of then would gain between sixteen minutes and one hour a day when they could be working (that's four to fifteen days a year). I misread the word *tidied* as *tie-dyed* at first. Now I had quite a mess on my hands. I couldn't figure out how tie-dying my home and office would help, but I was so desperate I was willing to try anything.

ENVIRONMENT: CLOSET

FIELD NOTES

If Oprah's professional organizer is correct about the sixteen minutes to one hour a day time savings, there might not only be happiness in cleaning and organizing my closet but perhaps an entire lifetime buried in there somewhere, like a hidden treasure. Either way, I could no longer resist my closet's plaintive cries to be organized. At least I thought it was my closet. It could have been someone trapped beneath the stacks of clothes, tote bags, and handheld electronic games that I stupidly bought and later had to stash away from my son. It could have been my son.

PROCEDURE

This was a huge task. I decided to begin by including "organize ten items in closet" on my daily list of things to do—just writing "organize closet" would have been too overwhelming. Even using this ridiculously pared-down expectation of myself, I was only able to cross it off successfully a few times.

Getting organized might be a far-off, crazy dream, but after all, someone carved Mount Rushmore and somewhere around George Washington's nose it must have started to seem like a ludicrous idea. On many days he must have said to himself, "I'll just do their eyebrows this year."

FIELD NOTES

I was drowning. This was a chamber of horrors for my OCD. I knew I wanted to keep the Kermit doll with the winter scarf sitting on the top shelf of my closet, but many belongings I just didn't know what to do with, such as my local Emmy. I kept it on the top shelf of my closet, because displaying an award seems kind of conceited to me. Plus it was a local Emmy. If I put it on the mantel in the ballroom, I'd get a lot of:

> **Guest:** You won an Emmy?
>
> **Me:** Well, no . . . yes . . . but it's a local Emmy.
>
> **Guest:** A local Emmy? I didn't know they had local Emmys.
>
> **Me:** I didn't either until I got it.
>
> **Guest:** What's it for?
>
> **Me:** A piece about a Picasso exhibit I did for local public television.
>
> **Guest:** What was it up against?
>
> **Me:** An episode of a cooking show that focused on rutabagas and a special about a man with only one kidney who tries to find work for feral cats.
>
> **Guest:** Don't you have room for this in your closet?

QUANTITATIVE OBSERVATION #1

Unfortunately, even though I'd been working like a dog, I was heavier than before I started the Get Fit experiment. Time was of the essence to get this top closet shelf right—another couple of pounds and I wouldn't be able to push my girth up on a step stool to access it.

FIELD NOTES

It was hell in my closet. I hacked through a jungle of clothing, like William Holden in *Bridge on the River Kwai*. I did find the strength to get rid of the last of my clothing with shoulder pads, a fad I confess to having participated in fully and of my own free will in the 1980s. I'd hoped that if I threw them out now, I could avoid explaining it someday. Future generations will ask questions of us, and my generation will someday have a lot of explaining to do:

Q: Why would anyone have wanted to stop gays from getting married?

A: Well, son, I know it seems odd now, but you have to remember, back then Christians were bored.

Q: Science proves beyond a shadow of a doubt that nutrition plays a large part in a child's ability to learn and focus. Good nutrition can even be a factor in reducing behavior problems in the classroom. Why did the public school system allow vendors like Taco Bell and Domino's to hijack the school lunch programs? Why didn't the cafeteria staff cook real food?

A: Well, I think, if you'll look back, you'll see we didn't teach science back then.

Q: Why did you wear giant shoulder pads?

A: To make our heads look smaller, of course.

Getting rid of all of my shoulder pads should have created a lot more space than it did.

QUALITATIVE OBSERVATION #2
Normal rules of physics do not apply to organizing.

FIELD NOTES
I moved on from my closet, not so much because I had finished but because I was suffocating. It required not just a winning battle strike but an occupying army.

ENVIRONMENT: BEDROOM/OFFICE

FIELD NOTES

Aside from a giant framed George Hurrell black-and-white photograph of Katharine Hepburn, a large framed movie poster from *Born Yesterday* and another from *Where Angels Go . . . Trouble Follows*, my bedroom couldn't really be said to be decorated. It would have been enough to drive Martha Stewart to the window ledge, although in my room she'd have to climb over some antique suitcases to get there. Still, there was barely an inch of wall space. An entire wall was filled with shelves of videos. I find the pictures on the box to be ample decoration. Mostly the theme was, if it can fit there, stuff it in with the pretty part facing out. That's why there was a cardboard box full of jewelry crammed under one of the wood planks that I used for a bookshelf, even though I hadn't worn jewelry since I got a grip on myself. I actually had diamond necklaces and bracelets with precious gems. Jewelry doesn't make sense to me anymore. If I want to hang shiny baubles on something, I'll decorate a Christmas tree. I'm not one of those doomsday types. I don't stockpile arms or have a bunker, but I do want to be free of anything dangling from my neck in case I have to run for it someday.

Alley used to get a kick out of trying on my jewelry and wondering whom it belonged to. I couldn't bring myself to get rid of it. So there it was in a brown cardboard box, pretty side out, alongside a few dozen photo boxes.

I didn't take that many pictures of my kids when they were little, because I'm a single mom with two hands, but I always had a lot of copies made when I got them developed. So we had tons of mostly duplicates. I just put different dates on the back and told the kids their growth spurts were late and that we visited the same places lots because they were our special places.

"Mom, this picture of me in a wheelbarrow in October of 1999 looks the exact same as this one from 2001."

"You sure did love that wheelbarrow."

The one thing I had going for me was that I never had to agonize in Bed Bath & Beyond over which floral-patterned linens would best bring out the burgundy in the complete set of *The Waltons* videos that took up the whole bottom shelf on the wall by the door. I didn't own a bed. I slept on a sheet, which I spread onto my floor each night and folded and re-placed in a large cardboard box each morning. I liked the floor. You couldn't fall out of floor, and besides, if I'd had a bed, I knew I'd never get out of it.

It's a lucky thing, too, that I didn't have a bed, or my room couldn't possibly have fit the three black art portfolios, unzipped, stuffed, and overflowing with many years' worth of my kids' schoolwork and artwork. They belched dust when I moved them, the way Little Nell's London spewed black industrial smoke. I couldn't do much in the way of organizing them, though, without losing whole days reminiscing, and getting rid of them would have meant tossing out a largess in hours of laughter.

ENVIRONMENT: BOOKSHELF

FIELD NOTES

I thought I'd try to whip the bookshelf in my bedroom into shape. How hard could that be?

I've found that having arrived at a certain age, I use a different criterion for which books I keep. First of all, now that I am, by any mathematical measure, and despite having recently choked down a serving of kale, closer to the end of my life than the beginning, rereading is out. Still, I like to keep *Homegrown Democrat*; *The Idiot*; *The Trial*; *From Beirut to Jerusalem*; *Good Grief, Charlie Brown*; *David Copperfield*; and an Archibald Cox book about the Constitution, all of which I have already read, so that if anyone has unauthorized cell phone photos of me reading *A Is for Alibi* at the airport, I can easily refute accusations of my lack of depth.

However, I was happy to toss a book called *The Explosive Child* that a friend gave me. The author, a therapist, recommended engaging in a type of dialogue with your "explosive child" that was supposed to teach him empathy and compromise and make him feel heard. Every chapter told the story of how a different family was helped by this technique. It even included sample dialogue that took place in the midst of a child's violent, raging tantrum:

> **Desperate parent:** I see that you are very upset.
>
> **Explosive child:** I don't want to do my homework!
>
> **Desperate parent:** You don't want to do your homework?
>
> **Explosive child:** I want to play with Joey!
>
> **Desperate parent:** Playing with Joey sounds like fun. I'm having a problem, though, and I hope that you can help me with it. I'm concerned that if you don't do your homework, you'll get behind in school.
>
> **Explosive child:** I could get started on my homework and then take a break to play with Joseph.

> **Desperate parent:** That sounds great. Thank you for your
> help.

I had tried this technique with my son repeatedly, but he wouldn't
say his lines:

> **Thomas E:** I WANT TO USE THE COMPUTER! I WANT TO USE THE
> COMPUTER!
> **Me:** You seem upset.
> **Thomas E:** No fucking shit, I'm upset. I WANT TO USE THE
> COMPUTER!
> **Me:** I understand you want to play with Joey.
> **Thomas E:** WHO THE HELL IS JOEY? WHAT THE HELL IS THE
> MATTER WITH YOU?
> **Me:** I have a problem. Can you help me solve my problem?
> **Thomas E:** NO ONE CAN HELP YOU WITH YOUR PROBLEM!
> YOU ARE INSANE.

QUALITATIVE OBSERVATION #3

Books about parenting written before the invention of video
games can go straight in the mulch pile.

FACTOR

It was hard to do any organizing that required making a mess in
the process and then resetting it all because we were deep into
the last quarter of the school year when barbecues, beach days,
award ceremonies, parties, exams, book fairs, and jog-a-thons
fractured each day's schedule. The minute I temporarily stacked
books from big to small in front of my bedroom door, it was time

to take enough healthful snacks for sixty students who don't like healthful snacks to the fifth-grade beach party, which thanks to the proceeds of endless after-school nacho sales, was in Monte Carlo this year. Once I pulled everything out so I could finally reach the "I'm Sorry" note that I made Toshia write to me when she lied about her homework in the first grade and that had been out of my reach since then, down behind *Defending Everyone: The History of the ACLU* for several years, one of my kids called from the high school. "Today is Teacher Awareness Day so we only had Spanish for fourteen minutes. Can you come get me?"

FIELD NOTES

I found a copy of my book, *There's Nothing in This Book That I Meant to Say.* I couldn't possibly get rid of that. It's autographed:

> Most of this book wouldn't have been possible without you.
> Yours,
> Paula Poundstone

QUANTITATIVE OBSERVATION #1

There were enough dust bunnies among my shelves and stacks of books to do a live production of *Watership Down*.

ENVIRONMENT: BEDROOM/OFFICE DESK

FIELD NOTES

Maybe I could be a professional organizer! My shelf was looking great! This is the fountain of happiness. If the rest of the world knew about this, the war on drugs would come to a halt. Derelicts would wander libraries and bookstores sorting and straightening.

I found that the surfaces in my room are interconnected, so I allowed the natural flow of the process to lead me to work on my desk. From past experience I knew that I could clear my desk at a rate of about one inch per hour.

CONDITION
Currently, by the measure of the purple ruler that my son broke during a rage precipitated by a time limit on video gaming, the stack covering the three feet by five feet desk surface was a whopping twelve inches high.

FIELD NOTES
I sorted papers for three solid hours and thought that it might be time to establish the "negative hep" measure. I was hemorrhaging heps of happiness. I hated not knowing if I needed to keep a paper or not, like the contract from Alley's orthodontist, which listed the cost of each procedure in order. She was done with everything, so I didn't know what I might still need the contract for. I didn't think an orthodontist's work could be guaranteed. Still, this is just the kind of thing that trips me up. I'm telling you, the day after I put the orthodontist's contract in the recycle bin, Alley will wake up with teeth so misaligned she won't be able to chew gum, and of course, without the contract there won't be a damned thing I can do about it.

I still have vaccine records for cats that died years ago. You never know what advances they may make in veterinary science. If the cats can be restored to life, I don't want to pay for shots they've already had.

Statements from my accountant seem to come like Harry Potter's first letter of welcome from Hogwarts School of Witchcraft and Wizardry, meaning frequently. There were piles of them. They used to come monthly, and I never read them. Now they came weekly, and I never read them. I was afraid to. I spend more than I make. I've heard on the news recently that that's bad. I always thought it was amazing. When a guy in a tux does something like that with a top hat and a bunny, we applaud, but I earn a grand and buy two grand's worth of stuff and it's bad? How can that be?

Now that I was getting organized, I took a vow to start looking at my financial statements, although I thought it certainly risked jeopardizing the chances of organization being the key to happiness. Just yesterday I got an ad in the mail for some sort of seminar about personal finance. It said it was "by women, for women," as if that would make it more clear to some of us. I think it's a leap to assume that a woman personal finance instructor will speak to another woman in a way that a man could not.

"Let me see a show of hands. How many of you have Hello Kitty on your business checks?"

"This is a minus sign. It make us sad, doesn't it?"

"Now we are going to make what's called a 'budget,' and we're going to put it way in the back of our underwear drawer, where it will be safe."

I'm terrified of Suze Orman. I have to remind myself that the people she talks to on the phone initiated the call, otherwise I can't get to sleep.

QUANTITATIVE OBSERVATION #2

I found enough paper clips on my desk to support the fastening habits of my entire neighborhood. I don't think I've ever bought a box of them. People must give them to me. It's probably going to cause me tax troubles.

FIELD NOTES

I could definitely explain where all of the school photos came from. I found another envelope of school photos every few inches of desk layer. School photos were never good, but in the old days photographs of one's children weren't as easily come by. School pictures didn't have to be good. The parents only wanted to give cross-country friends and family a rough idea of what their kid looked like. It was more for size really.

Now school photos are obsolete. Cameras are everywhere. My toaster has a camera. It's not good for close-ups. They come out blurry, and your face might get burned, but my point is that there are tons of ways and means of photographing our kids. We have no use for school photos. Nowadays parents only buy school photos so that we don't hurt our kids' feelings. The photo companies know it, too. They have the nerve to keep coming back throughout the year. I swear Thomas E had picture day three times this year. I know because he brushed his teeth without me telling him twice. It's not the sort of thing I would forget.

The photo company has a menu of "packages" for buying photos. Just filling out the order form is too hard for me. In package A you get one eight-by-ten-inch, plus fourteen one-by-one-inch photos for fifty dollars. In package B you get five two-by-three-inch photos, plus some stickers with your kid's face on them. In package C you get four one-by-ten-inch photos plus a class picture, with your choice of any three children blacked out. If you can fill out the school photo order form, you can do your own taxes, and there aren't enough people who understand how to do their taxes to even fill the president's cabinet.

PROCEDURE

I distributed the school photos of each kid into their personal three-ring binder.

QUALITATIVE OBSERVATION #4

I felt powerful, productive, and hopeful—approximately a hep and a half of happiness. If that reaction doesn't seem totally understandable to you, perhaps it's because I haven't told you that the three-ring binders contained "pocket pages."

PROCEDURE

I moved on from the desk. It was looking pretty good and also because while returning the cross-cut saw that I found under some papers toward the back of the desk (which finally explained the sawdust in my sleeping area) to the garage, I found bags of toys.

ENVIRONMENT: GARAGE

FIELD NOTES

I was squeezing between bicycles, boxes, garden tools, and some big black bags when one of the bags came open, exposing Talking Battleship. I was shocked to find our nanny had put tons of toys into trash bags and then deposited them in the garage. I guess this seemed like a logical step to her, like giving away clothes that no longer fit. It didn't seem like a logical step to me at all. I immediately started to remove Talking Battleship to restore it to a shelf in the house, until I realized we haven't played with it for years. *Still*, I thought, *I'm alone a lot during the day, and it* does *talk*. I shuffled back and forth across the garage floor holding the bag. *I'm supposed to be getting organized*, I told myself. *I have committed to the totally unscientific study of the search for human happiness, and this could be the key.* I closed my eyes, secured the bag around its contents, and hoisted it to the car.

ANALYSIS

It killed me to get rid of my children's toys, even the ones they never really enjoyed. I think it's the pictures on the boxes that rope me in. They always show happy families, seated around the game board, with looks of surprise and excitement: all good-natured winners and losers. It looks so doable. No one is spilling a drink, flipping the board in a rage, shoving a playing piece up their nose, slipping themselves a five-hundred-dollar bill from the bank, or yelling, "It's your turn. Will you go-o-o-o!" Scenes we'd never played a game without.

Getting rid of those games and toys, to me, was an admission of failure. We couldn't even keep the batteries in the Simon, let alone follow the music and light pattern successfully when it was working.

My son did not have a wealth of frustration tolerance when he was a pup. Why I ever thought to bring the game Perfection into our home, I can't figure out, even in my moments of deepest reflection. Remember Perfection? It is a plastic box with a timer. The outside of the box has holes of different shapes. The player takes pieces of corresponding shapes and puts them into the holes. The object is to get them all in before the timer goes off, but failing that, the pieces that have already been put in spring out when the timer expires. I believe there was a loud ticking noise as well.

We played Perfection exactly once. I never even found all of the pieces to put them back in the box afterward. Those that I could find have been in a zipper-lock bag in a drawer in the kitchen, in case I ever needed spare parts for a new Perfection game to replace the one Thomas E smashed to a fine powder after the timer went off and the plastic shapes sprung from it. I think there is still a hole in the ceiling from where his head shot through.

FIELD NOTES

I did snatch back the Game of Life from the clutches of the Hefty bag. We get a kick out of playing it every so often, but the only realistic part of the game is that my plastic pink peg gained weight and can't fit in my plastic car playing piece anymore. The rest may be giving the children the wrong impression of adult life. First of all, only one event can befall a player per space. You might land on a space where you have to pay taxes, a space where you lose your job, a space where you have to pay for your child's music lessons or some medical expense, but it's one at a time. You can't land on a space where on tax day you can't go to work because your child broke your front teeth with an overzealous cello bow stroke, and because you didn't go to work you got fired. In real life, things often happen all at once.

FACTOR

Playing the Game of Life with my kids was often a jumping-off place for conversations with them about real life. For example, there is an odd rule in the game that dictates that when a player gets a baby, each of the other players must pay that player five thousand dollars. I stopped the game for a lecture when that came up. I said, "Listen to me. This is important. No one gives you five thousand dollars when you have a baby. In fact, do you want to know what happens when you have a baby? Put all of your money in the middle of the board. Okay now, Thomas E, go get the matches . . ."

We must have four versions of Monopoly, and I don't think we have ever completed an entire game. It's an interminably long game to begin with and we added an extra hour arguing because more than one of us always wanted to be the hat, or Mowgli in the Disney version, or Paul in the Beatles version or the Corrupt Governor in the Chicago version.

CONSTANT

Just as I was reinforcing, with tape, the corners of the Game of Life box, which I rescued from the trash bag in the garage, I got a call from my son's school counselor saying that he did not yet have his school planner book. Santa Monica schools call it the "Binder Reminder." This is an assignment book with a photograph of the school on the cover, pages on which to write assignments, and daily inspirational platitudes such as "Aim high," "Be a friend," and "Follow your path." I have been forced to buy these books from the school for each of my kids every year, even though Toshia and Thomas almost never write down their assignments. Every year the Binder Reminder gets more expensive, and filled with more unnecessary stuff. The high school has gotten so bad that its Binder Reminder has blanks for the student's drug dealer's phone number. The school argues that it's easier to teach responsibility with something they like.

I finally just made one for Thomas E. I bought a plain spiral notebook and wrote my own inspirational platitudes in it. On the first page I wrote, "Write down your assignments," and on the next page I wrote, "Write down your fucking assignments," and on the following page I wrote, "In the name of all that is good on the fucking planet, write down your assignments." Several pages in I wrote, "How about you do your assignments now?"

FIELD NOTES

The only thing not in my garage was a car. The garage was especially hard to organize because the sole uniting theme of its contents was that we didn't know where to put them. I started with just a corner. It was like one of those Take Back the Night marches community members undertake to regain control of their neighborhood when it has fallen into the hands of gangs.

EQUIPMENT

I began by buying a cheap vacuum cleaner. We owned a few, but they were in the garage. I couldn't find them.

LABORATORY ASSISTANT

My friend Wendell uses my garage for his tools. My assistant of many years has left, so Wendell works part-time as my assistant now. He is a brilliant engineer-builder type. He's extremely funny, a naturally sarcastic man who not only sees the glass half-empty but also suspects that someone may have spit in it. I often accuse him of being in the Negative Club. He has been fixing things for us for years. In our last house, he had our garage so organized we had our Ping-Pong parties in there. It was fantastic.

CONDITIONS

That was our plan when we first moved here, but our garage suffered the brunt of the trauma of the bag and box pileup caused by the bigger-house to smaller-house move. The Partridge Family used their garage for band practice, and it always looked so nice. There was never an episode where Danny freaked out because he got cobwebs in his hair, or Laurie wouldn't touch the mic chord because she found rat poop on it. I got so jealous that I could barely watch it anymore.

FIELD NOTES

It was almost impossible for me to clean the garage without Wendell's help, because I couldn't even identify most of what was out there. Time and time again I'd spend hours cleaning some important-looking metal thing that turned out to be packaging, or I'd pull from the wall what appeared to be a jagged piece of metal trash, only to hear a groan of wood and see the entire garage list to the left.

Wendell came over to help and he mocked me mercilessly over the new vacuum. Especially when he watched me sweep and then whisk-broom each section before vacuuming, so as not to stress the vacuum or overload its small canister. I'll tell you, though, on the happiness scale, whisking that debris into the dustpan was unbelievable. After about my third dustpan full, I said to Wendell, "For me, this is better than sex."

And he said, "I don't think you've been doing it right."

That is no doubt true, but if cleaning the garage felt this good, why bother?

CONDITIONS

Two large mysterious filing cabinets filled the corner of the garage. I didn't remember purchasing them. I thought they were there when we moved in. They were old and rusty. It looked like maybe down underneath the drawers, there might be an undisclosed treasure of California history, an original Raymond Chandler manuscript, a picture of John Wayne with a toy poodle or of Ronald Reagan making out with Linda Ronstadt and signed "Let me be your Desperado-do-do-do." I really had no idea what was in those cabinets. I had never had cause to open them before.

FIELD NOTES

Now, in the pursuit of the totally unscientific study of the search for human happiness, I grabbed a handle, pinched the button with my thumb, and pulled open a long drawer packed, *packed* with papers. I tugged out paper after paper from the folders, which took very seriously their job of holding the papers. Some papers tore in half before I could wrench them all of the way out.

It turns out my former assistant had been using these file cabinets. I often saw her make copies of papers and sometimes she told me that she had this thing or that on file. I always assumed she meant the small file cabinet near the big desk at the business end of the ballroom.

She kept copies all right. She had saved children's clothing catalogs, with the items I had ordered circled and dated from when they were toddlers. It's a damned shame I'm not a beloved historic figure. This cabinet contained all of the elements of a fascinating Paula Poundstone Museum.

"If you'll step this way, you'll see Ms. Poundstone's catalog orders. As you can see she dressed her children in almost exclusively Disney garments, and historians believe this is due to her unfulfilled desire be a bear in the Disney World parade in Orlando, Florida, instead of working the graveyard shift at the IHOP there.

"No need to crowd, you'll all get to see."

One folder had instruction manuals for cars I didn't, at first, even remember owning. Fortunately, my former assistant had clipped careful documentation, including photographs, of every dent, ding, sideswipe, and bumper loss each vehicle had sustained. She even kept the old key fobs.

"This room contains almost a complete history of Ms. Poundstone's automotive life. I hope you can hear me in the back. Are there any questions?"

"Is it true she pioneered the modern "driverless car"?

"Well, not exactly, she pioneered the need for the driverless car. She also did jump out of a moving car once, but that was only in her driveway. She forgot a soda and went back inside forgetting that the car was still in drive. Perhaps that's what you're thinking of. Anyone else?"

"Would it be all right if I just clicked one of the key fobs?"

"Certainly. For those of you who want to come to a closer understanding of what it was like to be Paula Poundstone, you can come up here, pick a car key fob, and click it a few hundred times, which she often did in parking lots when she lost her car. Her neighbors said they'd frequently heard the car chirp several times hours after she went into the house, because she couldn't remember if she'd locked it.

"She used this fob here to open the wrong car door and curse loudly, pretty much every morning. She was a beloved member of her neighborhood."

I felt like a champion when I got a whole corner of my garage clean and organized, but even as I worked on the file cabinet, the scrap wood, broken electronics, and tools that had to be hidden from my son to keep him from dismantling me in my sleep, seemed to multiply. I almost filled the ninety-six-gallon recycle bin in our alley with papers. I got about four book boxes of papers that had to be shredded, for security purposes. Although I don't know why I should worry about identity theft. I dare someone else to be me. They'd collapse like a marionette with its strings cut before they even made it to the Best Buy to run up a bill.

ANALYSIS

It took me weeks to clear a corner of space in the garage, during which time the several areas I had busted my ass to organize in the house were in disturbingly similar condition to that which they'd been in when I began months and months ago. Organizing was driving me insane. I felt like such a loser. I'd find Ping-Pong balls in the drawer with my toothbrush no matter how many times I returned them to the garage. It was a goddamned tragedy, that's what it was. My closet seemed like a hill that neither side could hold on to in a war. Currently, it has, again, fallen into the hands of the enemy. The gleaming surface of my desk has disappeared beneath a tide that includes scattered bits of paper bearing inklings for jokes like, "Justin Bieber, football and prayer," "Touch where you want to sit," and "predictable nipples." Mixed among the inklings are travel itineraries, correspondence, receipts, warranties, reminders—a six-inch depth of disgusting paper bilge.

QUALITATIVE OBSERVATION #5
It's the "*stay* organized" that's the kicker.

QUALITATIVE OBSERVATION #6
Science sucks.

QUANTITATIVE OBSERVATION #3
There is no way I can do this alone.

CONCLUSION
EXPERIMENTAL ERROR

THE
GET REEL
EXPERIMENT

IN OLD SCI-FI movies, there is always a girlfriend who worries about the young increasingly mad scientist.

"I don't like it when you spend so much time in your laboratory."

"Darling, it's for science."

"You're different now."

"Why, whatever do you mean?"

"You're using yourself as a human guinea pig. I heard screaming down there last night. I'm frightened."

"You meddling fool! Now you know too much!"

CONDITIONS

My kids started looking at me funny during my cascade into madness caused by the first Get Organized experiment.

"Mom, you're never going to get the cats to sleep in alphabetical order."

"Why, don't be foolish. Of course I can. Brittle, sit. Clue, come here . . ."

It took months to recover. During that time, though, Thomas E did have an encouraging academic breakthrough that lifted my spirits. He had been doing poorly on tests left and right. I had always told him, "You've got to write down when you have an upcoming test and prepare for it." He would look at me with such suspicion, as if I were telling him some wild superstitious ritual, asking him to swing a dead chicken over his head or wear a clove of garlic around his neck during the test. But just recently, he actually told me that he had a test coming up. I was so proud. I said, "Good for you, Thomas E! What's the test on?"

He said, "I don't know. I'm going to ask the teacher."

It's a step! At least the fact that there is a test won't come as a total surprise. Prior to this breakthrough, every test, no matter how much its arrival had been heralded, was a pop quiz to my Thomas E. He sees no patterns in the routine of life. He is surprised by every school day, every meal, every bedtime, every parting. It's all pop. He experiences pop Christmas, pop seasons, pop spring, pop winter, pop twenty-first century.

Last night, Alley had fifty AP history questions that covered half the textbook. She said it was just assigned yesterday, and the class had to complete it last night because they had to turn in their textbooks today. This is quite within the character of her AP history class. It is crammed in so quickly as to be pointless. She wanted my help and asked me a lot of questions about what caused this war and that. What caused the Revolutionary War? What caused the Civil War? What caused the war with Mexico? The short answer is, of course, money, but I told her to always include the phrase "People were irked" so that it sounded as though she really knew the material. One question was, "Where did Lee surrender?" I told her we didn't even need the textbook for that. It was right near the Union troops, I would imagine.

I feel sorry for kids studying history now, because there's so much more of it than when I was a kid. Half our AP history book was only twenty questions. Alley asked me a question about Watergate one day. I thought it was for her current events class. She said, no, it was history. I said, "It is not."

Alley is a good student. I like helping her because she actually listens to what I say and follows directions. This delights me. I say it, she does it. I'm like an ape with a flashlight. I just can't get over that it happens. I'd never experienced that before.

Some of my favorite times with Alley were when she'd ask me to help her with math. We'd wait till the others were in bed and my chores were done, and then we'd sit on the living-room floor and I'd give what aid I can. One night not too long ago, she asked me for help, and after spending several minutes flipping through a few different textbooks, I announced that we had come to the day that I had long dreaded, a kind of rite of passage. We had reached the point where instead of being a mom who could help with math, I had become an elderly woman who could sit beside her while she did math.

HYPOTHESIS

Alley will be leaving for college soon. For better or for worse, there's not much time left for us all to be together. So in the aftermath of the crash-and-burn Get Organized experiment, when my kids begged me to make good on a promise to watch movies all day, it sounded pretty fine to me.

CONSTANT

Television is not allowed in our house. My kids may only watch videos or DVDs, and never during the day and only on non-school nights. So this idea of all-day viewing was an especially exotic one.

ENVIRONMENT

I'm not proud of this, but the idea of sitting in a chair for a happiness experiment very much appealed to me. Although my living-room chairs by most people's standards are uninhabitable, they were once beautiful custom-made, comfortable, stuffed chairs. Two were covered in green-and-white thick striped chintz fabric and two were covered in a thicker fabric, with a burgundy floral pattern. In recent years, they've been customized by cats. My cats have gone way beyond tearing holes in the fabric sharpening their claws. They've torn out the stuffing, which is just as well, because they've thrown up or peed on so much of the stuffing, we're better off without it.

I've gone to the trouble of purchasing chair covers, but of course, it doesn't help much with the smell. I spray copious amounts of Nature's Miracle on the chairs and elsewhere each day, trying to combat the smell, but I am losing the battle. The chair covers don't even come in nice colors. They are chair shrouds, and in our house they are generally covered in cat hair or, of course, actual cats. If one has the strength to lift our twenty-pound cat, Matilda, off a chair, she will squall pathetically, because she doesn't like to heft that twenty pounds either, before she moves to another chair.

Now we're down to three chairs, because one was so rank

with pee there was no miracle of nature that could save it. The miracle is that I still have cats after what they have done to our living space. In fact, we've recently gotten a few more. I did finally replace the shredded oatmeal color carpet with some green carpet. I purposely got ugly carpet, so I don't care when they throw up on it. It's interior design genius.

I don't have much else in the way of furniture. I use a large dog cage for a coffee table, which works fine, since I hate coffee, and I have a shiny, painted, wooden sculpture of a butler, who holds a small tray with enough space for a couple of diet sodas.

Then, of course, there's the forty-inch flat-screen television, which sits atop a glass stand. On the stand, beneath the TV, there is a collection of machines, buttons, boxes, chords, and remote controls that frighten me, all with a faint smell of cat pee. We have a laser disc player, a VCR, a rewinder, a DVD player, a Blu-ray disc player, and a box with buttons that you push depending on which device you're using. Buzz Aldrin couldn't figure out the sequence of buttons to push to watch a movie in my house.

The glass stand is in front of a shelf that holds poster paints, a tie-dye kit that we've never gotten around to using (except that one time during the first Get Organized experiment), a couple of books of third-grade-level quiz questions that say "fun for the whole family" right on the covers, yet many of the questions are too hard for us, which some of the family doesn't find fun; a stack of laser discs, three family photos that prove that we were happy, three times, for at least as long as the shutter speed, and a few badminton birdies that, when hit back and forth with the accompanying plastic drum paddles, make a wonderfully satisfying sound. Our top sustained rally, by the way, was seventeen.

Between the shelf and the glass stand is a mass of cords that looks like the snakes in Indiana Jones's archaeological dig where the ark is hidden in *Raiders of the Lost Ark*.

FACTORS

Toshia will generally go along with Alley, but Alley and Thomas E argue about everything. They disagree for sport. It is the same no matter what we're doing. If I seek their opinions on where we should eat, for example, it adds hours to the decision, and yet they like the same restaurants. I once handed them each a piece of paper, told them not to say a word, but to just write down their top three dinner restaurant choices. They knew what I was driving at right away, so they hesitated, then stared at each other like poker players looking for an opponent's tell. They wanted desperately to write answers different from one another. I could see the wheels turning. "I like Border Grill, but Alley likes Border Grill, so I'll say Chuck E. Cheese's, even though I don't like Chuck E. Cheese's . . . No, she'll probably say Chuck E Cheese's, because she knows I don't like Chuck E. Cheese's. No, I'll say Ed's Slop House . . . No, she'll say Ed's Slop House, and then we'll have to eat at Ed's Slop House. Wait, no, I'll say the Just Past the Expiration Date Cafe. If she says that, too, we'll go there and she'll get sick, like the last time. No, wait, I got sick the last time."

They sat there, gripping their pencils, trying to read the other's thoughts. They began to sweat. It was high noon for restaurant choices. Finally, I could see them each concede mentally that it was easier just to play this one straight. They jotted down their top three restaurant choices and there they were, the exact same. They chose Toscana, Border Grill, and the Daily Grill. I said, "So that's where all of our time goes," and we dined at the Just Past the Expiration Date Cafe as a punishment. It was yogurt night.

VARIABLES

We have tons of movies. I know one can do something computery to get movies or use Netflix, but I like seeing the picture on the box. I still have a VCR. People often make fun of me about that, but the VCR still works, even with cat pee in it. I don't understand why everyone else got rid of theirs. If people get rid of their VCRs, how will they watch their videotapes? When digital photography came on the scene, did everyone throw out their old photographs? In addition to the two walls covered in shelves of videotapes in my bedroom, there's a floor-to-ceiling shelf of DVDs in the hallway. Some are still wrapped in cellophane, because I like to have them, but I certainly don't have time to sit around watching movies all day. Until now.

Despite my bountiful supply of movies and television shows, Thomas E and Alley wanted a different selection, so on the night before the experiment, I took them to a video store and allowed them each to choose a couple of films. This seemed fair. Normally, when we watch a movie, I insist that they find a movie they can agree on. I do this because cock fighting is illegal.

The minute we entered the store, I realized I had made a mistake. In my children's efforts to each be their own person, they gravitate to ghastly film choices. I thought I heard Thomas E ask the clerk directions to the Unwatchable section. They felt the need to make a deliberate break from the bondage of years of happily viewing Abbott and Costellos, Harry Potters, the *Toy Story* trilogy, Broadway musicals, *Star Wars*, and beloved Disney films to the world of salacious and violent films. It didn't occur to me to give them any guidelines for their film choices, so they seemed to choose them like weapons, looking for the film that would do the most harm to the other viewers. Shall we say *I Know What You Did Last Summer* at dawn?

FIELD NOTES
The morning of watching movies all day:

8:30 A.M.
I got up to do my chores. With my bed folded, the dogs and cats fed, the litter boxes sifted, the breakfast prepared and eaten, the dishes done, the visible territorial cat pee wiped up and sprayed, the dogs put out, the dogs brought in, the cats' food filled, water bowl emptied and replaced with clean fresh water (into which they moments later dropped more kibble), I was ready to turn the living-room chairs toward the big screen and begin.

10:09 A.M.
We put on my choice first: *Hugo*.

10:10 A.M.
I let the dogs in.

I didn't know what it was about ahead of time, but it was an oddly appropriate film for our experiment, as it told the story of people whose lives were uplifted by film and filmmaking. The ending was quite moving, so Thomas E had to raid the pantry for potato chips, chomp them loudly, crinkle the bag, and put his face in mine and ask, "Are you crying?"

12:09 P.M.

Thomas E couldn't wait to whip out *The Immortals*, the first movie he had chosen. I had no idea what it was. Alley said it was violent. I looked at the jacket. On the front there was a picture of lots of Greek soldiers in armor, angrily swinging swords. I scanned the synopsis on the back. "Power-hungry Hyperion (Mickey Rourke) and his ruthless army march across Greece, leaving burned-out villages and the corpses of the innocent in their wake." I said, "*Hugo* doesn't exactly dovetail into *The Immortals*, Thomas."

"But you said . . ." he responded, which is one of my least favorite kid arguments.

I try not to make promises I can't keep, but occasionally there are unforeseen circumstances that preclude being able to make good on a plan. Thomas E has no concept of this. I could fall into an unfortunate coma and my son would lean over my bedridden body and say, "But you said you'd . . ."

"Thomas, yes, I said you could choose a film. I didn't think I had to say that it couldn't be mindless, senseless, life-devaluing, exploitative violent crap that I have never allowed into our home. Just because we are taking the unusual step of watching movies all day to see if it will make us happy, which I think I know the sad answer to already, doesn't mean we're throwing our taste and sensibilities out the door."

We finally talked him into his second choice. His second choice, unfortunately, was *Fast Five*. Thomas E coached me as I studied the cover carefully. "It's about racing, Mom."

12:20 P.M.
We pushed Play to begin viewing: *Fast Five*. The choice of theatrical version or extended version appeared on the screen. Alley, Toshia, and I almost blew Thomas E out of his chair eagerly shouting, "Theatrical version!" at the exact same time.

12:35 P.M.
There's been almost no dialogue, but a man was roped around the neck and pulled from a speeding car in the desert. Vin Diesel punched several people. The handsome lead had to wrestle away from a man trying to blowtorch his face. There was more punching, and then Vin Diesel and the handsome lead had to drive a car over a cliff, where they landed in the water, were taken captive by several indiscriminate angry, sweaty men and suspended by chains in a dungeon, from which they were able to escape and punch some more people. A threat was made about someone's sister.

Thomas E is trying desperately to enjoy this. I could hear his frontal lobe stop developing.

12:55 P.M.
There's been no racing.

1:03 P.M.
Vin Diesel just said his third line.

1:12 P.M.

I made some buttered popcorn, ate it, and watched my thighs grow. When I looked up, many unidentified characters were dead and I fit less comfortably into my chair.

I can't go on. I know this is unfair. I know some people like this shit, but after fifty minutes of car crashes, gunshots, macho monosyllabic grunts, and some sort of inferred tormented backstory ("I don't like to talk about what happened in Reno"), I begged Thomas E to turn it off. I said, "If you can explain to me what's good about this, I'll listen. Is there a story?" I tried to explain to him what qualities go into a good movie. "There's a message. The characters go through something that makes them better people, we see ourselves in their struggles, or they lift our hearts with laughter."

I could see he wasn't getting it. I said, "Let me make the definition of a good film simpler. Vin Diesel's not in it."

1:15 P.M.

I let the dogs out.

1:30 P.M.

We argued, and argued and argued. Not a hep of happiness in sight.

1:45 P.M.

Alley took a turn playing a film of her choosing: *Crazy, Stupid Love.*

As soon as he saw the cover of the film, Thomas E, who lives in fear that the rest of the world is constantly engaged in a sexual conversation so cryptic as to be behind his back, in front of his face, asked eagerly, "What's 'stupid love?'" I said, "It's like sixty-nine, but it's added incorrectly."

I trust Alley. However, in this case, that was a mistake. *Crazy, Stupid Love* did not make me happy at all. It stars Steve Carell. I love Steve Carell, but now I don't trust him or Alley.

In our family, we take a certain personal pride in the films that we like, as if we wrote, produced, directed, and starred in them ourselves. I confess that I also judge, quite harshly, the film preferences of others.

Toshia once said her favorite actor was Patrick Swayze. I asked her when she ever saw a Patrick Swayze movie and she said, "At school, we watched him in *A Street Car Named Desire* in English."

I couldn't believe it. Toshia's high school education has been almost criminally negligent. There were instances of egregious teaching practices, but if I sued the district, I wouldn't confuse the judge with any of those examples, of which I have dozens. I would simply say, "Your honor, they showed her English class the Patrick Swayze version of *A Street Car Named Desire*. I rest my case," and I believe we would receive the full extent of damages awarded in such cases.

1:56 P.M.
I let the dogs in.

2:27 P.M.
This film may have permanently damaged my relationship with my formerly beloved daughter Alley. She was a fan of Olsen twin movies when she was little, but she outgrew them. This, though?

She'll be eligible to vote in just a couple of years, and she's making me sit through *Crazy, Stupid Love*?

In this, as in many movies, mysteriously, no one in the story seems to have to work with any particular schedule. Steve Carell and Julianne Moore play a couple who split up and then receive counsel about love from their thirteen-year-old son, who doesn't require any support at all to cope with their divorce. For most of the first half of the movie, the screen was obscured from my view by our new kitten's butt. I let Thomas E choose a kitten at the animal shelter. He named it Theo. Theo is a very friendly kitten, with gas.

From what I could see of the movie, the first half included lots of scenes of a pickup-artist character telling Steve Carell that he couldn't get women because he didn't dress the right way. Anybody who has ever seen even a few minutes of Jerry Springer knows that's not true. In the beginning of the film, Steve Carell's wife had an affair. The only explanation the film offered is that Steve Carell wore sneakers and drank from a straw. Then, in the end, it turns out that Steve Carell and Julianne Moore are "soul mates." She simply hadn't realized this while she was having sex with Kevin Bacon. That can happen.

I moved stinky Theo off my lap about fifty times. It's going to turn out he's my soul mate. He might have been reviewing the film. Instead of "two thumbs up," Theo gives it a "breathe through your mouth for a while."

3:27 P.M.
I'm crazy with relief to say that, all of the soul mates in the film have been paired off, and it's over. I let the dogs out and apologized for making them sit through *Crazy, Stupid Love*.

ANALYSIS

This was turning out to be a far more challenging experiment than I had anticipated. Not so much as a hep of happiness had come my way. Even sitting in a chair wasn't all I had thought it would be. My tailbone was going numb.

3:30 P.M.

Having patiently waited her turn to choose a film, Toshia turned to the video shelf and reached for what I could tell was a Disney film. Obese Matilda was on my lap, so I could barely breathe, let alone see exactly which Disney film Toshia selected. I love Disney films, so I was relieved. That's a girl, Toshia! Then, as she walked past my chair, she wordlessly tilted the cover in my direction, like someone surreptitiously tugs up their shirt to expose the hilt of their holstered gun, and there it was: the animated version of *Cinderella*, perhaps the only Disney film that I loathe, and Toshia knows it. Toshia skipped a grade in passive aggressive class.

Of course, it's my fault for ever showing this movie to my kids, but in my defense, I had no way of knowing it would become Toshia's religion. She doesn't say it out loud, but Toshia seems to believe that she is Cinderella and therefore I am the evil stepmother. For this reason, I really hate *Cinderella*.

3:45 P.M.

I'm not proud of this, but I couldn't hear the words from Cinderella's hit single, "A Dream Is a Wish Your Heart Makes," which my daughter eats up like sugary cereal, without rebuttal, and my entire lower region had lost blood flow, so I struggled from my seat, grabbed an imaginary ballroom partner, and spun around the room singing, "If your heart doesn't talk your brain and other body parts into doing some actual work, it can kiss its wish good-bye." Not one of my children took their eyes off of the screen.

"I'm going to close my eyes while my heart makes a wish. Now, I'll open them and see if my dream came true. Nope, *Cinderella*'s still on.

"There aren't even any lines in her hair," I said, plopping back down in my chair. "It's just a hair blob."

If they weren't listening, I could say anything I wanted. "I've been to her castle. There's mouse poop all over the inside. That's the drawback of hiring mice."

"Birds help her make her bed? How hard is it to pull up some sheets and a blanket? She has to have birds help her? I'll bet it's bad for their beaks. They don't show it, but I'll bet just out of camera range their beaks fall off, and they flap on the floor in bloody agony. PETA should target Cinderella."

"Isn't she a grown woman? Can't she leave anytime she wants? But, no, she has to hang around whining and forcing woodland animals into domestic service. If she's so miserable in her stepmother's house, why doesn't she try sitting on a stool in the corner of the bus station?"

"See? To me, the Fairy Godmother is an enabler. If Cinderella, a grown woman, sits in a corner and cries, she gets her wish. Perfect."

"Glass does not make good footwear."

"What kind of mileage you think that pumpkin gets?"

"What do you do if your pumpkin breaks down? Better have Farmers Insurance."

"So she lies to her stepmother. Uh-huh."

"One dance and they're ready to marry. They must have talked fast. On their second time around the ballroom he asked her if she likes the toilet paper roll to unwind over or under."

"I'd rather marry Vin Diesel."

My children paid no attention to me at all.

5:10 P.M.

Cinderella was over. When that glorious THE END sign came up, it was like hearing the doctor say, "We've stopped the internal bleeding." I was certainly happy that it was over, but this was not the kind of happiness I'd had in mind when we began this experiment.

5:13 P.M.

I let the dogs in.

5:15 P.M.

Mercifully, it was my turn to choose again. It was like waiting for my up at bat. When I produced my videotape copy of *The In-Laws*, and of course, I mean the Peter Falk/Alan Arkin version, all three kids complained and asked suspiciously what it was about. I said, "You just have to watch." Thomas E's cart is permanently hitched before his horse. He reads the last page of a book first. I had to repeat "Just watch" several times. Part of it was, of course, because his film choices were so soundly vetoed that he felt the need to find fault in my choice. But also, he's just like that. He wants to get to the part where he says he doesn't like it as soon as possible.

Alley is of a mind that if a film was made before she was born, it can't be good, which is weird coming from a kid who plays classical music.

They were all determined not to enjoy anything I chose.

It was shocking what a bad time we were having. Thomas E became obstinate. I asked him not to eat cereal in the living room. He sat right beside me and ate four or five bowls of Rice Krispies. Crackle just stared at him.

I deemed it best just to get the film started as fast as I could, but my legs had fallen asleep, so I had to commando crawl to the VCR. I popped in the tape, and my heart made a wish.

Within minutes we were laughing. I want to give credit where credit is due. Alan Arkin isn't capable of not being funny (except in *Wait Until Dark* where he plays a vicious killer and torments Audrey Hepburn while she's blind) and we will repeat our impression of Peter Falk saying, "This man. Sheldon Kornpett, I call him, 'Shelly' . . . ," for months, I'm sure, but I also think the stress of hours of "family time" had to find relief eventually. It's possible that we would have laughed at *Cinderella 2: The Step-Mother Moves into the Castle* by then, but I did feel a sense of satisfaction that it was my pick that finally cracked the nut.

6:49 P.M.
I let the dogs out.

7:00 P.M.
Perhaps because of the success of *The In-Laws* viewing experience, we were able to agree on *Willy Wonka and the Chocolate Factory* for our next film, and in it went.

7:15 P.M.

We saw that Charlie's life seemed bleak, but he was able to keep a positive attitude nonetheless. As if to make clear that he was impenetrable to any film's message, Thomas E began to whine that there was a glare on the screen. Not wanting to lose the fraction of a hep of happiness that we'd managed to nurse along after the healing dose of *The In-Laws*, I switched seats with him. I noticed he had spilled some juice on the floor and then ignored it.

"Could you clean up the juice you spilled?"

"I didn't spill any juice."

"Yes, you did. It's right by the chair that you were sitting in."

"Where?"

"Right here by the overturned cup."

"I didn't spill it."

"Well, then, perhaps you just don't know how to use a cup. It works better with the closed part at the bottom, like this."

"Mom, we can't hear the movie."

"Well, Thomas spilled some juice on the floor."

"You are so OCD."

"It's not particularly OCD to not allow juice to puddle on the carpet. Thomas, I wouldn't even mind that much cleaning it up, but this thing where you just say you didn't when you clearly did is infuriating!"

"Okay, I spilled it."

"Great! Clean it up!"

"But you said . . ."

"Well, yes, if you had admitted it to begin with, but not now!"

"Shuuush! We can't hear."

7:40 P.M.

The gluttonous Augustus Gloop character just ate the interviewer's microphone.

Thomas E headed for the kitchen to get some ice cream. I said, "Is any of this ringing a bell?"

7:55 P.M.

Gene Wilder hobbles out of the chocolate factory. "God, I love him," I say. "Remember when he was there when I hosted the Art Directors Guild Awards? That was a fantastic night. I was coached by Carl Reiner, heckled by Mel Brooks, and kissed by Gene Wilder."

"Shuuush, we can't hear!"

"I'm glad we're doing this. I feel so much closer to you guys."

8:45 P.M.

Theo was asleep on the glass shelf beside the laser disc player, and Tonks was perched beside the VHS player, which was covered by a thick layer of dust. Brittle, Hardy, and Severus were squeezed into the chair with me and were becoming perturbed by the onset of my restless leg syndrome.

I felt gross.

8:50 P.M.

Charlie has been given the deed to the chocolate factory and there was a permanent butt imprint in my chair. I had a raging headache and my knees stiffened, which was unfortunate because just before the closing credits rolled, I heard a cat throw up in the other room.

8:55 P.M.

I cleaned cat vomit off of the new Dr. Seuss print fabric on the rocking chair in the ballroom. I don't know which cat it was. I was feeling bitter toward all of them. By the way, the Dr. Seuss print fabric is *my* taste, it is no longer my children's.

The dogs were barking in the backyard again.

"Could someone please let the dogs in? Do you guys not hear them barking? I don't know why they ever wrote that 'Who Let the Dogs Out?' song. Clearly it was me."

9:00 P.M.

I could no longer ignore the smell coming from the litter boxes. I insisted we take a chore break. Someone recently calculated that if James Bond had drunk and had sex as often as Ian Fleming said he did, he would have died of an STD or alcohol poisoning within the pages of the first book in which he appears, but I reveal to you only a small fraction of the times I sift litter boxes. I sifted and felt better. It may be where my strength comes from.

The chore break was deeply satisfying. After convincing Thomas E that he had dropped his sock in the yard when he brought the laundry in off the line and must go get it, we put in *Harry Potter and the Goblet of Fire*.

My kids were raised on the Harry Potter stories. I read the entire series to them twice. They read some on their own. As I have mentioned, we have listened many times to Jim Dale reading them in the audio version. Plus, we saw each of the movies in the theater when they came out and purchased them for multiple subsequent viewings as soon as they were available on DVD.

This was a good thing, because my cat Luigi kept blocking the screen and no one would get up to move him. He's quite large. We often couldn't see Ron.

We weren't just watching the film. We were watching very carefully. "Why do the Durmstrang and Beauxbatons vehicles arrive before Dumbledore has explained the Triwizard Tournament?"

"Why did the vampire from *Twilight* just put his name into the Goblet of Fire?"

"Why doesn't Ron use magic to repair his dress robes?"

"Where do you see Ron?"

"Will someone get that fucking cat out of the way?"

"Why is Neville better looking than Ron and Harry?"

"That's not Ron."

"Why is Luigi better looking than Ron?"

11:00 P.M.

The conclusion of *Harry Potter and the Goblet of Fire* gave way to another round of snacking and dog entrances and exits. Thomas E asked me, with only thinly veiled outrage, "Aren't you going to make dinner?"

"No, because we've been eating all day, it's eleven o'clock at night, and I'm not Mrs. Weasley."

11:10 P.M.

Alley loves the show *The Mentalist*. She owns every season on DVD. I have begged her not to make me watch it, because I know once I start I won't stop. I haven't watched a prime-time television show since Radar left *M*A*S*H*, for just that reason. My middle child poisoned the minds of the others, however, and they presented a united front, voting to watch a couple of episodes of this Simon Baker vehicle.

11:15 P.M.

We dropped *The Mentalist* DVD into the tray and pushed it closed. Simon Baker stars as a consultant to a fictitious but elite branch of California law enforcement called the CBI and uses his skills as a con artist to solve its most vexing of crimes.

The murder scenes tend to be rather graphic, which I don't feel good about Thomas E seeing because he gets scared. In fact, he asked me nervously, "Mom, if I were killed, would the CBI investigate?"

I said, "No, honey, I think I would just confess."

It's probably not a wise idea in our house to celebrate the achievements of a con artist, but I have to confess, I really enjoyed the episodes and so did the others.

12:40 A.M.

I had never seen *Rio*, starring Jesse Eisenberg, but again my kids miraculously all agreed on it, so we spun the disc.

1:05 A.M.

Rio is an animated film about tropical birds in Brazil. My cats loved it. Ten of them were standing directly in front of the screen. Their tails were twitching, they were drooling and making that little "ack-ack-ack" sound that kind of slips out of them when they're stalking prey. They seemed to have no idea it's animated.

1:15 A.M.

This was a wonderful movie. We were laughing and enjoying it all the more because we were together. Funny things are funnier in a group. Jesse Eisenberg is fantastic, and he gets along with others much better than when he was Mark Zuckerberg.

I tried to use this as another teachable moment. "See, Thomas? He does much better without all of that computer crap."

"Mom, that's because he's a bird."

"Well, it's costly, but I'd be willing to work more for you to have the surgery."

2:20 A.M.

Rio was over. The birds were happy. We were happy. I couldn't help thinking, though, that this would have been an entirely different film if Hitchcock had directed it.

2:22 A.M.

My restless leg syndrome was so severe, I think my legs had simply hopped away on their own, leaving my torso no choice but to slide almost prone in my chair. By now we all had hair that was kind of matted to the back of our heads, and we smelled a bit. My back was killing me, but we weren't done.

We love *I Love Lucy*. Since Alley was very little, given the chance to choose what to watch, she'd ask for an *I Love Lucy*. The show is part of our DNA. So it makes sense, that after almost sixteen hours of searching for happiness watching videos and DVDs, we still had a craving for an episode of Lucy, Ricky, Fred, and Ethel. Being connoisseurs, we began with "The Saxophone." Being exhausted, I couldn't keep my eyes open. I can only assume that Ricky didn't want Lucy in the show. My head bobbed. I'd jolt awake, and try again to remain that way. I'd hear a kid say, "Mom, are you awake?" and just manage to get out an "Of course," before I dropped off again.

2:47 A.M.

"The Saxophone " was over. I woke up to the familiar "duh duh duh duh duh da da da" theme song and, incredibly the sound of my kids saying, "Can we watch one more?"

They selected "The Handcuffs." I insisted that this be the last and, despite being unable to stand, wobbled to bed with their assurance that when it was over, they would do the same. I could hear them laughing at Lucy pretending her arms were Ricky's. God, I love the sound of their laughter. I came back out because I remembered I had to sift the litter boxes and let the dogs out.

CONCLUSION

We're already planning another all day movie-watching event for sometime in the distant future. If we did it any more than once a year, we'd just be a houseful of lazy losers. It obviously didn't make us happy the entire time, but we're going to agree on the films in advance next time. We've pinpointed that mistake as our downfall. Besides, deep down inside, we all believe—and continue to believe—that this really could make us fantastically happy in the moment. During the most stressful parts of any ordeal, I've secretly harbored the idea that nothing can break me, because someday I'll just sit on my ass and watch videos all day. It's almost better that someday never comes.

THE
GET ORGANIZED
EXPERIMENT: PART TWO

CONDITIONS

If Thomas Edison's kids played sports and instruments, we'd still be using candles. Months have gone by since my last experiment. Alley's school and orchestra schedule have crowded out gymnastics. Thomas E left gymnastics as well and joined the Santa Monica rugby team. Now I drive him to a practice field a few nights a week, and Toshia and I walk Ramona while we watch and learn this very rough sport. Thomas E's coaches are all British. It always sounds like he's being yelled at by the Beatles. I'm pretty sure I've heard Coach James scream, "I am the walrus," after he shouts, "You've got to be faster!"

I've been haunted by the failure of my first Get Organized experiment and I wonder if the fact that I wasn't able to successfully organize my home is a contributing factor in the snail's pace of my happiness study. I feel like I have the pedal to the metal all of the time, and yet I never get anything accomplished. It's like I'm on a treadmill in space.

HYPOTHESIS

I never considered hiring a professional organizer because they're pricey and I heard they do absurd stuff like make you put everything you own out on your front lawn. But I had never been practically strangled by the tenacious vines of the kudzu of things in my closet before.

I needed help. Using a professional organizer could be just the ticket, and now that I was thinking about it, the look of my front lawn might be improved by being covered in everything I owned.

PROCEDURE

I walked right into the dragon's mouth; I interviewed professional organizers. The first woman had a business card bearing an illustration of a flower with a rhinestone center on it, which was a clue that we would not have been a match. I think I would have ended up with a lot of stuff stored in gingham-lined baskets. She seemed like she'd be the type to be all nice until she came across the stacks of jeans that I'm holding on to in hopes of someday fitting into them again. Then she'd make me put them on my head and sit in the front yard along with everything I owned.

It was fortunate that she had a business card. It was my only real clue about her. I was so nervous during the interview, I forgot to ask her any questions. After an hour, she knew all about my great-aunt Irene's speech impediment and that the fat on my hips itches when it's cold out. I didn't even know if she had ever had a job before.

I also passed on the severe-looking organizer. She was like Mr. Murdstone's sister from *David Copperfield*, and when I mentioned we were getting a new puppy, she shooed a cat, who was blocking her view of me, off the table and insinuated that I was some kind of animal hoarder. We did just get a long-haired kitten named Shamwow. People tend to assume you're a "crazy cat lady," when you happen to be a woman who owns a lot of cats. That's precisely why, as soon as we adopted Shamwow, I chose our new puppy, Sirius, who we'd bring home in a couple of days. If you own a lot of cats, people think you're a "crazy cat lady," but if you throw in a couple of dogs, you're an "animal lover," which carries no mental health stigma.

The interviews went on for days. After I made certain they didn't have Ben Stiller as a client, I described my life to each candidate. A couple of the interviewees told me that it looked as though I was doing really well staying organized, which is clearly an intentional technique used by the professional organizer for building the confidence of the prospective client. Otherwise, surely they would have mentioned the cat pee in the dog's crate in the living room and that I still had bottles of bubbles in four different places in my house, though my kids were twenty, seventeen, and twelve.

Simply talking to all these professionals helped me better tease out exactly what my problem was, and it wasn't just one thing. It was both organization and time management. Short of the arrival of the thirty-six-hour day and a catheter, there was just no way of cramming anything else into my weeks.

CONSTANT

A few of the professional organizers were advocates of the things-to-do list. Me, too. I'm the goddamned poster child for the things-to-do list. I actually have a list with "make list" on the list. The problem: the planned keeps taking it on the chin from the unplanned.

Yesterday, for example, Alley texted me, "Pick me up," which given the size of the world, I considered a bit vague.

Besides, it was the one day I thought I didn't have to pick her up, because she was getting a ride home from someone else, so I had planned to go to the post office, the accountant, the grocery store, and the library. But there you have it. What can you do? I picked her up.

QUALITATIVE OBSERVATION #1

There's no such thing as "time management" when you have kids.

LABORATORY ASSISTANT

I think I found the right one. I hired a woman who calls herself a "green organizer," which is right up my alley. She does, however, charge seventy-five bucks an hour, which is several blocks north of my house. She did the most brilliant thing, though. She brought in four collapsible boxes. One was for donations. One was for recyclables. One was for trash. One was for things to be relocated. Every profession should work with such a pure and efficient system. I have wasted a lot of time in therapy in my life, but I might try again if the therapist used the collapsible box system. One is for thoughts that don't help at all. One is for relationships that haven't worked. One is for stuff that worked, which you need to do again, and one is for mental health "disorders" that are not uncommon at all, needn't be a source of shame and, once recognized, can in many cases be managed effectively.

FIELD NOTES

On my first day with the Green Organizer, I stopped and reminisced a lot as we worked. If we unearthed a picture of my son in his gymnastics uniform, I'd tell a little story about him. I showed her the Ziploc bag with the snip of his great dreadlocks and pointed out how boingy and beautifully sun bleached they were on the ends before he cut them himself, back in the first grade. By the end of her first day my bill was over four hundred dollars. I vowed to take another approach the following week.

The next time the Green Organizer came to the door, I wordlessly motioned her and her collapsible boxes into my bedroom, like the third spirit in *A Christmas Carol*. I worked like a galley slave. If we discovered a picture, no matter how gorgeous, of any of my children, I said, "I've never seen that kid before." Getting professionally organized was costly. If I wanted an expensive hobby, I'd buy a horse. I was taking this seriously now.

The surface of my desk was desolate after the first day. But it wasn't because we sorted through everything; it was because the Green Organizer took what was on there and stashed it away somewhere. I had planned to ask her about it on her second visit, but at seventy-five dollars an hour, I couldn't afford to have the conversation. I suspected she was waiting to reintroduce the items later, with a little speech about how I had gotten by just fine without them and didn't I prefer a clean and tidy desk? Two can play at that game. I wasn't saying a word until she brought it up, but all the while I was quietly building my case for the return of the small toilet that my son sculpted out of paper, which had held paper clips for years.

At one point, the Green Organizer said we'd photograph the children's mementos, now stored in those large portfolios, blocking access to the back wall of my bedroom. She said we could upload the photos onto the computer, and then move the portfolios to storage. She hadn't seen my storage. There was a *Cat in the Hat* bathtub ring feeling to some of this. I kept wondering when she might bring out Thing 1 and Thing 2.

What the Green Organizer doesn't understand is that the portfolios can't just be put away somewhere. They have to be out and available when the urge to look at them hits. While I'm working in my room, Alley sometimes comes in and asks if she can go through those mementos. I'll be busily itemizing my cash expenditures from a road trip, when she starts laughing so hard she can't even tell me what she's laughing at. I have to pry the paper from her hand and read it myself, before joining her in peals of laughter, which invariably attract the others. We once found what appeared to be a first-grade assignment that had the instructions "Write a story about a snow man. You can use the back" in Ms. Suomu's hand, followed by several lines carefully spaced to accommodate the young student's large lettering. Alley had written only one line: "Jaguars live in a variety of habitats." I couldn't possibly get rid of those messy black portfolios.

How about Thomas E's math homework with this question: "If Bob buys carpet for a room that is ten feet wide by eight feet long, how many square feet of carpet will he need?" He answered, "Don't you worry about Bob." That's in there somewhere. Somewhere in those portfolios is Thomas E's "What I Did over My Summer Vacation" paper, where he has drawn us, in pencil, in a row in our bathing suits. I am in a two-piece with no potbelly. We are covered by a blue crayon wave and he wrote beneath it, "We swam in the oshion in Massachoosetts," (with Ms. Suomu's penciled-in correct spellings just below). I don't even want those organized. I want to just come upon the really great ones when one or the other of the kids occasionally goes through them. They should be all over the place, like the gold dust in *The Treasure of the Sierra Madre*.

ANALYSIS

There'd been a hep or two of happiness in getting organized with a professional organizer, but there is no shelf life to it. It's not a happiness that lasts. It's like gambling. It feels great when you are winning but absolutely miserable when you are losing, and the odds are stacked in favor of the house. It has not given me a lasting strength that could weather any storm.

CONDITION

A storm is brewing with Thomas E now that he has started middle school. He has six teachers. That's six times the homework lies of elementary school. Plus, his computer addiction is endlessly exacerbated by homework that teachers needlessly insist be done on the computer, which causes daily outbursts. There are days I long for a power outage.

CONSTANT

The entire world seems to be in denial about the effects electronics are having on all of us.

One perfectly nice mother of a very sweet friend of Thomas E's listened to me explain my son's violent, frenetic behavior caused by playing video games. Then she smiled at me, shook her head, and said, "It's their world."

It's a little early for parents to just let go of the helm. I'd say there are some steps that we could take. Would people respond that breezily if it were any other kind of addiction? "I'm trying to keep Thomas E away from heroin. He just got through a lot of the vomiting from the withdrawal. If you could kind of keep your eye on him, I'd appreciate it."

"My son is the same way. The kids love the smack, don't they? Oh well, it's their world."

Many of us have made the mistake of occupying our children with video games just to buy some time. I think tying them up would do less harm. It doesn't have to be cruel or menacing. Make a game of it. "There we go. That should keep you. I learned that last knot in the navy. By the time you get out of that, I should be off the phone." It's better than doing neurological damage. If that sounds too harsh, how about a corn maze in the backyard? Tending it could even be a family project, and once the plants are fully grown, you drop your kid at one end, call him from the other side, and run to do your errands.

QUALITATIVE OBSERVATION #2

Parenting is a lot harder than I ever thought it would be, whether your desk is clean or not.

ENVIRONMENT: CLOSET

FIELD NOTES

"What's this for?" the Green Organizer asked when she saw the three small tattered rubber boots hanging from nails just above a framed calligraphied blessing, which was balanced atop a stack of sweaters in my closet. She said it as if it were a big discovery, like when Basil Rathbone in a Sherlock Holmes movie found the linchpin piece of evidence that lesser minds had passed right by. I could tell she thought this was an easy place to begin the purge. So I explained. "When Thomas E was three years old, I bought him an authentic-looking firefighter costume for Christmas. He had had a few firefighter costumes before, but the jackets were plastic. They tore easily and a blow dryer could have melted them. Even a three-year-old could tell they were bogus. This costume had a thick quilted jacket and pants with suspenders. But, best of all, it had firefighter boots.

We were regular visitors at several fire stations. The firefighters kindly gave Thomas E a little red fire hat with every visit. He had stacks of plastic red fire hats almost as high as an extension ladder. We went so many times, he was way beyond, "Look at the big red truck!" The firefighters had started teaching him how to use the defibrillator and asking him for hazing ideas. On that Christmas night, when he was three, Thomas E slept with his new suspenders clipped to his jammies. Beside his bed sat his empty boots with the cuffs of his firefighter pants over the tops, and the pant legs telescoped within, ready to jump in with one smooth move, just like the real heroes. And for the next three years, at least, he wore firefighter boots every day of his life; hot or cold, hockey rink or the beach, tuxedo or shorts. He would wear them ragged, and I'd order another pair. The last time I cleaned out Thomas E's closet, I carried a dozen old worn-out firefighter boots to the trash in the alley. I saved just three. I hung them on these nails in my closet.

Oh, and a rabbi gave me that blessing when I did a benefit at his temple. We're atheists, but on the off chance we're wrong, a blessing is nice.

It cost me thirty-five dollars to tell the Green Organizer that story and she wasn't moved at all. I didn't let her touch the firefighter boots or the blessing.

Her next potential victim was our Buzz Lightyear action figure, whose foot broke off a couple of years ago. "His foot is broken off," she said as she removed him from his perch on the closet's top shelf, handed it to me, and waited for my response.

I said, "Yeah."

I think she thought I was going to throw him away. Jesus, there have been three Toy Story movies. Had this woman seen none of them? You don't throw away Buzz Lightyear because of a broken foot! My God, I hope I don't cut myself on the jagged edge of a tape dispenser while I'm working with her. She'll donate my body parts to science right then and there.

VARIABLE

Alley and I watched *Toy Story 3* while on a road trip to look at colleges. I recommend that when you take your child to look at colleges, you choose a different film. Perhaps *The Bad Seed*, something that will make the idea of parting more desirable.

ANALYSIS

I have spent much of Alley's high school career working on getting organized. I don't know if I can say that it has been the right priority. On the other hand, maybe she'll mention it in an application essay. "Although my mother was unable to teach me any marketable skills, her sweaters are stacked according to fluffiness." If the admissions officer who reads it has OCD, it could score Alley some big points.

CONSTANT

In our house, Alley is a rock star. She does amazing things, like bring her ID, which students are required to have to enter school, to school. With skills like these, I can't imagine what more she could possibly need from college. I guess she's going to go, though.

FIELD NOTES

I took a stand for Buzz Lightyear and continued to work for hours with the Green Organizer. I was going crazy with OCD and by the time she left I was sick to my stomach. She moved my underwear. I had my underwear in the same footlocker for thirty years, much of it the same underwear. She took everything out of the trunk and put it on a table in the ballroom. Then she held up each garment one at a time. It was as if they were appearing before the House Un-American Activities Committee. She would dangle them in front of me, with a look on her face that clearly expressed bafflement at how I could continue to wear something with so many holes in it. Alley makes me pay top dollar to buy her underwear that is no more than a couple of elastic strings, but if I wear underwear that started out the size of a tarp but I've worn down to a couple of strings, it's a disgrace?

Since I was paying this woman stacks of my hard-earned cash, I decided to go along and throw away some of the more tattered pairs. I told myself that if I had second thoughts, I could go through the trash when she was gone. I might even go to the Rite-Aid to purchase a fresh package of four. I hated to spend the money, but when she went through the underwear/sock trunk, she found a lot of socks that I didn't even realize were there. So, although I had already paid her a thousand bucks, it was offset by at least fifty dollars due to the sock find. I thought *green organizer* meant environmentally friendly, but it might be a reference to how much money she makes.

I was definitely able to reduce my inventory by working with the Green Organizer. After a few days, I was worn out and weakened. I just said okay to pretty much everything. I agreed, without objection, to get rid of a bracelet worth over a thousand dollars, as if it were an unused beverage cozy. She must have hypnotized me by swinging my old underwear back and forth. I swear I didn't realize the bracelet was gone until the next day, by which time she said she had already donated it somewhere.

I worked in a daze. We rapidly cleared whole sections of my house, as if we were lightening the load on a sinking ship. I had a large collection of misshapen sweaters that I was able to pare down to the three or four that I actually wore. I even had one with the logo of a golf resort on it. What could I have ever been thinking? I hate golf. The only good use of a golf club ever was by Tiger Woods's wife. I can't even remember how that sweater came my way.

ANALYSIS

I have lots of clothes that I hold on to just for the memories. I still have the hooded sweatshirt that I wore under a satin baseball jacket under a sweater during my Greyhound Bus trip across the country in 1980. I caught the Dog in Boston, Massachusetts, where I lived as a young adult, and it left me off in San Francisco. I didn't own any clothes without holes in them, so I wore a turtleneck, covered by a T-shirt, covered by my sweatshirt, satin baseball jacket, and the sweater. Each garment provided just enough fabric that all together they covered all of my skin by at least one layer. Today the hood only remains attached to that sweatshirt by a few threads and the shoulders are missing. The Green Organizer thought I should get rid of it. I don't know why. It no longer has enough fabric to take up that much space.

The truth is, I was afraid that if I got rid of all of the memorabilia from my past, I wouldn't remember it anymore. I already have a shocking level of short-term memory loss. I bought that Lumosity memory training game for my iPhone. I forget to play it.

If I got rid of the box with Thomas E's first Halloween costume, an Anne Geddes potted plant, I might forget the time I zipped it up his several-month-old body. The petals surrounded his head, and four-year-old Alley laughed the hardest I think I've ever heard her laugh. Halloween was always such a big deal to my kids that on Thanksgiving they dressed up like pilgrims and went door to door begging for yams.

FIELD NOTES

The Green Organizer didn't actually say, "Get real," but she definitely had a look that implied as much when she displayed five camisoles in front of me. I said, "Go ahead, get rid of the three with the orange foam stains from the padded hangers," but I was fighting dizziness and nausea. Then she said something that really struck me. She said, "People usually only wear about twenty percent of their clothes." I never felt so human. We had already weeded out about 30 percent of my high-fashion wear, but this notion inspired me. I loaded the collapsible "Donate" box with about 40 percent more. I used to have to muscle space on the clothing bar in order to hang anything. Now I ended up with enough space that the Green Organizer was able to hang my T-shirts. For years they have been folded in a treacherous stack, from which I wore about 20 percent.

Now she really had my attention. When she announced, "If you don't wear it, get rid of it," I listened. I appeared onstage at the taping of the weekly NPR news quiz show *Wait Wait . . . Don't Tell Me!* the following night in my Pilgrim costume. The host, Peter Sagal, was quite confused. He asked me why I was wearing a Pilgrim costume, and I explained that I was working with an organizer and that if I didn't wear it, I'd have to eliminate it from my wardrobe.

ANALYSIS

I'm hoping that the awesome spectacle of my orderly closet will be a shining example for Toshia, who is anxious to move to her own apartment soon. She is receiving independent skills training from an agency hired through the California Regional Center. Unfortunately, the agencies involved are either unskilled themselves or out-and-out corrupt. I overheard the woman who owns the independent skills training agency tell Toshia, "I can work for you for the rest of your life." I tried to make Toshia see that if the independent skills trainer worked for her for the rest of her life, it would mean, by definition, that she had failed as an independent skills trainer.

These people are not good at their jobs. It takes them five phone calls to even make an appointment, and then they call repeatedly to say they're stuck in traffic, as if traffic in Los Angeles surprises them every time. One day a morbidly obese trainer came to take Toshia to the park, less than a block away, to practice crossing the street more carefully. Afterward, they pulled up in the woman's car. I couldn't figure out why they hadn't walked to the park. Toshia told me that the woman wanted to go to the Jack in the Box. I said, "But the Jack in the Box is right beside the park and Toshia said, "Yes, but she wanted to go to the drive-up window."

I tried to point out to Toshia that this pushed the needle beyond "not doing a good job" and entered fairly significantly into the "shamelessly squandering governmental funds" zone and that therefore she should dump these people and request a competent agency. But my oldest daughter was an adult now, and she neither sought nor appreciated my sage counsel.

VARIABLE

Alley turned eighteen. It was bound to happen sometime after seventeen. I wish it hadn't, though. I'm going to miss that Alley. We're having cake tonight, and then I hope to surprise her with a huge bag of rubber bands. I don't think I can organize anymore. I never cracked the time management nut, although I can pick out the day's T-shirt wardrobe faster. I'm sure those minutes add up. On the other hand, the organizer moved the silverware into a drawer that makes no sense to me. We often eat with our hands now, which makes for a lengthy, messy cleanup.

CONCLUSION

The Green Organizer put my canned goods on plastic risers in the back of a shelf in my pantry, so no can is blocked by another. It looks like a can glee club. That was easily good for a hep of happiness right there.

I had moments of exhilaration from at last seeing the pressed wood-chip bottom of a drawer or carving out a bit of space in the closet. I loved having less clothing. The clothes I have now hang on velour-covered hangers, saving me oodles of time having to pick them up after they slid off those slippery plastic ones.

Instead of sitting in a basket in the ballroom, toys, clothes, and books that we've outgrown go into the trunk of the van the minute we realize that we've done so, and I drive by donation drop-off sites as needed. That makes a big difference.

Both my house and my heart feel lighter.

THE
GET ROLLING
EXPERIMENT

CONDITIONS

Toshia has left for higher ground. She feels strongly that the "services" for the disabled provided by the state will fulfill her needs. Thomas E insists that I drove her away when in fact she took the bus. I have made a lot of mistakes in my relationship with Toshia. People always say that with kids you've got to pick your battles. I chose rhyming and the weather.

Thomas E has noticed that I do many things wrong and is making a consistent and strong effort to bring it to my attention. I'm wondering how "Gee, and she tried so hard" will look on my gravestone.

Alley chose a college in Oregon. I drove her the seventeen hours from here to there in time for her freshman orientation before I realized, *I can't do this every day*. So I just left her.

I could feel her disengaging as we neared the school. She

started calling me "Mother" instead of "Mom," but fortunately, I'm familiar with that from *Bye Bye Birdie*.

For me, it was an ordeal similar, I imagine, to severing a limb, but Alley apparently didn't feel that way, so I kept it to myself. At the time, it seemed like a good place for her to be. Later I found out that some of the little faceless men had broken off the rod on the school's foosball table, and although they have a Ping-Pong table, there are no balls. So now I'm considering bringing her home.

HYPOTHESIS

I needed to do something drastic to score some happiness. Until now, I had experimented with what I thought would make me happy, but I was wrong a lot and this was beginning to feel urgent. I decided to ignore my own instincts and try a more mainstream idea.

I would rent a fancy sports car.

CONSTANTS

I am thousands of dollars in debt. I drive a minivan with many dents and scrapes. I don't know where the dents and scrapes came from. I am not a good driver.

FIELD NOTES

The only thing I knew about sports cars was that James Bond's went very fast. So on a Saturday afternoon, from high atop the bed in my hotel room in Troy, New York, I took a few moments out from reading a book about the banking crisis, of which I was understanding about three words per page, to Google "sports car."

Eventually, I found myself on the website of Carefree Life-style, a company that rents luxury cars. I figured a week should be a long-enough time to reap a balou or so of happiness from a sports car, if there was any to be harvested. The site had pictures of about twenty cars, most of which I wasn't familiar with at all. I ruled out names like Benz and BMW right away, because they didn't sound sporty, even when they add the numbers and letters to the name, like the BMW SG241. It's still just BMW to me, which are cars that therapists drive, using the money they saved when they got rid of their offices and started seeing clients in their homes, which is never too awkward, huh? "Come on in. My office is right upstairs, through the master bedroom. Just ignore the dog. He's friendly. Barney! No jumping up! Get down! She's here for therapy. She's fucked up enough already. Sorry about that. Go on up. Oh, and could you take this laundry on your way?" Anyway, I didn't want a BMW or a Mercedes. Ferrari sounded good, or Maserati, because of the Joe Walsh song.

At first I thought the numbers beneath each car picture on the website were serial numbers of some sort; then I noticed the dollar signs. These were sizable sums. *But*, I thought to myself, *this is for science*, and it was after all for a whole week.

I'm not much of a wheeler-dealer, but I thought there was a possibility that since I'm not rich the luxury car rental business simply wouldn't charge me that much money. It made sense to me. You can't get blood from a stone.

You were supposed to be able to reserve a car online, but despite my newly found internet savvy, I still couldn't fill out a form online. Every time I pressed Submit, whatever it is bounced back telling me I didn't fill in my private information correctly.

By the way, if they already know, then how private is it and why do I have to bother typing it in?

I got the phone number from the website and called. That worked. A guy with a thick, been there, done that New York accent answered the phone. He told me his name was Darren, so I said, "My name is Paula Poundstone."

"What? You're kidding? *The* Paula Poundstone? I love your work."

I'm in like Flynn, I thought. This was perfect. If the guy liked my work, he wouldn't charge me full price. He might even just give me the car. I explained what I was doing. I didn't hint either. I just laid it out. "Darren, I am not rich. I'm writing a book. It's an experiential book about searching for happiness." I paused, but there was no response.

"I know you're probably thinking, 'You're a performer, of course you're rich.'" Uh-oh, I was getting nervous. Here we go. I would never stop talking. "Yes, I'm a performer, but I'm best known for my work on NPR. It's public radio. I get paid in coffee mugs.

"I bring home the unused portion of my hotel shampoos, double-wrapped in plastic bags so they don't leak in my suitcase, and then I drip them through a funnel into a large shampoo bottle at home.

"So, I'm not rich, but I am writing a book in which I do experiments with what I thought would make me happy, like I got fit, well, I'm not fit anymore. I gained a lot of weight during my first Get Organized experiment. I was so enamored of the new unobstructed view of my canned goods, I kept returning to the pantry where I also found chips and 3 Musketeers bars.

"I also became computer literate, although I couldn't navigate your website, but you get the idea. So, now, you know how people always think they'd be happy if they had a sports car? I never thought so really, but I thought I'd rent one for a week and just see."

Nothing.

"Darren?"

"Yeah. So, what car did you have in mind?"

"Well, originally I thought I'd do the Maserati for a week, because when I think fancy sports car, I think of that song 'My Maserati does one eighty-five da, da, da, da . . .'"

Nothing.

"But now that I see the prices for a week, I guess I'd better just go for whatever's cheapest."

"Dose prices ah fuh da day. Where do you live?"

"Oh my God, for the day? Santa Monica, but I rent."

"I guess you can tell where I'm from."

I figured I'd try one more time to win him over with my sense of humor that he's such a fan of. "Arizona?"

Nothing.

By now, he may have realized it was Ellen he liked.

"If you like da Maserati, why not go fuh da Lambo?"

"The what?"

"Da Lamborghini."

"Oh, yes, the Lambo. I was thinking the Mazi, but if you think I should do the Lambo, that's fine. I could do that, I guess. These prices are for the day, huh?"

Although there was a thin sheen of perspiration forming all over my body, my mouth was very dry. "How much would that be for the day altogether?"

"Fuh twenty-four hours, out da door, it'll be $1,576.93. Can I put you on hold?"

I assured him he could, and while on hold, a recorded voice asked rhetorically if I was feeling stressed and recommended I indulge in one of the many Carefree Lifestyle luxury rental services, which besides exotic car rental included limousine service, yachts, mansions, private jets, helicopters, penthouses, and armed security. Ironically, I wasn't feeling stressed until I began my indulgence.

When he came back on the line, I gave Darren my credit card number. He told me that if there was anything I needed at all, he was available to me 24/7. The rental car place was in Beverly Hills and I had an acting class not too far away from there on Monday night, so it made sense to pick up the car Monday evening and then shoot over to my class.

"I'm just over in Santa Monica. Could you have someone pick me up and bring me to the rental place?"

"Dat's gonna cost you a hundred dollars extra."

"Okay, then, never mind. I just thought when you said, you know, if there was anything I 'needed.'

"Wait, here's an idea, do you have any other customers coming from Santa Monica on Monday night? Maybe a member of the one percent or a rapper swinging by to pick up his yacht? Maybe he'd want to carpool. I enjoy rhyming."

Nothing.

CONSTANT

I don't know why I balked at an additional hundred bucks. The cash spigot was already open. I had decided not to give Santa Monica High School another bite at the Poundstone apple, so I enrolled Thomas E in a small private school this year. I'll never be solvent. I deal with money like a soft-hearted fisherman deals with fish. I catch it and throw it back.

FIELD NOTES

I was feeling a good deal of excitement on rental day. I planned to surprise my son and my assistant, Wendell, and I also called up two other friends to offer to take them for rides the following day.

QUALITATIVE OBSERVATION #1

Happiness is best when shared.

FIELD NOTES

I had to tell Wendell the surprise, because in order to let him drive the car, I had to include his license information on the form. I told him, "I'm renting a Lamborghini tonight, and I thought I'd let you drive it."

Without even batting an eye, he said, "I don't want to drive that car."

QUALITATIVE OBSERVATION #2

Qualitative Observation #1 is in no way a hard-and-fast rule.

FIELD NOTES

"That's a terrible idea," he continued. "Where are you going to drive it?"

"Around," I said. "To do errands."

In fact, I needed cat food and some of the loose arugula from the bin at the food co-op, and I was purposely waiting until I had the Lamborghini so I would have some place to drive it.

Wendell just plain frowned on the whole idea. He said the car was too powerful. I remembered years ago horseback riding with a friend who owned horses. I had only ridden a horse before while someone pulled it with a rope in a circle. This horse that I was riding had no one pulling it, and it was huge. It just sort of did whatever it wanted.

Now I was scared to drive the car. I pictured it with its powerful engine, zooming away, my feet flying out behind me while my hands held tight to the steering wheel. It takes me ten minutes to parallel park my minivan in front of our house. This Lamborghini would vroom right up on the sidewalk when I tried to inch it close to the curb during my twenty-point turn.

Science, I reminded myself, then called a cab to drive me to the rental place.

The dark-haired, slender woman who administered the paperwork at Carefree Lifestyle wore high heels and a tight black miniskirt but was oddly down to earth. She immediately apologized for having a cold sore, which I couldn't even see. I said, "My heels are dry and cracked," still hoping for a discount and because it seemed the custom.

She went over the credit card charges with me, and I pretended to be following along carefully. They took a deposit of thousands of dollars, but when she came to a charge—for what I don't know—of seventy-five cents, she said without a hint of irony, "You know what? Don't worry about the seventy-five cents." I thanked her.

I signed papers that looked a lot like what I would sign on Christmas Day when I would take the kids to Go-Cart World. I forgot to bring my glasses, so I really couldn't see most of what

I was signing. I'm not sure it mattered. If I screwed up this car, it was all over for me, no matter what I signed.

The woman handed me the keys, and seconds later I couldn't figure out which of my six cargo pants pockets or two sweat-shirt pockets I had put them in. Still, she and two very sweet instructors walked me out to the small parking lot to show me the Lamborghini. I attempted to look nonchalant while getting into the driver's seat. The driver's seat was quite low, though. Thanks to public toilets, I have enough balance and thigh strength to get down to about a ninety-five-degree knee bend, but after that I dropped into the seat, making a graceless plopping sound. I didn't have the leg or core muscle strength it took to then lift my feet into the car. So I scooped my hands under my thighs and dragged in all that was attached to them, like lifting an anchor to set sail. Kofi, one of the instructors, was already in the passenger's seat, waiting to familiarize me with the vehicle. It never occurred to me that there were any special operational instructions, but there were.

By now I was late for my acting class, I was very nervous, and it was dark. There were lots of buttons that had to be pushed, in sequence, to make the car work. The driver's side door was open, and the other guy was standing beside me, leaning in to give instructions. I was so scared. I was processing only about one out of five of their sentences.

"To put it in reverse, you pull this knob out, just to here. You'll feel it. Then you move this stick forward, count to about three, and give it just a little bit of gas, before you tap this button. You'll see it here, on this dial. No, this dial."

I decided to listen hard for the instructions, "To make it go . . . "

and then try to avoid ever having to back up. Several times Kofi said, "You'll feel it." I couldn't feel my legs. I knew I wouldn't feel some subtle shift in this monstrosity's idle.

I started to breathe funny. It was more like a traumatic thing that was happening against my will than the thrill of a lifetime. I was almost in tears. I finally blurted out, "This is the stupidest thing I've ever done. I should've just rented the private security." The guy on my driver's side tried to reassure me. He leaned in and said, "You are going to love this. You're not going to want to bring it back." Then he quickly added, "It's very important, though, that you push this button if you are going up a drive-way, or you will take out the underside of the car."

The car was parked facing a wall, so despite my clever plan, the first thing I had to do was back up. I inched back, Kofi coax-ing me as if I were a cat stuck behind the washing machine. He even stepped into the street to block traffic for me, while I backed out and paused to figure out how to make it go forward. I hoped he'd just jog alongside the car for the entire twenty-four hours. "How fast can you run?" I asked him. Finally I eased into traffic, like the Joads heading toward the angry grapes.

I carry a thermal lunch box with diet sodas and water every-where I go. I tried to put it in the backseat but to my surprise, there was no backseat, not even a well. There was just the one passenger's seat. It's no wonder people are happy driving a fancy sports car. You can't fit more than one kid in it.

So, there I was driving down Sunset Boulevard in Beverly Hills in a Lamborghini with the top down.

QUALITATIVE OBSERVATION #3
You can feel like a real dick driving a Lamborghini.

FIELD NOTES

I felt people staring at me, but I couldn't be sure that they actually were. Every bit of my attention vacillated between watching the road and trying to figure out how to turn on the panel lights, which I couldn't.

After a few blocks, I heard a guy on the corner yelling, "Fuck you, bitch. Fuck you, bitch." The seats in the Lamborghini were so low down that I couldn't possibly see the guy yelling. It was very possible that he meant me, but it was just as possible that he stood on that corner yelling, "Fuck you, bitch," every night. This was Sunset Boulevard in Hollywood. He might even have an agent.

I made it the last several treacherous blocks to the lot I usually park in for class and realized I didn't know how to put up the top. I spent another very sweaty twenty minutes pushing what I thought were the right buttons only to have the little rear window go up and down and Mexican music go on and off. I was cursing loudly when some kids appeared over the fence in front of me. They were snapping photos. I was miserable.

I eventually figured out that the little rear window lowered at the beginning of the sequence of movements when the top was going up or down. I was pushing the right button. I was just releasing it too soon.

When I finally burst through the door of my acting class, I said, "I'm sorry for being late. I rented a Lamborghini." Then I took a seat and felt like a dick some more.

As soon as I could, I called my son to tell him about the surprise. I said, "I rented a Lamborghini!"

"No! You didn't!" He was more excited than I'd heard him in years. "That is so cool! Oh my God!"

I was so happy to make him happy that all of a sudden, despite my first encounter with the car, it seemed great to me, too.

"I really did!" This was worth it. My teenage son was pleased with something I did. I would just work harder this year and not worry about the money. He was stoked. I was stoked. This was it. We could be happy together. I felt great.

Then it happened. "Can I drive it?" he asked.

"No, you can't drive it. You don't even know how to drive. You don't have a license. Drive it?"

"How long do you have it for?"

"Twenty-four hours."

"Oh, only twenty-four hours," he said, with his voice returning to his adolescent monotone.

"What do you mean 'only twenty-four hours'? 'Drive it'? I can't let you drive it! I don't even like you to sit in the front seat of the van."

"Okay, Mom, I get it," he droned. We hung up.

QUALITATIVE OBSERVATION #4
Qualitative observation #1 is a crock.

QUALITATIVE OBSERVATION #5
A fancy sports car can go from zero heps to sixty on the happiness scale in a second. But hit a wall at that speed, and you're dead.

ANALYSIS
I once saw a woman wearing a T-shirt that read, LUCKY MOM 24/7. I thought, "Define your terms." Did she mean twenty-four

minutes seven days a week? Did she mean she left her kids at the neighbors' during those time periods? Maybe she saw me at homework time and just felt lucky by comparison. Maybe it wasn't even a reference to raising kids. Maybe she had a gambling addiction.

FIELD NOTES

It was 11:00 p.m. by the time I returned to the car. With no one watching me, I was able to turn it on and get ready to drive a lot more smoothly. I put the top down, pulled out onto Melrose Avenue, and headed home. I passed a homeless guy on a corner and felt like an asshole again.

QUALITATIVE OBSERVATION #6

It's hard to be happy when others are suffering.

FIELD NOTES

Just after eleven o'clock at night, Wilshire Boulevard through the Westwood area is kind of fun to drive, even in my minivan. It's dog ugly during the day, but at night, with the buildings lit up and no traffic, it's hard to hate it, and in a Lamborghini it was fantastic!

That engine was powerful, and I was so close to the road I felt like I was one with the car. I was Penelope Pitstop, as long as I didn't have to back up.

I scored a hep or two of happiness.

Thomas E was supposed to be in bed when I got home, but he came out to look at the car. I said, "Go in the house, get a jacket for you and one for me, and come back out."

It wasn't a very long trip, because I didn't want him to be tired for school the next day, but we drove around the city of Santa Monica, laughing at each other's attempts at looking cool. I told him he's very cool, in any car, or without a car at all, and that when we returned this thing, neither he nor I will be any more or less cool than we ever were, and we were doing just fine how we were. I said it. He didn't listen, but I want to go on record as having said it. We went down past the Ferris wheel on the pier, past the Promenade, mostly making right turns, and back to park, as quietly as I could, in front of our run down rental house with the dead grass in front. It was nice. I felt happy.

I think I made a grunting noise when I got out.

QUALITATIVE OBSERVATION #7

It's hard to sleep with a Lamborghini parked in front of your house, especially when it's costing you $1,576.93 and you only have it for twenty-four hours.

FIELD NOTES

Thomas E was excited to ride to school in the Lamborghini. He didn't even pretend to fall back to sleep after I woke him, the way he normally does. He kept rushing me and got mad when I said I couldn't go without sifting the litter boxes. He said I was taking too long but was careful not to offer to help.

"As a priority," I explained, "cat waste trumps a Lamborghini."

When we got outside, my neighbor was looking at the car. I quickly said, "It's not mine." My house is falling apart. My backyard is a dustbowl. I wear the same cargo pants everyday. The address numbers on the front of our house are crooked and held on with Scotch tape. Good thing I cleared up the misconception that I owned the gleaming white Lamborghini in front of my house.

Thomas E was very anxious for people to see him riding in this car. I tried "The car doesn't make the man" to no avail. I was just hoping he would enjoy riding in the car. Stupidly, it never occurred to me that he would view it as a symbol of his own personal status. I think he thought he was going to pick up girls in it.

"Mom, could you keep driving but kind of duck down."

He reached over and turned the radio to a rap station. He can't seem to control himself when it comes to playing with the buttons on the dash, even in the van. "I didn't hear you ask," I reminded him.

"Mom, you gotta listen to rap in a Lambo."

I was trying so hard to share the fun of this with him, I said, "I'll tell you what, you can listen to this for five more minutes and then we turn it to music."

At about four minutes, I believe I heard, "In the pussy so deep, I felt a draft," coming from the radio.

"Time's up."

"That was only four minutes!"

"I'm sorry, I thought I could take it longer, but I can't. It's awful. Put it on classic rock."

"Classic rock?"

"Yes, classic rock. I'd rather listen to *Muskrat Love*, the opera, than hear one more minute of a station that would play a song involving pussy draft."

"Mom, you don't understand."

"No, not the actual physics of the pussy draft, but I have a handle on good taste. Besides, you like lots of rock songs."

"I can't listen to classic rock in a Lamborghini!"

"Thomas, you're fourteen years old and I've given you a chance to ride in a Lamborghini. How can you turn this into a miserable experience? Either put it on classic rock or get the fuck out of the car!"

"What's the matter with you?"

"What's the matter with me? You know what? Don't talk to me. Just don't talk to me."

I turned the radio off. I can't listen to music when I'm mad.

We rode the rest of the way to school in angry silence. When I got to the foot of the school's inclined driveway, I pushed the button so I wouldn't take out the underside of the car.

Lots of kids and parents came over to look at the car. I told each of them that it wasn't mine, that I rented it for a project I was working on, that I had to save up to do it, and that classic rock sounded especially good in it.

QUALITATIVE OBSERVATION #8

I like driving a Lamborghini a lot more than I like being seen driving a Lamborghini. If there were a way to sneak a drive in a Lamborghini, that would be best.

FIELD NOTES

I pulled into the grocery store parking lot to pick up some cat food and Diet Pepsi. I was feeling sheepish until I saw a Bentley parked a few spaces away. *That guy's the asshole*, I told myself.

I was headed to the food co-op after that. That's where I go for fresh produce and vegan cheese. Most people bicycle there, or crawl in a yoga position. Something told me this car might not go over so good there. I thought of parking far away and walking, but instead I bagged the idea for the time being. We could eat canned vegetables until I was, again, safely behind the wheel of my minivan. I made three rights and was off to the pet store for a couple of gallons of Nature's Miracle, cat-pee-odor eradicator.

QUANTITATIVE OBSERVATION #1

Rich people must not have a lot of cats. There's hardly any trunk space in a Lamborghini.

FIELD NOTES

Back home, I took a bunch of photos and made a little film of me and the car. It had to be quick because I had made a plan to give a friend a ride. I drove to Westwood to pick her up. I was into it now. I stopped at the light at Centinela and Olympic. I could feel people staring at me, but I was playing it cool, like it was all in a day's work. When the light changed, I hit the gas, the engine roared, and I didn't move an inch. I punched the gas pedal again, which took probably a gallon of gas. The noise doubled in volume, but I still went nowhere.

I began to panic. Several cars were lined up behind me. I sunk lower in the seat, now practically prone. I pictured myself approaching each driver to explain that this wasn't my car. There were easily twenty dials on the dash of this car. One was labeled Press, which I guess tells the driver how much publicity they're getting. I was relieved to find it was low. By chance, I noticed that the car was in neutral. Several more cars fell in behind me. There was some horn honking, which only further distracted me from recalling how to put the car in drive.

QUALITATIVE OBSERVATION #9

Being on the receiving end of a honk in no way improves my driving performance.

FIELD NOTES

Finally, I got the thing in drive and sped away. That's how I roll.

I picked up my friend Lynn and we drove up the Pacific Coast Highway with the Pacific Ocean shimmering to our left. I shouted, in order to be heard over the engine, that the overweight "independent skills" training woman had taken Toshia to the food court at the mall, telling her she was teaching her budgeting. When I asked my daughter how that was budgeting, Toshia told me, "She said, 'If you only have three dollars, you can't order two Whoppers because that would be spending beyond your means.'"

"I told Toshia," I continued loudly at a stoplight, "that a budget is a written document, a spending-and-savings plan based on your income. Burger King does not provide that service. Its cash registers have pictures on the buttons and the employees are not even required to make change.'"

Lynn said, "Just so you know, we're rolling backward."

We were, and I knew it, but I don't like to interrupt a story.

I returned Lynn to her house, drove off to give another friend a ride, and then zipped back to Thomas E's school in time to get a parking space.

FIELD NOTES

The second time I stalled at Centinela and Olympic, I must say, it didn't take me nearly as long to figure out what was wrong and far fewer cars piled up behind me.

QUALITATIVE OBSERVATION #10
Practice makes perfect.

FIELD NOTES
Thomas E's new school is also an animal rescue center for exotic animals. They have several alligators, a puffer fish, a bobcat, huge scary lizards, a couple of tortoises, and a dozen big colorful birds that they put outside in giant cages during the day. Whenever I pick up my son, I can hear a chorus of squawks; screeches; and "Hello," "Hello," "Hello." It sounds like a call center.

Jose, the parking-lot attendant at the school, smiled broadly as I raised the front of the Lamborghini and pulled into the lot in the afternoon. I waved and said my now-customary "It's not mine." line. I see the attendant every day. I always say hi to him, but I don't know him. We've only ever talked about parking spaces. His first language is Spanish, and I don't think his English is very strong. He seemed interested in the car, though, so I told him he could come and sit in it, and I would take his picture on my iPhone and send it to him. He was a little reluctant at first, but then he happily gave in.

I pushed the camera button on my phone and pointed it toward the car. "This'll take me a minute. I'm not so good with technology," I explained, chuckling and thinking I must seem so cool that he couldn't possibly believe I wasn't a whiz with technology. I backed up to fit as much of him and the car into the picture as possible. I was hoping I was coming off as a unique combination of hip and generous, when I tripped over the cement block at the end of the parking space and fell over backward into the chain-link fence. I tried desperately to remain on my feet, but my legs were tired from getting in and out of the car. Instead, I just pushed with my legs enough to slow my slide down the fence to the pavement, scraping my arm as I went.

I jumped up as quickly as I could. Jose sprang from the car to assist me. "I'm fine. I'm fine," I said. "I think I'll just hit the ladies' room for a minute. You go ahead and sit in the car. I've got to wait until I stop bleeding."

QUALITATIVE OBSERVATION #11
I am not capable of being cool.

FIELD NOTES
When I got back from the ladies' room, the students had been dismissed and Jose was directing traffic. I was too embarrassed to ask him for his email address. I'd totally humiliated myself in front of the guy and now every time he sees me he's going to wonder why I have a picture of him on my iPhone. I don't know how I'll face him every morning and afternoon.

I can only hope my son flunks out.

ANALYSIS
I was troubled by the idea that we were using the car to improve our social lives. For example, I let kids who never seemed to notice Thomas E or me sit in the car and take pictures of themselves. Still, it was fun. I pull up at the school in my minivan every day and none of the kids flock to sit in it and take selfies. I don't even think my friend would have been available if I had invited her to go for a drive in my minivan.

"You mean the big clunky thing with the annoying electric doors and the Pop-Tart crumbs?"

"That's right."

"Say, could you also tell me some little anecdotes about how the state is screwing over your oldest daughter, who wants to get away from you and is so unimpressed with your opinion there's nothing you can do about it?"

"You betcha!"

"Be ready in a jiff!"

FIELD NOTES

Once we arrived home after school, Thomas E and I only had time to grab a quick snack before driving to Hollywood to return the car. There was bumper-to-bumper traffic and we spent an hour and a half going an average of five miles per hour in the fastest car I'll ever drive. Every so often I'd let the traffic ahead of me move for a minute and then let her rip up to twenty miles per hour in the space that accumulated.

I remembered to push the button to lift the front end of the car when I pulled into the parking lot. I returned the car, I called a cab, and we left. It was a long, depressing ride back to find my pumpkin parked in front of our house.

CONCLUSION

The truth is, the Lamborghini is a terrible gas guzzler and the mere sight of it shines a glaring light on economic disparity at every turn. I wouldn't want to own one. I wouldn't want to be the type of person who would own one. Still, although I'm not proud of this, I sheepishly confess that I enjoyed several heps of happiness driving a fancy sports car. Not a bit of it lasted, though. In fact, the morning after we'd returned it, Thomas E and I couldn't help looking out the front window of our house at our Lamborghini's old spot and wondering what that minivan was doing there.

THE

GET UP AND DANCE

EXPERIMENT

A WHILE BACK, I was waiting for my daughters to come out of that intolerable Abercrombie & Fitch store, the clothing chain with the soft-porn posters; inescapably loud, bad music; and the odd smell that permeates the entire neighborhood. This is the store with the CEO who said they don't carry large sizes because they don't want fat people wearing their clothes. I was waiting outside because I try not to go places where I'm not wanted. Alley always insists they have clothes on sale in the Abercrombie & Fitch. I try to explain to her that when the original price was absurd, slashing it to merely unreasonable won't keep me up nights deciding what I'll do with all of the money I'll save. It's on the Third Street Promenade in the downtown area of Santa Monica, which is shut off to cars and hosts a lively array of street performers.

I happened to be waiting near a group of swing dancers. A sound system blasted that wonderful upbeat music and it appeared that anyone could join in. The dancers were swinging, stepping, hopping, spinning, sliding, and looked like they were having a fabulous time. I asked one of the participants how she knew how to do that, and she told me she had taken lessons with Rusty Frank and that there was a community of people who showed up at lots of swing dance events in the Los Angeles area.

It really looked like fun and I was going to investigate further, but Alley found a shirt she wanted at that horrible store, so I had to spend the next few months working extra to pay it off. I back-burnered the idea of learning to swing dance. In fact, I took it off the stove altogether and put it in the freezer.

Recently, I've been reading *The Moral Molecule* by Paul J. Zak, a fascinating book about the author's quest to discover what circumstances cause our bodies to release a "happy chemical" called oxytocin. One of his experiments was with people at a dance. He measured the level of oxytocin before the activity and again after the activity. Bingo! After cutting a rug, the dancers he tested received a generous boost of the good stuff. Zak pointed out that in the earliest of cultures, humans reached levels of ecstasy from a combination of tribal dance and music.

CONDITIONS

I'm on the road on average two nights each week, and I'm so busy when I get home, social life is a rarity. Okay, I'm so busy, and so socially undesirable, social life is a rarity. I wouldn't say that I have no friends, but I would say that I have no friends who want to talk to me or spend time with me.

I'm not a very good conversationalist. I don't watch sports on television. I don't drink coffee. I can't remember facts or song lyrics. I never saw *Seinfeld*. I don't cook. I don't have sex. Most of my spiritual references involve *M*A*S*H*, and I read really slowly. I have nothing to say, and yet I interrupt a lot.

Much of my day revolves around cleaning up after animals, and no one calls me to hear about that.

"Hi, Paula, it's Bob. I'm just checking in about that territorial cat peeing situation. How's it going?"

"Thanks for calling, Bob, it's driving me crazy. I'm about to hyperventilate from sniffing to find out where the smell is coming from so that I can clean it. This is just not the kind of life I had hoped to have. I keep thinking about the cat litter commercial where the woman opens her front door to guests, who immediately begin to sniff, then look scandalized. I feel so ashamed. But, Bob, how about you, was your liver transplant successful?"

"I don't think that's important right now. Do you?"

HYPOTHESIS
Gotta dance!

FIELD NOTES
I remembered the name Rusty Frank, the dance teacher whom the woman from the promenade had mentioned. I looked up her website, but the group classes were Thursday nights. I'm often on the road Thursday nights. I decided I'd like a running start at this swing dancing anyway. I knew it was cheating, but I wanted some private classes under my belt before subjecting myself to a group, just so I didn't look like an idiot, or not as much of an idiot, in front of other people.

Except in my kitchen, I've always had to be pretty drunk to dance. If I ever got any kind of natural high from it, it was drowned out by the unnatural high, which inevitably ended in some form of social disaster. It's not real dancing either. I do the kind where you just move to the beat of the music and try not to bump into people. My kind doesn't have any steps.

It just so happens there is a dance studio in downtown Santa Monica. It's called the Dance Doctor. I've walked by it a thousand times.

The Dance Doctor himself answered the phone when I called. His private classes were forty-five minutes each, and although he didn't normally work that early in the day, I was able to talk him into giving me a lesson at 1:15 p.m. on a Monday, so I could leave his studio early enough to head over to Thomas E's school to do paperwork in the parking lot before I picked him up.

I left my house at 12:45 p.m. on the day of my first lesson, which was a good thing because I couldn't find a space until I went all the way to the top of the nine-floor parking garage over the top of the Dance Doctor's studio. I sped quickly down the stairs, then past George's Shoe Repair, an old-fashioned-looking barber shop, the Central Parking office, through the glass doors, and onto the spacious wood floor of the Dance Doctor studio. The front walls are all glass windows and most of the inside walls are mirrors. There is a bench just inside the door where I sat looking at the TV hanging near the front desk and waiting for the good doctor to show up. The TV played clip after clip of the Dance Doctor's appearances on television shows and in dance contests. He teaches swing, tango, salsa, and ballroom. As in most doctors' offices, I waited quite a while for him and expected that soon the nurse would appear with my chart, and I'd have to put on the paper gown.

For my first class I had selected my navy-and-turquoise checked shirt, brown flat shoes, and the cargo pants that are part of my daily uniform. When the doctor arrived, he greeted me with a warm handshake. His name was John Cassese. He wore black pants, black shoes, and a black dress shirt. He looked like he might be on top of a wedding cake. I looked like I might climb it.

I explained that my goal was to be able to go to a public dance with other swing dancers and . . . well, dance. He did me the kindness of not scoffing.

The Dance Doctor showed me the basic step of the single-step East Coast Swing. It's a step on the right foot, a step on the left foot, and a back step on the right foot. It's step, step, back step. He put on a tame version of the 1960s song "The Letter," wrapped his right arm around my waist, raised my right hand, draped it over his left, and we stepped, stepped, and back stepped to the beat.

Once I had mastered that, he upped the ante to the East Coast Swing triple step. In this dance, you step right-left-right and left-right-left in the same space of time as you had in the single space, followed by the same back step. It's triple step, triple step, back step.

Like Mr. King's taekwondo studio, this place draws the attention of passersby. I didn't imagine I'd be much of a sales tool here either, though. Swing is supposed to be done with a smile and a bright attitude. I was doing it with a furrow in my brow and a grimace of very deep concentration.

QUALITATIVE OBSERVATION #1

The hardest part was finding where to look. I mostly looked at his shirt. It was just plain awkward standing that close to someone.

FIELD NOTES

At the end of my first class, the Dance Doctor wrote me out a prescription for two to three forty-five-minute private classes with him each week, and I labored up nine flights of stairs to return to my car.

QUANTITATIVE OBSERVATION #1

Although it wasn't a group, I might be onto something with this moving to music with another human being thing. I definitely garnered three to four heps of happiness from my very first class.

ANALYSIS

Swing dancing was up against a formidable challenge from my life these days. There was no topic about which Thomas E would not argue, and lately he'd wanted to bet on the outcome of every dispute. You'd think he had been raised in a back room at the Golden Nugget.

It dawned on me a while ago that boys might be different from girls, so I read a couple of books about the psychology of boys and about raising boys in our society.

The book *Raising Cain* reported that on average boys and men think about sex every thirteen minutes. Geez, every thirteen minutes? And it didn't say how many minutes the thought lasts. Twelve-minute-long thoughts would mean they only have about eight productive minutes per hour. Productivity-wise, women must run circles around guys. I think about sex every thirteen years, and I'm productive even then, because it's quite compatible with vacuuming.

In light of this new information I was afraid to talk to my

son. I wouldn't even say anything anymore when he stood in front of the open refrigerator door, just staring for long periods. I realized he might be having a "thought," and I didn't want it to back up on him or something.

FIELD NOTES

Not surprisingly, I looked forward to these dance classes.

Today I did a few spins, which was kind of exciting. Well, they were more full turns. I do them on the triple steps. When I was a little girl, I always thought it would be wonderful to spin and have my dress flare out around me. Cargo pants don't exactly have the same effect, but with a cell phone in each pocket, the centrifugal force of the turn caused them to fly out and make my thighs look bigger. Which I couldn't have dreamed of as a child.

ENVIRONMENT

There is barely a space on the wall above the mirrors that is not covered with pictures of the Doctor dancing with different women. He always looks dapper, usually in black; the woman, in a sequin gown or leotard, is on his arm, draped over his knee or at his feet. Her legs are wrapped around his waist, or she's perched on his shoulder. In some photos, the woman wears a tiara.

I almost always wear a baseball cap from the Tree People or my daughter's college, and I don't think he can lift me.

QUALITATIVE OBSERVATION #2

The Dance Doctor asked me a lot of questions while we danced, partly to get to know me and partly because being able to talk while dancing is a measure of how second nature the steps have become. I had a tendency to just stop dancing altogether and answer his questions. I needed both hands when I talked about how family life is treating me, so I could grind my fist into my palm.

FIELD NOTES

I was able to talk and dance a little more today:

> **Dance Doctor:** Do you have any pets? (*triple step, triple step, rock step*)
>
> **Me:** I have sixteen cats. (*triple step*)
>
> **Dance Doctor:** How did you get sixteen cats? (*triple step*)
>
> **Me:** (*rock step*) I had fifteen, and I got one more. (*twirl, stagger*)

I was such an incompetent dancer that we didn't use any of the characteristic joyful swing music, because it would have been too fast for me. He was playing the slow version of "The Letter" at an even slower speed. It sounded like the artist's voice had been altered to protect his identity in public testimony, and yet I could still barely keep up. Think Peter Boyle in *Young Frankenstein*.

These were the easy moves, too. If he'd added any steps at all, we would have had to dance to funeral dirges or the "O-Ea-Yah! Eoh-Ah!" march of the Wicked Witch's Winkie guards.

Today I learned a new step. We turned to face the mirror, clasping one another from behind, with our inside arm. Then we stepped toward the mirror, inside legs at the same time and outside legs at the same time. On the outside step, we swung our outside arms out and snapped, and on the inside step we swung our inside arm across our front and snapped. Then he turned me facing him. I kicked between his legs with my right foot, to his right with my left foot, we turned away from the mirror and each kicked right and left to the side. I hoped it wouldn't happen very often.

QUALITATIVE OBSERVATION #3

I feel like a total idiot a lot.

FIELD NOTES

The Dance Doctor showed me some sort of heel-toe-kick-twisty thing today, watched me try it a couple of times, and then with a worried look on his face, he walked over and turned the music off. He said, "Let's go to the bar." I thought he was throwing in the towel, and I wouldn't have minded a drink about then myself, but he walked to the ballet barre and repeated the step very slowly.

It's step right, twist left, step left, right toe, twist right, heel, twist right. No, twist left, right toe. No, that's not it. It's twist left, right toe. No, it's twist right, left heel. No. I had it before. Anyway, that was how I did it.

QUALITATIVE OBSERVATION #4

By the time I got home, I didn't remember any of this.

FIELD NOTES

Today I learned the Charleston. It's supposed to be a snappy step, but we're doing it to "Fire and Rain." It looks like tai chi when I do it.

I got the footwork, eventually, but you're supposed to swing your arms as well, which for my brain, is a deal breaker.

QUALITATIVE OBSERVATION #5
When the Dance Doctor added any kind of hand movements, snaps, or arm swinging, I couldn't do the footwork.

QUALITATIVE OBSERVATION #6
When you dance without arm movement, you look like a big dancing stick.

FIELD NOTES
I learned a new step called a "boogie walk." It is several swivel steps forward, with open palms facing front, about a foot to the side of each thigh. I think you're supposed do it with a come-hither look. I look like I'm chasing chickens.

ANALYSIS
I garnered a few heps of happiness from each class. It did tend to settle by the end of the day, though.

Sometimes I tried to practice my swing dancing while walking down the street or waiting for Thomas E after rugby practice or school. If he caught me, he'd get mad.

"Mom, what are you doing?"

"I'm bringing the joy of dancing into my life."

"Please don't."

I hadn't done it yet, but at these moments I often feel like saying, "Gee, doesn't time just fly? It looks like another thirteen minutes has passed. Why don't you go that way and have a thought, while I go over here and dance happily."

Perhaps my expectations were unrealistic, but in *Mary Poppins*, when the mother danced, the children joined in.

Man, the teenage years just suck. That's why cats die around fifteen. Though there's the occasional cat who lives longer, argues a lot, and doesn't plan well, mostly they cut out before nature puts them through pointless emotional hell.

I was a miserable wretch of a teenager. Plus, I was just plain stupid. I used to stay up for days on end, having no idea that sleep was an enormous component of emotional health. And I wish I could tell you I was up studying, writing, or even thinking. I wasn't. I was taking lots of NoDoz, which gave me gas, desperately trying to stay awake so I could go to school the next day and tell anyone foolish enough to listen that I hadn't slept. I guess it was a cry for help, but help with what I couldn't say. "Help! I live in a lovely suburb in New England, have plenty to eat, and go to a good school."

I'm sure I caused my parents enormous amounts of undue pain, but in general I think we parents today have it far worse than most other generations. I would rather tote our water from a faraway river than have to forever police my son's computer use. But there was no escaping. The private school, which I was "dancing as fast as I could," so to speak, to pay for, now used online tutorials for almost every class. I assumed that in its online PE class the students logged on to a program that had an avatar that played a sport for them while tracking their personal contribution to the obesity epidemic. Instead of writing research papers, they were required to do PowerPoint presentations, which is where, for example, a student might, on the topic of tortoises, stand in front of the class, with a computer screen, showing a picture of a tortoise and the word *tortoises*.

The student would first turn to look at the screen so that he'd remember to say, "I did my report on tortoises." Then a few uncomfortable moments would pass while he tried to get the next image to come up on the screen. Another picture of a tortoise and the phrase "many kinds of tortoises" would appear, and the kid would say, "Um, okay [glancing quickly at the screen] there are many kinds of tortoises." Another few minutes would drag by while the kid messed with the computer and the other students and teacher checked their email, and then a picture of a dry landscape would come on the screen, with the word *environment*. The student would look at the screen and say, "Oh, yeah, environment" before leaning over the keyboard for another few minutes, to produce a tortoise picture, looking suspiciously like the first, with the sentence "Tortoises live in dry environments." By now, many of the presenter's fellow students would be texting one another, which the teacher wouldn't notice, because he'd be posting on his Facebook page a funny picture of the world history teacher in a loincloth at the most recent "Cash Bash" school fund-raiser, which would lead to the world history teacher's dismissal and a possible Supreme Court battle.

In a few minutes, the same tortoise picture would flash onto the screen but with flames coming out of its mouth this time and the kid would say, "Tortoises don't really shoot flames out of their mouths, I don't think, but this is kind of a cool thing I learned how to do on the computer."

The PowerPoint presentation is the enemy of education and intelligent oration. I long for the days where a poster, propped on a chair, occasionally fell over during an oral report.

FIELD NOTE

I learned a move called a "sugar push" today. It's really fun. The Dance Doctor twisted me one way, and I triple stepped, and he twisted me the other way, and I triple stepped. He said I did it well. I'd rather he not have said it with that surprised look, but still, I guess I was good at the sugar push. This could be my thing. Sugar Push might be my new nickname or something. "Ladies and gentleman, please welcome this year's Kennedy Center honoree, Paula 'Sugar Push' Poundstone!"

Actually being good at a step provided a few heps of happiness. I practically flew up the nine flights of stairs to my car and didn't really mind the traffic on the thirty-five-minute drive to Thomas E's school.

ANALYSIS

I had tried getting out of my car and talking with the other parents in the parking lot at Thomas E's school, but I felt alien. Some of them just plain didn't like me because I hip-checked them out of the way to get to the "napkins" slot on the potluck dinner sign-up sheet, but with most I just wasn't fitting in. They seemed to be able to motivate their children and still have the time and energy to volunteer at the school. I didn't know how they did it. I caught my son taking someone else's writing off the internet and using an app that tells him what words to change to make it "original." When I told him he couldn't do that, he said, "Mom, it's not the forties." I often have zero energy left after dealing with my son.

I did volunteer to be in charge of a bulletin board near the main office in Thomas E's school, because in December it still featured an announcement about Back-to-School Night.

On one-half of the bulletin board I posted a picture of FDR and some facts about the years that he served. I made a little cardboard frame to enclose the number of televisions in use at that time and put the title "Frame of Reference" above it, because I don't think dates give kids enough of a sense of time. Beneath that I put this series of quotes:

"Let us never forget that government is ourselves and not an alien power over us."

"For God's sake, Eleanor, chew your food."

"Yesterday, December 7, 1941, a date which will live in infamy . . ."

And "Dude, you sunk my battleship," followed by the question, "Which of these are quotes from President Franklin Delano Roosevelt?"

On the second half of the board, beneath a YOUR BUDS ARE NOT YOUR BUDS sign, I put information about the workings of the inner ear and how earbuds risk causing permanent hearing loss.

The whole project took me hours. In the thank-you note that the principal emailed me, he wrote, "I hope the kids look at it." That concern never crossed my mind. It's right in the main hallway. How could they not look at it? I read the Back-to-School Night announcement every time I walked into the main office. The guy was so tech-whipped, I thought, that he couldn't even be sure what had been communicated without seeing how many "likes" it got.

FIELD NOTES

I watched some swing dancing on YouTube. It was amazing. It also looked nothing like what I do. I had a "Rocky" moment. Remember when he watched the Apollo Creed fight film and realized that not only could he not beat the guy but he would be lucky to go ten rounds with him? It would take me years to be able to swing dance well enough to really dance with others, so I decided to just take the dive into the icy cold waters of a group class.

I went on Rusty Frank's website and signed up for a beginner class. I'd been with the Dance Doctor for months, so I was not technically a beginner at this point, but this is where the genius of my plan kicked in. I'd be just that much ahead of my new classmates. This was my chance for Paula "Sugar Push" Poundstone to shine. The other students might come to me and ask for tips.

As it happened, Rusty had a series of beginner classes just starting, and I had a rare month with most Thursday nights available.

QUALITATIVE OBSERVATION #7

I do not look like a dancer to anyone. When I told people I was going to take a group swing dance class, I might as well have said, "Thomas E's school is really expensive, so I thought I'd give some blow jobs for cash over on Hollywood Boulevard."

ANALYSIS

I found myself closing cabinet doors in the kitchen with my feet as I moved around the floor preparing meals. I liked having a skill that no one expected of me.

FIELD NOTES

The Dance Doctor taught me "kick-ball-change." He held my right hand and rotated while I did a right kick with my hand on my left hip. Then I swiveled on my left foot and kicked right again, continuing the step around the circle.

It could be that this secret capable feeling I was occasionally experiencing these days was coming from running up and down the nine flights of stairs at the parking garage near the Dance Doctor's studio. It wasn't coming from the kick-ball-change, I could tell you that.

I didn't tell the Dance Doctor that I was going to take an additional class elsewhere, because I enjoyed taking classes with him so much. I didn't want to risk offending him.

ANALYSIS

Thomas E's school is going through the Western Association of Schools and Colleges accreditation process. Basically, three WASC team members came to observe the school and interview students, parents, administrators, and teachers. I went to one of the meetings. All of the participants sat in a circle and each of us talked about our experience with the school. Some of the founders spoke about how the entire school started out fifteen years ago with just one student. In a few minutes, one of the WASC members observed enthusiastically that many of the private schools that they visit have declining enrollment, so she was quite impressed that our school's census was continuing to grow. I looked around the room hoping to find a puzzled look on at least one other face, but there was none. Everyone else seemed pleased with that assessment. So I raised my hand and said, "The school started out with one student. The bar for enrollment growth was set fairly low." They all glowered at me. My bulletin board job may be at risk.

I'm so frustrated with the state of education. In truth, though, it's hard to suss out how much is failure of the schools and how much blame should go to the families and students themselves, in this case, my son and me. When we first visited the school, I was very taken by the animal rescue aspect of the program, and I assumed Thomas E was, too. Among other things, it is a great resource for their zoology classes. During our tour, Thomas E was allowed to hold a chinchilla and he seemed totally enraptured.

I realize now he fooled me completely. We were also shown the computer room, where he was told he could take video game design classes. Thomas E was smart enough to feign only a mild interest in the treasure trove of electronics. So when we got back to the car and he was wildly enthusiastic about going to the school, I was naive enough to believe he had fallen in love with the animals. I've seen far too many Disney movies. I had a whole *My Friend Flicka* thing going on in my head. "He was always such a sickly child until he started spending time with that chinchilla." But, no, it was the fucking computer.

FIELD NOTES

My first group class took place at the Rebekah Lodge in El Segundo, California. It's nowhere near where I live, but surely happiness is worth an hour in the traffic of multiple freeways. The Rebekah Lodge is a typical community center kind of a room. It's got a large wood floor, a few tables with folding chairs, and a kitchen with an opening through which one might be served from a large vat, at another type of function. At this function, Rusty herself leaned through the opening, collecting a small fee from each of her dance students. I watched as she happily issued everyone a name tag in a plastic cover, which they pinned through their garment somewhere on their chest and stepped away, nervously adjusting. A number of people had come as a couple, which gave me pause, but I had specifically read on Rusty's website that partners were optional. I got my name tag and hoped it wouldn't leave too large a hole in my Cookie Monster T-shirt.

I had only chatted with a couple of people before we were called to circle up on the floor. The couples stood close to each other. I looked around wondering which single guy I'd be forced upon. I was one of the oldest people in the room. There was one guy who might have been older than I. I only guessed that because he had kind of a shoe-polish hair-dye job. His name tag read FELIPE, but with that much shoe polish on his head, I don't know why he'd use his real name. For the sake of the happiness experiment, I was trying hard to be more outgoing than usual, but my anxiety was rising like the federal deficit.

In just a second, Rusty came out of the kitchen to join her dance partner, Gio, in the center of the circle. She was a ball of fire, and they were adorable together. They both wore headsets with microphones to amplify their spoken directions and banter.

Rusty is a short, bubbly woman with cropped red hair. Gio is tall, with broad shoulders and dark hair. I would never have guessed either of them were dancers, which just goes to show how much I know. They danced for a few seconds, long enough to prove that they were the real deal. They were. Their dance was animated and funny. It was high energy and uplifting just to watch. If there was a procedure that was to swing dance what stomach stapling is to weight loss, I would have paid to have it done, no matter the cost or the danger.

Rusty told the men and any women who wanted to lead to step into a second circle inside the larger circle, which made about twenty couples. A guy named Aleck appeared before me. He was young and thin, with brown hair and a sweet, funny smile, and he didn't seem to mind being stuck with me at all. With a lively back and forth of words, Rusty and Gio now demonstrated how the "leader" holds the "follower."

Perhaps because I knew this part by heart already, Aleck and I were one of the first couples ready. His right hand was around my waist, and my right hand was draped over his raised left. I looked around the circle and wondered how long it would take these newbies to get this. *There is a bond that develops between dance partners*, I thought. Aleck and I already had so much in common. Our name tags drooped at a similar angle. I tried to guess how many minutes it would be before the others cleared out of the way and applauded supportively while Aleck and I whirled around the floor.

My experiments had not been for nothing. Surely I had found the secret to happiness. I didn't want to rush things, so I would wait a couple of days before introducing Aleck to Thomas E, but no doubt they'd come to love each other for my sake. Maybe they'd throw a ball together in the backyard, and Thomas E would soon forget about the computer. Toshia and Alley would be dying to meet him over the holiday break and all three kids might take up the dance themselves once they saw what it was doing for their mother and new father.

There would be no sex in my relationship with Aleck. We wouldn't need it. We would have swing dance.

"Okay, that's great," I heard Rusty call through the sound

system. "Now, leaders, you rotate. Followers, you stay where you are."

So that's how they do it.

Aleck moved on to the next follower, and there before me was a beefy, sweaty guy named Chuck. And so it went for the entire evening. They rotated every minute or so. It was like being a factory worker turning a wrench on an assembly line. As soon as I'd completed a move with one guy I had to reset for the next. The class lasted an hour. I couldn't help thinking about my newfound knowledge that men think about sex, on average, every thirteen minutes. I'm sure not every guy was having a thought every time we were partnered up. In fact, I'm so nonsexual that maybe I was a nice break for them but statistically speaking, it would have had to occur occasionally. In any case, whatever happened, happened fast. I never got out more than a "Hi, Jason" or "Hey, you're back again, Dylan!" or "Good for you for learning to lead, Michelle" before Gio or Rusty called out, "Switch!"

We started with the basic step, step, back step, at which Sugar Push Poundstone prevailed. Then we moved, with similar results, to the triple step, triple step, back step. There was upbeat swing music on the sound system. I was on fire. "Don't worry about it, Jordan. You'll get it."

"You're getting better, Felipe! Remember, triple step, triple step, back step. Oops, you got a little black stuff on my shirt. Don't worry about it. I'll soak it when I get home. Just listen to the music and you'll be a natural by the next time we're together."

"Of course you're as good as me, Claire! Are you kidding?

You're doing great. Triple step, that's it! Triple step, back step. See you in a bit."

Then something happened that I absolutely hadn't expected. Rusty and Gio demonstrated a "swing out." I'd never heard of a swing out. You're at the end of the leader's left arm, and they pull you toward them. You take two steps in and triple step. They turn you, take two steps back and triple step, I think. I was lost. I knew nothing. I stumbled. I apologized. I sucked.

I sucked with Jason. I sucked with Dylan. I sucked with Michelle. I sucked with Aleck. We broke up, by the way. I sucked with Bryan. I sucked with Chuck. I thought I got it once with Claire, but I didn't. I sucked.

When the hour came to a close, we stood in one big circle again. Rusty asked for whom this was their first dance class and my hand shot up.

Many of us stayed for the class that followed in the next hour. I got marginally better, but no one remotely suspected that I'd had any prior experience.

At the end of the night I told Rusty that I would have to miss the next class because of work and she mentioned that she taught private lessons as well. I pretended that the notion of taking private lessons had never occurred to me. I had raised my hand as a newcomer, and I sucked as badly, or worse, than anyone in that room. I couldn't possibly tell her that I had taken private lessons for months. Don't get me wrong. The Dance Doctor is a wonderful teacher. It's just that here we didn't do the steps that he had taught me. I made an appointment for a private swing dance class with Rusty.

ANALYSIS

Thomas E enjoyed hearing about how my group class went. I love making him laugh. I'd be shot out of a cannon if I thought it would amuse him. Come to think of it, I'd be shot out of a cannon anyway. That has always seemed like an interesting job to me.

Anyway, after I told him about my dance class, I made him read aloud to me from *Pride and Prejudice*, because he was supposed to be reading it for school, but I knew he was not.

The following morning I left for the airport early to go to work in Sellersville, Pennsylvania, a town, I assume, founded by people who sell things and where a common greeting is, "What can I interest you in today?"

Before I went on that night at the Sellersville Theater, I got a call from Thomas E asking if I knew where his copy of *Pride and Prejudice* was. I said, "You just had it last night. Did you take it to school?"

"No," he answered, like it was the dopiest question he'd ever heard; why would anyone take a book to school?

I said, "Well, then, it's in the house. Go look for it."

He said, "I did," because he doesn't know yet that the way you know you finished looking for something is that you've found it. Looking isn't all higgledy-piggledy and random. There's an end game to looking.

Then he said what he really called to say in the first place: "The teacher says we don't have to read the book. We can use SparkNotes, which is a computer version of the Cliffs Notes of my childhood. That got me.

"Oh really," I said. "You mean there isn't yet a thumb-drive thing that you can just stick in your ear and download into your brain, so you can have more time to sneak playing video games, which let's face it, is where the real jobs will someday be? How unfortunate for you. What a cruel and unfair world for you. You know what? If you actually have a teacher who told you you could use SparkNotes instead of reading *Pride and Prejudice*, I hope Jane Austen reaches out from her grave and gives this teacher's computer consternation and vexation."

"What's that?"

"I rest my case."

FIELD NOTES

I took Thomas E and the girl we carpooled with to school, slept outside the Burger King for half an hour, and drove to Rusty's small studio in El Segundo. She has lots of old movie stills and publicity photos from the thirties and forties on the walls, and closets full of retro clothes. She used to be a tap dancer and she switched to swing because, as she says, "It's like a party every time you practice." Rusty has been a driving force in keeping this genre alive. Not that I needed more convincing, but her enthusiasm was contagious.

She fired up her playlist full of cool swing music and we practiced swing outs, both six and eight counts, a distinction I pretended to understand. She was complimentary about how after only one lesson I was doing so well. She simply marveled at it. I felt awful for the deception, but I just couldn't tell her the truth. After all, she thought it was amazing, but she certainly didn't think it was unbelievable. I mean, she still wouldn't have guessed that I'd had months of training. Even so, I was having a hard time receiving credit where credit was not due.

After leaving, I drove an hour or so to the Dance Doctor, where I continued to work on entirely different steps. I then drove to Thomas E's school, took him home, bought his lies about having no homework, gave him dinner, and drove him to rugby practice. All the while, I was feeling guilty about telling Rusty I'd had no dance lessons, so I sent her a note ratting myself out.

CONSTANT

When I picked up Thomas E from rugby, I told him the saga of my deception. It clearly illustrated the folly of dishonesty and the importance of taking responsibility for your mistakes, even when you're a mom. To my surprise, he softened some and said that he had a confession to make. He took a breath and blurted out that he did have homework and that he was sorry he lied to me.

"I really appreciate your telling me. That really speaks to your character. It takes courage to be honest sometimes," I said, beginning to tear up. "What homework do you have?"

"I'm supposed to play World of Warcraft for a couple of hours for history."

"Thomas, that's not a history assignment."

"You want to bet? You want to bet?"

FIELD NOTES

In tonight's group class after a few minutes of practicing the swing out, Rusty explained the protocols of the social dance. She gathered us together in the corner of the lodge floor and talked about proper manners at a social dance. No sleeveless shirts for the women, so guys don't stick their hands in sweaty arm pits. Men needed to bring a change of shirt. No garlic. Shower first. There were a lot of admonitions about sweat and body odor. It was like a junior high PE teacher's speech. She seemed reluctant to say these things, but clearly she'd been given cause.

She told us that the men (leaders) asked the women (followers) to dance and that the women stood on the side of the dance floor to indicate availability. When asked, the woman responds, "I'd love to," then extends her arm for the man to walk her onto the dance floor. After the dance, we applaud the band and the man returns us to where he found us.

After she had informed us of all this, she asked us to practice. I hadn't sweat all that much while dancing, but I was dripping with perspiration while standing on the edge of the dance floor waiting to be chosen. At least the men weren't encouraged to lift us up or pull back our lips to look at our gums before they chose.

I was the last person chosen, me, Paula "Sugar Push" Poundstone.

I was thrilled to get back to the rotating circle. We were still wearing name tags, but I remembered some of the guys. Most of them stumbled through the dance steps apologetically, just like me. There was the occasional bright spot when a guy would start with an enthusiastic "We got this!"

Then there was Chuck, who seemed to have enough previous experience to be dangerous. We were supposed to be practicing swing outs, but Chuck knew some other moves that he was hell-bent on putting me through. When Rusty and Gio would yell, "Switch!" and Chuck would appear before me, I knew I was in for trouble. At one point he wrapped my arms around me and pinned me to the front of him, facing out. He said, "Do you know this one?"

"No, Chuck," I said, "but it seems oddly like some form of restraint." He seemed to think I was kidding.

It's hard to trust a guy who is supposed to be leading a swing out and pins you to the front of him instead. It'd be like if you loaned someone your lawn mower and they used it in the ocean.

I was so grateful to again hear, "Switch!" Everyone else was pretty enjoyable to be with. There were a lot of very sweet engineers and computer nerds in the group, but when I'd looked up and saw the circle rotating Chuck toward me, I felt like Batman when the Penguin's unpleasant henchmen tied him to a table with a circular blade saw spinning gradually toward his crotch. Except he had a secret Bat laser that could burn the ropes.

PROCEDURE

I continued to take lessons several times each week. I don't know how many times I drove from Thomas E's school to Rusty's little studio in El Segundo to the Dance Doctor in Santa Monica and back to the school. I do know that I often drove by a strip mall with a store called A Little Romance, which sold sex toys. It was right beside a karate studio with kids' classes. I always imagined a guy dropping his kid off for his karate lesson and saying, "Son, you head on into your dojo, your mom and I are gonna go next door and price a cock ring."

Rusty hosts a dance club at an Elk's Lodge every Wednesday and also on the first Friday of every month. She had been telling me about it for a while. They have a live band, a bar, a big crowd of swing dancers and an old-fashioned ice cream man.

They even have half an hour of beginner and advanced instruction, with a variety of guest teachers.

I was ready to enter the final phase of the Get Up and Dance experiment. I would attend my first social dance on Friday night.

FIELD NOTES

I arrived at Rusty's Rhythm Club early, so I slept in the car for about thirty minutes before I looked in the rear-view mirror and, in the dark, slapped on some red lipstick. I think I put it on my lips. I also, somewhat sheepishly, slipped on a brand-new pair of black-and-white dance shoes with suede soles for a smoother spin. I was hoping no one would notice that I was presumptuous enough to invest in dance shoes. I was also hoping the shoes knew all of the dance steps.

I joined in the beginner class, secretly believing that this time I couldn't possibly look like a beginner. In fact, I was pretty good in the beginner class. There were about twenty students, and again, we used the rotating circle method. The teachers assured us that knowing just these basics would be enough to dance all night.

QUALITATIVE OBSERVATION #8

Some dance teachers lie.

FIELD NOTES

Rusty had told me that a good leader will figure out the follower's "ceiling" and won't lead beyond it.

QUALITATIVE OBSERVATION #9

Not all leaders are good.

FIELD NOTES

The band was fantastic and the dance floor filled quickly. There were lots of hats, suspenders, and two-toned shoes.

As instructed, I stood on the edge of the dance floor, where I was approached by a man who asked me to dance. I dutifully responded, "Why, yes, thank you." He took my arm and walked me out directly in front of the band. For some odd reason, this didn't bother me, because I somehow thought I was about to dance. I did, too, for a second. My bright red lips broke into a wide grin. I triple stepped, triple stepped, rock stepped, and right after that everything I thought I knew fell out of my head. I don't know what happened. All of a sudden I just knew nothing. My ceiling was so low that to not lead above it would have meant that the leader and I stood on the side of the dance floor and tapped our feet.

After that, I changed my "Would you like to dance?" response to "Yes, but I suck."

I'd taken dance classes for months with two different teachers, but I didn't recognize half of the steps, and the half that I did recognize were over before I could pull them off. The band didn't play "Fire and Rain" the whole night.

These poor guys pushed me and shoved me, trying desperately to nonverbally direct one unfamiliar move after another. They were like cowboys taking turns trying to break a horse. One guy sort of tipped me up onto his hip and hobbled in a circle, looking at me expectantly. I said, "Did you just make that up now?"

Another guy, Nutty McBuddy, I think his name was, took my hand and dragged me around the entire dance floor. I noticed he had a small felt carrot dangling from the crotch of his pants.

By the end of the night, abandoning protocol entirely, when

someone asked me to dance, I'd just lean on his shoulder and whisper, "Help me."

QUALITATIVE OBSERVATION #10

My dog plays Jenga better than I swing dance.

ANALYSIS

On my way home, I listened to a voice mail from Thomas E telling me he refused to play in Saturday's rugby game because, I assumed, he'd rather stay home and argue. Then I added half an hour to my travel time because I was so addled that I got lost, even with a GPS. I don't know when I've been so depressed.

QUALITATIVE OBSERVATION #11

Dancing is really fun. Not being able to dance while others can is not nearly as much fun. It's like watching people swim on a hot day when you don't have your bathing suit and you're wearing wool. So, until I can really dance, which is a long-term proposition, it's tough to wring a lot of heps of happiness out of it. One night of relentlessly beginner social dancing is not a proper test.

CONCLUSION

Dance lessons provided me several heps of happiness over this months-long experiment, and I plan to continue because I really believe that once I have any kind of mastery, which will take me years, it'll be a blast.

THE
GET WARM AND FUZZY
EXPERIMENT

CONDITIONS

Thomas E is not the only one with a jones for screens. If I checked my post box as much as I check my Gmail, my neighbors would do an intervention. I still enjoy Twitter, but I check that compulsively as well.

If you look up from your screen for a few seconds, you'll see everyone is staring at their flat things everywhere they go. If Robert Frost had lived today he would have written, "Whose woods are these? I think I'll Google it." It's causing distraction, isolation, and loss of humanity. What really frizzes my hair is that people think technology is keeping them "connected." We are in trouble. I am longing for real connection.

HYPOTHESIS

Someone needs a hug.

PROCEDURE

I am going to hug as many people as I can. I haven't read anything about the etiquette of hugging. So I'm not exactly sure how to proceed.

FACTOR

Many of us have bad hug memories. I had a guidance counselor in high school who always had her hands on people, not in a sexual way but in a way that made you back into the wall and sign up for classes you didn't want, just to get away from her. Why else would I, or anyone else, have taken a class called Introduction to Fife and Drum, Appliance Instructions as Literature, or Beginning Sports Injuries? She had huge thick glasses, too. Now that I think of it, she might not have been just touching people to touch people. She might have been locating them.

Hugging has evolved, though. When the first President Bush announced Dan Quayle as his running mate, the Republican vice presidential nominee came out on the stage and hugged George Herbert Walker Bush. The nightly news was immediately filled with reports condemning the hug as "un–vice presidential." Now high-government-official hugging is quite common. Dan Quayle was ahead of his time. Perhaps we owe him an apology.

VARIABLE

Thomas E was mortified when I told him about this new experiment. He wailed, "Oh, Mom, don't do that." You'd think I had told him I was going to run naked through his history class, where let's face it, buried in their online education, no one would even see me. "I got an A on my gif of the Kent State shooting."

PROCEDURE

I had invited Thomas E to accompany me on a trip to do the National Public Radio weekly news quiz show *Wait Wait . . . Don't Tell Me!* at Red Rocks Amphitheatre in Colorado. I figured I would start the experiment on the first day of our trip.

To soothe his angst about me besmirching the family honor by hugging people, I told him to feel free to step away from me at any time and pretend he doesn't know me.

Alley agreed to stay home to take care of the animals. She's home for the summer! The part of me that pays for college feels the college school year is remarkably short, but the part of me that misses her so much is thrilled to have her back. Every time I see her coming down the escalator at the Southwest baggage claim, and after I check that she has no tattoos, I am so happy.

She has become a vegan, which means she only eats plant-based foods. I think it's great. I can't feed her, but I do think it's great. I make dinner for Thomas E and me; and she just sits at the table and sucks on a wicker chair. She is right, of course: a vegan diet is healthier for the individual and healthier for the planet as a whole, and it is, obviously, also more humane. I'm just too lazy. It takes a good deal of willpower and commitment. I fall short of her standards. She made me buy cat food that hasn't been tested on animals. My cats took one bite of it, spit it out, and yelled, "Did no one test this?"

Thomas E and Alley are still often at odds. They mostly only talk to each other through me. He seems to have become more carnivorous since she's been home.

FIELD NOTES

The night before our trip, I set my alarm, as I usually do, for 1:45 a.m., 2:15 a.m., 2:45 a.m., 3:15 a.m., and 3:45 a.m. I turned it off at 1:45 a.m., 2:15 a.m., 2:45 a.m., and 3:15 a.m. At 3:45 a.m., I got up. I do this because I love to fall asleep, and if I only set my alarm for 3:45 a.m., I only get to fall asleep once.

I stepped out of my room, crossed the amazing minefield of vomit left by the sixteen cats during the three hours of sleep I was able to manage, and made my way to the cleaning products. I finished my chores, sprinkled some birdseed on the table for Alley's breakfast, and woke Thomas E. I don't very often take him on the road with me, but when I do, I always hope the experience of getting up so early "like Mom does" will give him some kind of empathy for me. So far, it hasn't.

Wendell arrived to take us to the airport at 4:15 a.m.

PROCEDURE

Technically, I should have hugged Wendell, but we work together in my house a few days each week, often at side-by-side desks, and I'm concerned about setting a hugging precedent. We both struggle to stay focused to begin with. I'm afraid if we start hugging, minutes of getting nothing done will grow to hours. I don't know what the rules are. If we hug when he arrives for work, should we hug when he leaves? What about when he picks me up or drops me off at the airport? What about when one or the other of us has an achievement? "There, I spelled that right. Give me a squeeze." Tick, tick, tick, tick.

FIELD NOTES

With the bags loaded in the car, we joined the relentless flow of LA traffic to the airport, where I performed my first hug.

QUALITATIVE OBSERVATION #1

It takes a lot of courage to hug someone you don't know. Especially when your sixteen-year-old son is standing a few feet away, cringing and rolling his eyes.

QUALITATIVE OBSERVATION #2

TSA agents hate hugging.

FIELD NOTES

If I got any boost of happy chemicals in my brain at all, it quickly evaporated when I had to explain to the TSA agent, whom I had embraced, that I had simply misinterpreted the pat down.

Thomas E walked ahead, way ahead.

I went to the gate, where I scanned the passengers looking for someone I might engage. Surely there was an enormous burst of oxytocin perched on the edge of my brain just waiting to fire. I found two gray-haired women, wearing *Jersey Boys* T-shirts. I couldn't just spring forward and grab one of them, so I put a big smile on my face and asked, "How was the show?"

"What show?" they asked before I appeared to point at their breasts.

"Jersey Boys," I said quickly, but they still didn't seem to understand and were looking at me with alarm and suspicion as if I were *that person*, the one the voice on the airport loudspeaker constantly warns of, the one who introduces "foreign objects" into the luggage of those who don't keep their bags in close proximity.

They seemed so spooked by me, I decided it would be cruel to hug them or even put a gentle hand on their shoulders. Besides, I couldn't risk another run-in with security. I think I'm already on the national Do Not Hug list.

PROCEDURE

I decided to adjust my approach. When hugging didn't seem appropriate, I would simply smile and make eye contact.

FIELD NOTES

I walked slowly around the gate area using this new procedure.

QUALITATIVE OBSERVATION #3

When you walk around the airport smiling and trying to make eye contact with people, you look like Carol Channing panhandling.

FIELD NOTES

Thomas E walked to another gate and tried to board a flight to another destination altogether.

ANALYSIS

Once Thomas E and I were seated together on the plane, I was impressed that he chose to use his time well. He was filling out an application for a Mexican restaurant called Poquito Mas, one of places to which he was applying in hopes of landing a summer job. This was new for him, so he had some questions.

"Mom, what's my previous work experience?"

"You've had none, honey."

"Do I have any degrees?"

"Thomas, if you don't remember receiving a degree, that's the same thing as not receiving one. Do you want a doctor who has no memory of going to med school?"

"They asked what percentage of English I speak and I accidentally checked the seventy-five percent box. Should I cross it out?"

"No, leave it. You mumble."

He had another application for Bed Bath & Beyond. It had essay questions. Like any applicant would be, Thomas E was stumped by "Why do you want to work at the Bed Bath & Beyond?" It'd be a breeze if it weren't soon followed by a signed sworn affirmation that everything you'd written on the application was true to the best of your knowledge. It's a diabolical question.

I said, "Well, the honest answer is that you need a backup in case you don't have enough degrees to sling refried beans at the Poquito Mas, but I don't think that honest answer will get you a job. How about, 'I've always been interested in the Beyond?'"

FIELD NOTES

In the airport in Colorado, I missed a lot of opportunities to connect with people. Every time I approached someone I'd think, "Hug this guy! This is the one. Hug him!" Then I'd pass the person and think, "Aw, I should have hugged him." It was like watching balls go by my bat in the strike zone. I lost my nerve. I was in a slump. I couldn't even make eye contact.

Once we got to the hotel, Thomas E wanted to eat lunch. I was afraid I'd fail to hug someone again, so I gave him some money to go by himself. I ordered from room service and had them leave the tray outside the door.

ANALYSIS

I had huggers' block. I was really starting to feel like a failure.

FIELD NOTES

At about 5:30 p.m., I'm sure I received a hep of happy chemicals when Thomas E and I joined my fellow *Wait Wait . . . Don't Tell Me!* panelists in the lobby of the hotel. I hugged Brian Babylon (who does a killer Obama impression) and introduced him to my son. Then Thomas E and I both hugged Tom Bodett. They know each other because Thomas E and I were guests at Tom's house in Vermont once. We were still on West Coast time in Vermont that night and we stayed up after Tom and his family had gone to bed. When we finally went to turn out the lights, we couldn't find the switch. So we left the lights on at Tom Bodett's.

On this night in Colorado, we'd met to ride over to Red Rocks Amphitheatre for the taping of the show.

ENVIRONMENT

I am lucky enough, and have been for thirteen years, to be a regular on NPR's weekly news quiz. Way back when I had never even heard of the program they called to invite me to be a panelist. They sent me an audiocassette tape of an episode and I left it on the island in my kitchen, where one of our nannies saw it and said, "I love that show. You've got to do that show."

I listened to the tape and found that it was a wonderful program, with Peter Sagal as the host; Carl Kasell as the announcer/scorekeeper; and three panelists each week who answer questions, make jokes about the latest news, and vie for the mantle of that week's most informed. There are about fifteen panelists in all who rotate appearances on the show, in no particular order that I know of.

When I first participated, it was not performed in front of a live audience. Everyone was hooked up via wire. Peter was at the show's headquarters in Chicago. Carl was in Washington DC, where he still was an NPR *Morning Edition* newscaster, and the rest of us went to the NPR station nearest to where we lived. Not too long after I joined, they found a permanent home for themselves in an auditorium in the basement of a bank in downtown Chicago, where the show is performed—and recorded—in front of a wonderfully intelligent, fun, and very live audience. Except about once a month, when the show travels to a venue in another city around the country.

The panelists have no scripts and we are all encouraged to jump in and make jokes whenever we feel like it. It is a joyous free-for-all. Since the first time I sat onstage, several feet away from Peter Sagal's host podium, *Wait Wait* has been one of the greatest pleasures of my life. We've never talked about it, but I've always had the sense that Peter finds me something of an oddity. I think he loves me, as I love him, but he has absolutely no idea why I say most of the things that I say. He is a Harvard graduate, extremely sharp witted, the perfect host for the show, and watching the look on his face while he tries, unsuccessfully, to figure me out gives me delight.

FIELD NOTES

We arrived at the Red Rocks backstage entrance. Some of the most legendary performers in the world have worked at this place: Ray Charles; Peter, Paul, and Mary; the Beatles; Willie Nelson; Jimi Hendrix; and the Grateful Dead, to name a few. I suspect I was the only performer ever there who hugged every member of the Red Rocks Amphitheatre production staff.

QUALITATIVE OBSERVATION #4

The Red Rocks Amphitheatre staff, who are very nice to begin with, are even nicer when you hug them. Every one of them asked if they could bring me something to eat.

QUANTITATIVE OBSERVATION #1

Hugging causes weight gain.

FIELD NOTES

I hugged every one of the *Wait Wait . . . Don't Tell Me!* producers and staff, even though I was behind, as usual, in memorizing the answers to the most likely vexing lightning-round questions about the week's news (Afghanistan . . . Iraq . . . lemurs down his pants . . .) and couldn't really spare the time.

The show was a blast. The place was spectacularly beautiful. When Peter Sagal, Brian Babylon, Tom Bodett, our new announcer/scorekeeper Bill Kurtis and I walked out onstage, our mouths hung open. There were around eighty-five hundred audience members, and each and every one was fantastic. They could have been auditioned and handpicked.

After the show, the cast usually stays onstage and meets audience members, but on this night we had to attend a backstage reception with staff and members of the sponsoring radio station. As the others made their way backstage, someone from the audience wanted my autograph, so I stopped and asked if I could give her a hug. Thomas E shifted nervously behind me.

"Mom, you have to go to the reception."

I ignored him. A cluster of people gathered around to take photographs, get autographs, tell me when they first saw me onstage, and tell me what they were usually doing while they listened to the radio show or how much listening to it meant to them. Some told me that they had just moved to Colorado and weren't quite hooked up there yet. Some told me they thought they had a son like mine. One woman told me she'd recently lost her husband. One little girl told me she'd be entering middle school next year and was interested in politics. I begged her to learn quick and see what she could do for us. One family had a high school boy who hoped to be a comedian.

I hugged every single one of them, and more and more showed up. It felt magical.

Thomas E paced like a caged animal. "You've really got to go, Mom."

I was rooted to the spot.

When I thought I had connected with every last person, maybe a hundred or so, I turned backstage to go to the reception. But Thomas E stopped me. He pointed out a few people I had missed. I apologized, talked with them a bit, and hugged them, too.

VARIABLES

The reception was friendly and fun, but the hugging there wasn't as easy. Red Rocks Amphitheatre is in one of the most beautiful places in the world, and those of us who hugged outside underneath the Colorado night sky may have had an advantage. There might have been a moon, there probably was, but I never once looked up that high. I looked into the eyes of each person, often with my hand at rest on their shoulder. Inside, at the reception, people wore name tags that snagged on my jacket and they held wineglasses that bumped precariously against my shoulders. These hugs required technique and strategy. I dodged more than one chocolate-covered strawberry to complete an embrace. These conversations were longer, making the timing of the hug more difficult to judge.

I tried not to squish people with my hugs, nor hold them hostage. One advantage to hugging a hundred people in a row is that I found a rhythm. Those waiting knew the hugging conventions by the time they were up. Everyone seemed to know when the hug was over. In a hundred people, I didn't get more than one or two of those male defibrillator hugs, where they grab you and give a quick pound to your shoulder blades, like they are embossing metal.

At the backstage reception, however, I received a wide variety of unfortunate styles of hugs. Perhaps as a result of the longer conversations, liberties were taken, beyond the standard unspoken contract of the social hug. Several could've brought up a chicken bone lodged in my throat. When I stepped back from hugging one public radio board member, he had a little rabbit puppet in his hand, which he said he'd pulled out of my ear. Liberties. I hugged one woman, and deeming it the right time to release, I withdrew, but she held on to my hand, which I tried gracefully to extricate, leaving my guard down for her to grab my other hand. It was like hugging flypaper.

QUALITATIVE OBSERVATION #5

Some hugs fill you up, and some hugs suck the life out of you.

FIELD NOTES

Still, it was a truly blissful night. We slept fast and then it was off to the airport in the morning. I gave Thomas E my first-class upgrade and I took a middle seat in steerage, sensing an opportunity to connect with my fellow passengers.

QUALITATIVE OBSERVATION #6

You can't hug from the middle seat. You can't even put your hand on your fellow passenger's shoulder and look into their eyes, unless you're sliding out to use the bathroom.

FIELD NOTES

I talked a lot to the men in seats 35A and 35C, figuring I'd create a bond and then hug them at the baggage claim. They were greeted by family and friends, so I hung back, looking for an opening to approach them. I saw them each glance nervously my way once or twice, clearly noticing that I was watching them. When it began to take on a stalking quality, I gave up and retreated to home. Besides, I was exhausted. I usually sleep on planes, but I stayed awake for this entire flight, doing hug reconnaissance.

CONCLUSION

Hugging may be to people what running up to speeds of ninety miles per hour is to cheetahs. They only have the energy to do it once a day. I had a peak hugging experience outdoors after the show at Red Rocks that one night. It was sweet. I think I garnered a whopping two balous of happiness, but I couldn't re-create it. I read a tweet on my "Notifications" feed a day or two later: "Paula Poundstone hugged everyone in line after *Wait Wait . . . Don't Tell Me!* It made me smile and fired up a residual hep of happiness. I'm assuming they meant it as a positive observation, not a CDC alert.

Even Thomas E said he had a great time on that trip. It may have been the result of a contact high from the hug fest, or maybe it was because he got my first-class upgrade while I sat in coach.

THE
GET PURRING
EXPERIMENT

CONDITIONS

Thomas E's private school is an expensive disappointment. It turns out the building is too frail to accommodate Bunson burners so the students can't do a lot of science experiments. I talked to the head of the school about it once. He said that students have to take chemistry again in college, anyway, so the goal of this school was just to get students interested in chemistry and science. He said the school tries to encourage curiosity, to get them thinking and formulating questions like scientists. Questions, I guess, like, "How come no one is actually teaching us science?"

I might have even overlooked that, but the school's plan for next year is to provide a laptop for every student. I don't think I should pay a school to give him brain damage. So Thomas E will be transferring to Santa Monica High School, which are words I'd hoped never to utter. After Alley and Toshia graduated and Toshia and I brought fondue to our last potluck IEP there, I thought our family had escaped their halls forever.

Alley is thriving, working for another summer at the Santa Monica Food Co-op. I shop there occasionally. They have bins of grains and seeds that you scoop, bag, and write the code on the twist tie yourself, and it's still pricey. I can never figure that out. I'm doing half their work for them, and it's costlier. If I harvested it, ground it, and trucked it to their store, a bag of cornmeal would put me out on the street.

A few weeks ago, we were driving to the airport in Boston, coming home from our traditional one-week vacation in Manchester-by-the-Sea, Massachusetts, when I casually asked Alley to check the Santa Monica High School's website to find out when Thomas E started. She looked and said, "Tomorrow." It was two weeks into August. Kids must wear flippers and floaties for the first week. I felt stupid that I didn't know, but why would I have even checked in the middle of the summer?

My computer is chock-full each day with emails from the school announcing that the principal did the "ice bucket challenge," that it's not too late to buy Spirit Wear before the first pep rally of the year, and that the school is desperate for donations, but it never occurred to anyone there to send one along that mentioned the start day.

VARIABLES

Toshia is getting her sea legs in apartment life. I miss her, but she's fine.

CONSTANT

I have to remind myself that the words the Reverend Mother sings to Maria in *The Sound of Music* are not "Follow every rainbow until you find my dream for you."

CONDITIONS

Thomas E has already told me that he had to write a tweet for English and that his teacher liked his rough draft.

Alley's summer break is over, too. I drove her back up to school in Portland, Oregon. I miss her, but I know she's alive by the Starbucks charges on my MasterCard bill.

I worked more this summer than I have in summers past, and I've got lots more coming up. I'm doing interviews, packing, unpacking, grocery shopping, cleaning, driving back and forth to school, signing syllabi to say that I know what is required of my son in his classes (I also know that he won't do it, by the way, but there's no space to sign for that), sifting litter boxes, letting dogs in and out, and tripping over cats.

I look longingly at my cats before I pass out at the end of the day, but it occurred to me recently that I almost never spend any quality time with my animals. My dog Sirius sleeps in front of doors constantly now. Because he's so attention starved, being stepped on is the closest thing to being petted he can hope for.

When Alley was home, she would sit for hours petting them or bobbing the feather on a stick toy for the cats. In fact, in her absence her cat Harrison often stands outside her door crying. I'm just the cat's waitress and chambermaid. Most of them don't come anywhere near me anymore.

HYPOTHESIS

They say pet ownership is good for the heart. I think they mean the part where you are actually interacting directly with them. It couldn't be the part where you pick up their waste or heave enormous bags of their food onto your shoulder. They even bring animals to the bedsides of hospital patients to help with their recovery. I'm sure they don't say, "Mr. Simmons, this is Skippy and he's come to visit you. He also just pooped over there behind your heart monitor, so here's a bag. Let's have you get up, hold your gown closed in the back, and clean it up. Skippy is so happy to see you."

I am going to see how many heps of happiness I can get from spending a day with my cats and dogs.

FIELD NOTES

I dropped Thomas E off at school, cleaned the kitchen, looked around at my son's filthy room, sighed deeply, and wondered how high I was when I decided to have kids. I checked my email and found one from the high school with the subject line "Parent Involvement Survey." I didn't click on it. That should give them some idea.

EQUIPMENT

It must have been some time after the first Get Organized experiment when I received a box in the mail from a kind fan. Inside was a cat toy called a Cat's Meow. It has gathered dust on top of the antique suitcases in my bedroom for a long time. It consists of a plastic disc with a motor that moves a stick at three different speeds, all under a yellow, nylon cloth.

After seeing my show, in which I talked about my cats, another audience member sent me a shallow wooden box packed tight with short pieces of vertically standing cardboard. This pet toy, too, has been stored in my room for quite a while.

In my safe, I have buds of catnip in Ziploc bags, also gifted from a generous audience member. I received them a couple of years ago and had originally put them in the freezer to keep them fresh, but one day my son took one out and tossed it on the table in front of me, sanctimoniously bellowing, "Look what Alley's been doing!"

"Thomas, it's catnip."

He was pretty revved up when he thought he'd caught his sister with pot, so it took him a minute or so to process the disappointment. I started to put the bag of catnip back in the freezer, but I thought better of it. I'm pretty sure he believed me that it was catnip, but I also wondered if he might be tempted to try to sell it, as if it were contraband. So I stuck it in the safe in my bedroom closet. Now, sometimes late at night, I can hear the cats in there slowly turning the dial trying to decipher the combination.

FIELD NOTES

10:00 A.M.

I put the Cat's Meow toy on the living-room floor and knelt beside it. My dogs, Ramona and Sirius, and my neighbor's dog, Jack, loved the Cat's Meow toy; however, the cats would never come near it amid the rowdy company of the big, lunkish canines. I had to uninvite the dogs. I got up, put them outside, and again sat down on the floor beside the toy.

QUALITATIVE OBSERVATION #1

Our rug really needs cleaning.

FIELD NOTES

Cats are nocturnal, and the cats that I could see in the living room were sleeping, as they often are at this time of day. They were under the pinball machine, draped across the TV stand, and curled up on the chairs.

QUANTITATIVE OBSERVATION #1

Fuck, I have a lot of cats.

ENVIRONMENT

The chairs are vacuumed almost every day, and still I have to offer an adhesive "lint lifter" to any guest who sits on one, which might be one reason I don't have many guests.

FIELD NOTES

My cat Belle, a large, friendly silver tabby, approached the toy as soon as I dumped the dogs. Several times she batted at the mysterious thing beneath the yellow nylon cloth, before lying down and blocking its further passage, which caused the machine to make a high keening wail. I think it is supposed to replicate the sound of a small creature of prey begging for mercy.

Tonks, Luigi, Harrison, Brittle, and Theo began to take an interest and crept forward haltingly, kind of like R. P. McMurphy's fellow mental hospital patients when he pretends to give color commentary on a World Series game in *One Flew Over the Cuckoo's Nest.*

Belle backed up when Tonks moved in on the toy. Tonks is

a scrawny Siamese, who aspires to be the head cat but has no leadership skills nor charisma on the stump. Instead she's an erratic bully. I think she is responsible for much of the territorial peeing. Because she is not an inspiring leader, other cats see a power vacuum there and try to make a move into the top spot. There are constant territorial disputes, involving marking, scratching, yowling, large tufts of fur flying, plus the age-old cat karate move where one cat grabs another cat's head with its front paws and rapidly kicks it with its hind paws. It's like an endless primary season, but not as ugly.

10:05 A.M.
My twenty-pound cat, Matilda, made plaintive squeaks from a chair, so I brought her over to where I was sitting. Matilda does not carry her weight well. She is so fat, her legs just stick out of her bulbous torso. She looks like she was drawn by a kindergartner. Clearly she didn't win the genetic lottery in terms of body type. I don't really see her at the food bowl more than the others. Of course, I don't see her throw up, either, which is clearly how the others keep their shape. If she could talk, I'm sure she'd say, "I gain weight just looking at kibble," but I only have so much sympathy for her. She doesn't do anything to help herself. She barely moves. She hasn't chased a ball with a bell in it for years.

I began to pet Matilda, and several others crept over to enjoy a bit of petting.

QUALITATIVE OBSERVATION #2
Cats are greasy.

FIELD NOTES

10:20 A.M.
My hands were covered in just enough cat grease to make a thin layer of cat fur stick to them, which in turn stuck to my face. It goes without saying that my T-shirt was covered.

10:25 A.M.
The phone rang. I got up from the floor. I make a grunting sound when I get up now, like my dad used to. What with all the residue on my hands, I could barely grip the phone. It was a robocall. The voice said, "Congratulations! You've been selected to win a trip to the Bahamas." I said, "Fuck you, I'm petting the cats," and I sat back down.

ANALYSIS

Even while petting the cats, I find it hard to just sit. Maybe it's the walking cautionary tale of Matilda, or maybe it's because when I slow down I'm consumed with anxiety.

I worry about my son almost constantly. Teenage boys are difficult. I read that their frontal lobe, the part that handles planning and reasoning, doesn't even come in until between twenty-five and thirty. Sometimes I check on him at night. There is a divot there. It hasn't even started. I wonder if there's some kind of a lobe-growing kit you can buy at Hobby Lobby or something. That's where I got my contraceptive kits. You make them out of felt and pipe cleaners.

I heard an ad on the radio for an instructional audio series on family relationships, created by a wife and husband who are both therapists. In the ad, the woman therapist says, "I will never forget the day my son, Jeremy, slammed the door and said, 'I hate you!'" I thought, *Really, that stands out in your memory? Shit, that's a good morning in our house. And he slammed the door, huh? That must have been awful.*

I saw *The Exorcist* on TV recently, and except for the holy water and the green vomit, it looked awfully familiar.

FIELD NOTES

10:30 A.M.
I got out the FURminator, an industrial-strength brush for pets. I brushed Shamwow, who is our only long-haired cat. I brushed Rutherford, who is living proof that medical science is a money-making hoax. She is so old and skinny, she must be down to one organ. There simply isn't room in that frame for any more than that. It turns out, we don't need organs. She's fine. I brushed Hardy. I brushed Jem. I brushed Severus. I brushed Matilda.

11:00 A.M.
I had a pile of cat fur the size of two whole cats. I'd have to reassemble some of it to get Shamwow back. There was a horrifying moment when I realized I had brushed all of her fur away, and there was no cat.

The phone rang. I struggled to my feet to answer it. This time, a voice said I had been selected for a government program providing me with a discount on solar paneling. I had fur in my throat. I tried to clear it, but I just made a raspy noise and hung up the phone.

11:01 A.M.

The sun was beating down through the skylight above us, which is what attracts my cats to the living room at that hour. It made me hot, sweaty, and reflective.

As much as I dread Thomas being at Santa Monica High School, I thought, *the teachers have been more involved and responsive than they ever were with either of the girls.*

Toshia ended up in summer school one year, and one morning, in frustration, I asked her if this time the teacher was finally correcting her writing. She said, "No, we do peer editing."

I nearly choked on my instant oatmeal.

I said, "Please tell me that you mean that the teacher corrected it at that place near the boardwalk on the ocean with the Ferris wheel. Please tell me you don't mean that you handed it to another kid, who's stuck in summer school because she can't write, and asked her for her thoughts on your work."

"It looks gud to me."

For a while after Toshia moved out, I felt like I was doing most of the phone calling. I didn't want to nag her, so I let her know I was "leaving the ball in her court" in terms of our relationship. Now she never calls. Every month or so I call her and ask if she understands what the phrase, "leaving the ball in her court" means. She seems to.

I continued petting. I pet Clue, a calico who seems far down in the cat caste system. The other cats won't usually allow her into the living room. Anytime I start to pet her, she meows and whines for more. It's never enough. Perhaps that gets on the other cats' nerves and she doesn't pick up on the social cues.

We named Clue after Inspector Clouseau, the delightfully

funny Peter Sellers character from *The Pink Panther*, whom all of my kids love. But Clue is nothing like Peter Sellers. That's the problem with naming. You name someone, and then later you find out who they are. I should have named Clue "Clyde's Sister-In-Law," from *Bonnie and Clyde*, who was played by Estelle Parsons and was quite whiney, but who knew?

11:15 A.M.
I let the dogs back in, and the cats scattered in all directions. They came out again slowly, like Munchkins, while I brushed Sirius.

11:20 A.M.
I thought I'd better take a quick break to read the emails from the high school, because if school started in the middle of the summer, then surely Winter Break would commence in late September. I don't want to be caught off guard again.

11:25 A.M.
Luigi, a huge gorgeous silver tabby with large white patches and beautiful blue eyes, rested comfortably in my lap until my dog Ramona moved. Despite years of living together, if there's a cat in my lap, every time a dog so much as stirs, the cat leaps up, digs its claws into my copious thighs for traction, and begins a Paul Revere dash around the house. "The dogs are coming! The dogs are coming!" Luigi has carved his name in my legs.

11:27 A.M.
I put the dogs out, bandaged my legs, and brought out the wooden box with the side-up cardboard packed tightly within.

It's designed to be a scratching toy but my cats just stared at it, so I went into my closet, spun the safe dial left-right-left, and grabbed the Ziploc bag with the catnip. I sprinkled it liberally on the top of the cardboard in the box. They lined up like the disciples at the Last Supper.

11:30 A.M.

Theo stretched out across the top of the box, belly up, and fell asleep. There was another brief flurry of activity over at the Cat's Meow, but this time not one cat could catch the revolving stick under the yellow nylon cloth. They were satisfied to lie on their backs and look at it. I pushed the button to increase the speed and the looks on their faces seemed to say, "Fuck, that is just amazing . . . whoa . . . I'm gonna let that one live for now."

Oreo came for the nip. She never comes close enough for me to pet her. She seems to feel she's really depriving me and takes great pleasure in that. I got close enough to Mrs. Fezziwig to grab her, wipe her eyes, and clip her nails. We have a strictly business relationship, but it's warm compared to the one with my cat Wednesday, who rarely comes out of the bathroom cabinet behind the litter boxes. Every time she sees me she gets a horrified look, as if to say, "It's the large one!" and scrambles out of the way. I only clip her nails when they get so long they snag on the carpet and she can't get away from me. In short, Wednesday uses me. I think she spends most of her time in the cabinet wondering what she'll inherit when I die. The answer, of course, is the same as what my kids will get—debt.

1:00 P.M.

I had been petting for hours. I was filthy. My living room was covered in fur, claw clippings, and catnip. I was dizzy from watching the stick turn under the yellow nylon cloth on the Cat's Meow. The cats were all asleep, and it's no wonder: some of them had been awake for over an hour.

I was drowsy myself. Mostly because of the sun. Petting my cats isn't all that relaxing, because although they enjoy attention and insist on it, if I am sitting near them, they also bite after every several strokes. It actually makes me kind of edgy. There's a Russian roulette element to the whole enterprise.

ANALYSIS

The dogs had been looking in miserably from the back door for quite a while. I was feeling guilty. Plus, I was glancing at the clock every few minutes, nervous about how long it would take me to make the living room livable again before I had to get Thomas E from school. I don't like any distractions during our homework argument. Last week I got caught up doing the dishes and I let a "she said we don't have to know what it means" slip by unanswered.

I'm not sure I would call this happiness.

FIELD NOTES

1:30 P.M.

The phone rang. I had an interview with a public radio station in northern California to promote a show I'm doing there. The host asked me about the devastating drought in California, and whether or not I thought northern California should secede from southern California. Thinking quickly, I said, "I have sixteen cats." That show should sell out.

Comedy and public radio don't always mix. They do real journalism on public radio. They sometimes have the same guy interview me that they had interview a hostage or someone from Doctors Without Borders in a war zone. I get a lot of questions like "What's funny about the conflict in Gaza?" or "Burkas. Anything?"

2:00 P.M.

The dogs started to whine and I couldn't take it anymore, so I grabbed their leashes from the closet (and endured the routine of spinning and jumping that is triggered by even going near the closet with the leashes), saddled them up, and took them for a walk. I hate walking the dogs. I wouldn't mind if we simply walked. I just don't enjoy the tour of the famous canine pee spots the way they do. I think it's how my son felt when I took him to the Smithsonian.

2:45 P.M.

I returned from the walk and picked up as much fur off of the rug as I could with my hands. I then vacuumed, emptying the canister three times. I dare Mr. Dyson to come to my house.

I shoved the toys, the brush, and the clippers back in their respective places before jumping in the car to get Thomas E.

CONCLUSION

Ramona, Sirius, Jack, Rutherford, Matilda, Brittle, Clue, Jem, Oreo, Hardy, Belle, Harrison, Severus, Luigi, Tonks, Theo, Wednesday, Shamwow, and Mrs. Fezziwig provide me with a steady stream of low-grade happiness every day. I love watching them. They give my home a kind of comedic baseline. If they stood in one place when they threw up, they'd be even more lovable.

Spending hours with them in my living room on a hot day gave me no more than a hep or so of happiness. I prefer the time we spend intermittently throughout the day. If I added up all of the quick head pats, the chin strokes with the top of my pen, the toss of the ball with the bell in it, the times I wished I'd had my camera, and the snuggles in bed, it would probably come to a sizable slice of my happiness pie. Maybe happiness doesn't come in bulk. Maybe it's sprinkled in.

THE
GET POSITIVE
EXPERIMENT

I'VE BEEN AWARE of the concept of "positive self-talk" since I was young. For my fifth birthday, I received a Burl Ives record album that included the song "The Little Engine That Could" about the determined train who sang, "I think I can. I think I can," to power a heavy load successfully up a steep hill. I also got a set of toy pots and pans. Neither message really took. All of these years later, I generally think I can't, think I can't, and I don't cook.

It does seem possible that the dialogue in my head could be influencing my happiness.

CONDITIONS

I've been on the road every weekend for months. I'm about to go stir-crazy in the hotel rooms. I try to keep room service on the phone for the social life.

"Fries or chips? Hmmm, that's a tough one. How many chips would I get? Do you know where the potatoes come from? Are they free range? I was just working in Idaho. I wasn't sure if I should say anything about potatoes in front of the audience because maybe it's a sore subject. I mean, Californians don't like to talk about the Kardashians and Missourians are sensitive about meth, but then, when I flew into Idaho, right in the middle of their baggage claim they had a giant statue of a potato. Um, I guess I'll have chips. They don't seem as heavy."

"Okay, that's a veggie burger and chips. We'll have that up in thirty minutes or less."

"Thank you. I'll miss you."

I'll do anything to avoid being alone with myself. I'm sick of myself.

HYPOTHESIS

Although negativity is practically my native language, I am going to replace my negative thoughts with positive ones.

PROCEDURE

I looked up "positive self-talk" on the internet. There were several articles by therapists and life coaches, who I imagine burn incense and play didgeridoo music in their offices.

A few of the articles suggested specific affirmations for the novice in "positive self-talk." I include myself in the beginner group, so I jotted down some of the lines.

Believing any of these would be a bigger stretch for me than when Mr. King held my heel over my head in taekwondo. I had to skip the ones that defied reason, such as "My intentions create my reality." That's the kind of logic that got me thousands of dollars into debt. If my intentions created my reality, not only would I not have enough shelf space for my Pulitzers and Nobels, but my dog Ramona would hold the world's record for duration on her sit/stay, and she doesn't. I'd put my intentions up against Mother Teresa's. It was her follow-through that kicked my ass.

I nixed "Each step is taking me where I want to be," as I have no sense of direction and have therefore taken many steps toward where I do not want to be.

I had to put the kibosh on "My life is unfolding beautifully," for obvious reasons.

"I feel energetic and alive" seemed to be low-balling it.

"I know who I am and I'm enough" sounded like an affirmation for people recovering from a brain injury.

I scrapped "I always observe before reacting" before I even thought about it.

Many of the self-proclamations were further proof that one can't just believe anything they read on the internet.

It's not like these were quotes from Martin Luther King Jr. or Mark Twain. They're mostly written by women who sit on mats, breathing, in front of tables covered with batiked cloth and who started blogging after their divorces. I say, "I just plain suck," to myself several times a day. Replacing it with "My body is my vehicle in life; I choose to fill it with goodness" just isn't gonna fly. I could do, "My body is my vehicle in life; I'll never pass the smog inspection," but where does that get me?

I narrowed down the affirmations to those that wouldn't require just plain lying to myself. I wrote them on index cards and slipped them into my back pocket, where they made my butt look even bigger. I wrote them on poster boards and taped them up all over my house.

In a bold move I put "Today I choose joy" on my video shelf above the wheelie cart my computer is on and beside where I sleep on the floor. I put "I can find balance in my life" above the calendar that takes me two hours to hand-write in marker each month. It's on newsprint and every square is packed with time entries and symbols, including little airplane illustrations for the days that I travel and symbols like poorly drawn drum kits to mark the nights Thomas E has drum lessons. It has days that start at ridiculous hours and spill into the next box. I think I've already found balance in my life. I never take any days off. That would tilt it.

I put "I am strong" on my bedroom door. I had to modify some of the messages. I put "Stress is leaving my body" on the inside of my front door. Then I crossed off *body* and wrote *house*. That seemed easier to believe. Stress is in my body, but it comes with me when I leave.

I put "This too shall pass" down low on the living-room wall, where the cats will likely pee on it. I think of it as "This too shall piss" or "Piss too shall pass." Either way, I can believe that.

I posted the vague and haunting "Today has limitless possibilities" higher up on the living-room wall. Then I took a shot at a few of my own and hung them under it. Like "I thought it was going to be a lot worse than this" and "I can handle any crap that happens."

I put "I breathe in peace" on the living room window. In truth, I know that, even if I do breathe in peace, I'll cough it out right away. Still, it might help.

Obviously, "I can find my happy place" went right on the

mirror in the bathroom, where the four cat litter boxes are stationed and where I spend many happy hours.

Finally, I stared at "I'm doing my best" for a while before posting it in its rightful place, across the front of my car's glove compartment, where it can help to hold back the tidal wave of criticism that comes my way from both my passengers and fellow drivers on the road. It even covers the latch on the glove compartment. So when a cop pulls me over, I have to reach beneath the "I'm doing my best" sign to access my registration.

Happiness, at this point, will just be a matter of following directions.

FIELD NOTES

I had a feeling of excitement from the moment I woke to see the "I choose joy" sign. I stared at it, trying to take it in.

That's right, I choose joy, I thought, quickly pushing *Shit, my back hurts* out of my consciousness. I dressed, hobbled to the cats' bathroom, and began to sift the litter boxes, while repeating aloud to myself, "I can find my happy place."

QUALITATIVE OBSERVATION #1

It's so easy.

FIELD NOTES

I received notice in the mail from the Department of Motor Vehicles that I had to renew my driver's license, and I thought that meant I had to retake the written test. At first I thought, *Uh-oh*, but I caught myself, reviewed the index cards from my back pocket, and tried to internalize "I can stay calm under pressure."

Remaining calm, I thought I remembered that here in Santa Monica people who don't test well can opt for a project instead of taking the written test. I was considering making a papier-mâché car wreck. Just to be on the safe side, though, and because I am strong, I Googled "California DMV written test" and began to practice. It all seemed so new. I kept reading the answers, mumbling things like "Really? A full stop, huh?"

QUALITATIVE OBSERVATION #2
I could see that I did have a choice about how I felt.

FIELD NOTES
On the way to an appointment, while merging onto the 405 Freeway, another driver honked and barked something at me. There wasn't time to rifle through my index cards, but fortunately, by now I had begun to commit some positive self-talk to memory, which is the idea. They should become a part of you. I quickly lowered the window and yelled, "I choose healthy relationships." When he flipped me off, I screamed, "I briefly drove a Lamborghini."

QUALITATIVE OBSERVATION #3
Not everyone supports my positivity.

FIELD NOTES
I parked on a side street to wait for Thomas E to get out of school. I thought about how I had sworn to myself that I would step back this year and allow him to sink or swim on his own, but I was failing already. I had made a big deal about how he had to set his own alarm clock in the morning and that I wouldn't

wake him. Yet I've gone into his room every morning. First I pretend that I accidentally went into the wrong room, which probably isn't all that believable, given the small size of our house and the fact that we've been here for twelve years. "Oh, sorry. I thought this was the breakfast nook." When that doesn't work, I pretend I just stopped by to enjoy the smell of moldy clothes.

These were very negative thoughts. I had to stop. I punched on the news on public radio. I listened to a guy with a British accent report on Boko Haram. I could have sworn they were a seventies rock band. It turns out they've committed horrible atrocities in Africa.

ISIS, which must be a band I never even heard of, has captured cities in Iraq.

There were more bomb blasts in Israel. As near as I could understand from the report, it was in retaliation for some horrible thing Israel did, in retaliation for the bomb blasts in Israel before these, in retaliation for some other awful thing that Israel did. There was more, but I lost track.

"I can find inner peace," I repeated to myself.

QUALITATIVE OBSERVATION #4
Outer peace would be nice, too.

QUALITATIVE OBSERVATION #5
Don't tell me that I said so, but when this positive self-talk doesn't work, I feel even more like a loser.

VARIABLES
Thomas E showed up at the car.

ANALYSIS

He seemed agitated. When we got home, he insisted that he needed to use my computer right away. I told him he had to wait. All hell broke loose. While he was banging on my door, he yelled, "Are you choosing happiness now?" This is the behavior of someone suffering with electronics addiction.

When things were calm, I came out of my room, took down all of the signs, emptied my back pocket of the index cards, and put them all in the recycling.

CONCLUSION

What the hell was I thinking?

THE
GET OVER HERE AND HELP
EXPERIMENT

IN THE 1800S theology professor Henry Drummond said, "Happiness . . . consists in giving and serving others."

Nineteenth-century educator and civil rights activist Booker T. Washington said, "If you want to lift yourself up, lift up someone else."

Eighteenth-century Swedish philosopher, scientist, and theologian, Emanuel Swedenborg said, "True charity is the desire to be useful to others with no thought of recompense."

Of course, if I'm seeking my own happiness, technically that would be recompense, but let's face it, Emanuel Swedenborg was always a bit of a downer, and his words, though sometimes inspirational, needn't be followed to the letter.

I've long been familiar with the idea that true happiness is found in helping others, and I've always meant to get around to it. I just had to make sure it wasn't found in a Lamborghini first.

CONDITIONS

After speaking with the handful of electronics addiction experts around the country, I decided to take Thomas E to a wilderness program in Utah, where he'd live outside in the mountains. He was probably, even now, desperately trying to get a signal. In a program like this, kids backpack and learn survival skills. They make their own shelters, using a piece of canvas and a length of thin rope. They learn to make fire by rubbing sticks together. They talk and hike. They learn to read facial cues because they look at each other, sometimes, when they talk. They eat with spoons that they carve from wood. It is not a program specifi-cally designed for kids with electronics addiction. No such pro-gram exists in the United States at this time. This is a stopgap arrangement, not nearly enough to solve the problem, but the virtue of a wilderness program for us is that the kids don't go anywhere near a building and mercifully, they are completely relieved of screens, phones, or electronics of any kind.

So I drove my son ten hours to Utah and drove home, with a short stay at a Comfort Inn off the freeway, where I found, after a couple of hours and multiple pillow arrangements, that I couldn't sleep. I left a twenty-dollar tip for housekeeping on the nightstand by the table-tent advertisement for the Denny's All-You-Can-Eat Pancake Extravaganza, where I wished I could leave my useless, aching heart.

He'll be there for about ten weeks. Some experts recom-mended six to eight months without any electronics. Given that we have not yet colonized the moon, it's uncertain whether or not we'll be able to pull that off but if we don't, his future is not looking bright.

There's not a hep of happiness in sight, which couldn't be a better laboratory for another happiness experiment.

HYPOTHESIS

I am going to devote as much time as I can to helping others. I'd like to say I'm going to forget about myself and only think of others, but my memory is a little too good for that.

PROCEDURE

I decided to start by donating platelets, which are cells made in the bone marrow that circulate in the blood to help it clot. Donating platelets is a lengthier process than donating blood. I wanted to go the extra mile in my giving. I called the UCLA Blood & Platelet Donation Center. A nice man answered the phone and told me I could sign up online.

QUALITATIVE OBSERVATION #1

Aaaaaaaaaaah!

PROCEDURE

I begged him to just let me make an appointment over the phone, since we were already talking on it. He scheduled the appointment, told me to eat healthfully, and not to take aspirin for a couple of days before. Then he thanked me.

QUALITATIVE OBSERVATION #2

I hadn't even done anything and I was being thanked. I liked this.

FIELD NOTES

I pulled up to my house today and found a couple with their car's back end being hoisted by a tow truck. I didn't know them, but they were right on my curb. Although, to be honest, I was wincing internally when I did it, I said, "Do you guys need a ride somewhere?"

I really didn't feel like driving strangers anywhere, but in the interest of my experiment, I knew it was my duty. They pointed to another car, explaining that it was the woman's car that was being towed and that the guy had come to pick her up, but they thanked me enthusiastically.

QUALITATIVE OBSERVATION #3

I'm enjoying the heck out of just intending to help.

FIELD NOTES

After negotiating frustrating one-way streets, I paid eight bucks for a parking space and made my way to the UCLA Blood & Platelet Donation Center. I had eaten a spinach-filled breakfast so as to donate the highest-quality platelets.

I walked up the stairs, gave my name to the woman at the desk in front of a poster with a drawing of a drop of red blood with eyes and a happy smile. I couldn't help wondering who their target donor was.

I received a clipboard with pages of questions. Did I use needle-injected narcotics? No. Had I had sex in England? No. Had I had sex in Africa? No. Had I had sex in France? No. Had I had sex in Haiti? No. Had I had sex in Mexico? No. Had I had sex in the rough section of Canada? No. Had I had sex on Dummkopf Street in Germany? No.

Did I have tattoos or piercings? No. Had I had sex with anyone who had tattoos or piercings? Did I have anything against people with tattoos and piercings? No. I was tempted to take aspirin.

If there were two small blank lines on which I could write the time and place of my sexual encounters, I could have made this a lot quicker.

When I finally completed the form, I was ushered into a small room, where a nurse asked me some of the questions again. I guess this is because they want to make sure the blood is healthy and they think that if someone lied on the form, they might crack there in the little room.

I stuck to my story, because it was true, but I was expecting them to use good cop / bad cop techniques soon.

Nurse 1: Thanks for coming in to donate platelets.

Me: Sure, I'm happy to.

Nurse 1: See my tattoo? Do you like it?

Me: Yeah, sure, it's nice.

Nurse 1: Excuse me a minute. I'll be right back. (*leaves the little room*)

Nurse 2: (*enters the room*) So, you *do* like tattoos!

Me: No, I was just . . . I didn't want to hurt—

Nurse 2: You have had sex in England! You have fucked the Rolling Stones! You *have*! Say it! *You have!*

I was relieved when the nurse only pricked my finger, took my blood pressure, pulse, and temperature, and I was surprised that my blood pressure wasn't higher. I was then led into a room full of machines and beds, where I suspected for a moment they might place a British guy with tattoos in a bed beside me, just to measure my reaction. They didn't.

I climbed up on a bed. In front of it was my own screen with a list of movie titles. The nurse gave me a headset, showed me how to select a movie, and asked if I wanted a warm blanket, which I accepted. They heat their blankets. He asked if I needed anything else and I asked him to please pass me my diet soda. Then he handed me a ball to squeeze while he stuck a needle in my arm. I hate needles, but the nurse was good at it. Plus, I was lying in a bed with a warm blanket and a beverage, watching *Flight*, starring Denzel Washington, which I never saw when it was in the theater. Nurses kept coming over to ask me if I needed anything. I was so comfortable, I felt guilty. I was supposed to be helping others.

The whole thing was over in about two hours. Denzel Washington was fantastic. Before I left they gave me two free passes to the movie theater and insisted I eat some cookies. "Oh, well, if it's part of helping others, you talked me into it."

I took out my calendar and scheduled another donation appointment for the following week. This time I hope to get a Disney cruise.

QUALITATIVE OBSERVATION #4
I love warm blankets.

ANALYSIS
My house is fairly quiet. Sometimes all I can hear is my cats throwing up. Not that I was ever a great cook, but without kids in the house making a meal seemed pointless.

A friend bought me a Vitamix blender. I used it for my first time today. The cover of the instruction manual reads, "Welcome to the Vitamix family." I wasn't planning on adding family members. I'm not doing that well with the ones I have now. Soon my new Vitamix children will be telling me that I dress funny, and I'll be driving Uncle Vitamix to the hospital for outpatient procedures. I really just wanted a smoothie.

PROCEDURE

After enjoying a healthful fruit beverage, I began to work on an additional way to help others.

I have always been afraid of the elderly. I know that's not right. It's true, though. I don't really know why I feel that way. They can be cranky, but so can people of any age. I can't explain it. I've just always been afraid of them, but given that I'm unalterably gravitating toward that direction myself, I decided that I should face my fears and make this the very population upon which I focus my helpful efforts.

I made a list of nursing homes in my area and called several. I left messages at most and spoke directly with only one person, who when I suggested volunteering, said, "What would you do?" I said, "I could read to people or talk to them." It was worrisome how unfamiliar these ideas seemed to her. "Talk to them? No, we don't, ah, use, ah, volunteers. Talk to them, huh? No." I thanked her and hung up.

In a short while, the activities director from one of the places I had left a message returned my call. She had a thick accent, which I thought was maybe Russian, and she was extremely grateful and enthusiastic about my interest. "What would you like to do?" she asked. I said, "Anything. I'll read to people, or just talk to them. Whatever you want."

To my relief, she said that would be wonderful. I asked if I could come by. I hadn't heard back from the other nursing homes I called. I thought I'd just check out this one before I committed.

ENVIRONMENT

The facility was about a mile from my house, in a residential area. It had a well-groomed garden out front and didn't look offensively institutional on the outside. The inside bustled with doctors, nurses, physical therapists, custodial staff, and aides. Essentially, it was a small hospital. There were school-type seasonal decorations, including cardboard leaves and acorns, on the walls. Between the wheelchairs, the stainless-steel carts full of plastic disposable cups of yogurt, and the oxygen machines, there were more wheels than at the Tour de France. There was a holiday donation box at the front desk, made with a bit of wrapping paper around a large cardboard box. I could clearly see GAUZE stamped on the box beneath the paper. I stepped up to the nurse's station to ask for Katherine, the activities director.

FACTOR

Katherine appeared a moment later. She had a warm sideways smile, wore a white uniform jacket with a name tag, and couldn't have been more welcoming.

ENVIRONMENT

Katherine showed me around the place. There was lots of metal. Even more metal than wheels. Dr. Simon Bar Sinister, the arch villain from the old *Underdog* cartoon, once tried to rule the world with a giant magnet. He could have brought this place to a screeching halt. We walked past metal trays, metal canes, metal oxygen cylinders, metal crutches, and metal pans. The walls have framed, old-time Santa Monica photographs every few feet. We toured the dining room, the outdoor patio, and the physical therapy room, and walked past lots of rooms with beds, and easy-to-clean surfaces. Occasionally, we went by a room with pastel plastic-pan decor and a bed whose occupant appeared lifeless, with thin, stringy hair and ancient Chinese papyrus skin. This was my worst fear.

We ended up back at the activity room. Don't let that word *activity* fool you.

VARIABLES

Katherine introduced me to the eight or nine people in the room. They were all in wheelchairs, surrounding two large round tables. One or two had oxygen tubes wrapped around their faces, which fed into two short parallel nozzles that went up their noses. A few of them were using colored pencils—there was a box in the center of their table—to color in pictures of horses or princesses. A bunch of newspapers were distributed around the second table, including a copy of the day's *Los Angeles Times*. Here and there, people stared at open copies of the *Santa Monica Mirror*. I figured they used those to sedate the excitable patients. I live in Santa Monica, and even I don't care about the "news" of Santa Monica. I didn't imagine that the gripping cover story, about the high school holiday production of *Annie*, would light a fire among the old folks. "Say! Would you take a look at this? Daddy Warbucks may be replaced because he's failing algebra."

"Where? Where? Let me see that!"

"I have it next!"

"My God, now I'll never get to sleep."

FACTOR

It was obvious that Katherine truly cared about the people in the activity room. She both served their needs with upbeat energy and spoke to them with kindness and respect.

FIELD NOTES

She told the group I was to be their teacher and had come to read to them. I had never said anything about teaching anybody, but privately she explained to me that several of the clients had some dementia, which could make them childlike and that the dynamic would resemble that of a teacher and student. She said they couldn't follow a novel and that I should read children's books, which the facility provided. "Great," I said, and told her that I'd be back the next morning.

QUANTITATIVE OBSERVATION #1

There wasn't a patient in that activity room who didn't have a gauze bandage somewhere on their person. They must have emptied that big gauze box they used for gift collection in less than a day.

QUALITATIVE OBSERVATION #5

Aging can really suck.

ANALYSIS

This was pretty depressing. End-of-life issues bring up difficult questions and the answers are elusive. Obviously we can't all live forever, but must we crawl to the finish line?

CONSTANT

Alone and back at my house, I found myself starting to talk to my cats and dogs like the Dustin Hoffman character in *Papillon* talked to his pigs when he was in isolation on Devil's Island.

FIELD NOTES

I arrived the next day, nervous but looking forward to reading to the group. Again, Katherine welcomed me with bubbly, warm, undeserved gratitude. As she ushered me in, she announced my arrival to the room, where in addition to yesterday's pursuits, some of the occupants were now staring at *The View* on a television, which dangled from a metal arm on the wall.

QUALITATIVE OBSERVATION #6

Aging can really, really suck.

FIELD NOTES

Katherine pointed a remote control at the screen, said, "Let's turn this off," and clicked the button. The screen darkened. There's nothing more heroic than turning off *The View*, anywhere, and perhaps especially here, but still, I was terrified. I thought, *Great, now they're going to hate me.* I pictured them with their oxygen tubes, slingshotting their colored pencils at me, and yelling, "We were perfectly happy watching *The View*!"

"What did you do that for? Rosie O'Walters was on!"

"Ya whippersnapper!"

But most of them just turned from the screen with silent resignation.

Katherine then proclaimed, in a big, happy voice, "Your

teacher is going to read for you some wonderful story!" With that, she placed three third-grade-level nonfiction books on the table in front of me and stepped out of the room. I looked at the titles:

Georgia: A Pictorial History of the State,
Fast Food,
and *Soil.*

I picked up one book after the other, flipping through its pages and trying to think how I could possibly make these books remotely interesting to anyone. There was no way I could read a book called *Soil* to old people confined to wheelchairs in a nursing home.

I nervously reached to the center of the table for a copy of the day's *Santa Monica Mirror.* There was a weather section. We don't have weather in Santa Monica. The closest thing to weather we have is when a water main breaks. I threw it back into the center of the table. One or two people began to snore. Olga, at the other table began to moan, "I fall down." I looked at her, and said, "No, you're not, Olga, you're in your chair, at the table. You're fine." She stared at me silently for a minute and repeated, "I fall down."

I figured I'd just bring up a topic. I said, "Does anyone here like the Olympics?"

"No."

"The what?"

"I fall down."

I was dripping sweat.

Mercifully, Katherine returned and asked how it was going. I said I thought I needed to try something else and she suggested trivia questions, which sounded like a fantastic idea to me. So she brought out a notebook filled with sheets of questions in plastic page protectors. I scanned the questions, looking for something I thought might grab them, while occasionally answering "I fall down" with "No, you didn't."

I wouldn't call them "trivia" questions in the strict sense of the word. For example, I tried "Name three red fruits."

Margaret, a stocky woman sitting across the table, stared at me like I was the stupidest person she had ever met and said, "Well, a strawberry is red."

"Great!" I yelled like a game-show host. "Anybody else got one?"

Nothing.

"A red fruit," I repeated, as if I were really thinking about it, too.

"Well, an apple," Margaret answered, now sort of shaking her head with wonder at me and using her "isn't it obvious" voice.

"You betcha! Great, Margaret! Anybody else? A red fruit . . ."

"Fish!" said Elaine.

Now I had a situation. I wasn't sure how to break it to someone if she got it wrong. I hadn't thought it through, and if I had, I wouldn't have thought I was going to stump someone with "Name a red fruit."

With a big, silly, "wha'the heck" face, I said, "Oh my gosh, Elaine, I don't want to eat at your restaurant. I'll order a fruit tart, and you'll serve me fish heads in a puff pastry. How about raspberries? They're red fruits, aren't they?"

Elaine smiled and nodded. It seemed as though she really was remembering that raspberries were red fruits.

Margaret burst out laughing.

I gave it another shot. "Name something with wheels."

"Chairs."

"Chairs."

"Chairs."

"Chairs."

"I fall down."

"No, you didn't. You're good. You're sitting at the table. Chairs! Those are great answers. Under the circumstances, it's almost cheating," I said, smiling.

Again, Margaret let out a really hearty laugh.

I believe I was getting a clearer picture of the challenge. This place was like a one-room schoolhouse. The residents were at wildly different cognitive levels from one another. Some of them were even at varying cognitive levels with themselves at different times of the day. Most group activities were virtually impossible.

QUALITATIVE OBSERVATION #7

John-Boy and Elizabeth Walton's teacher was a goddamned genius.

FIELD NOTES

Michael, a tall, balding man with a bruise on his forehead, had already told me his name twice, but I forgot it again. I apologetically asked him to repeat it. "My short-term memory is shot," I explained. "I've driven past our house more than once. My kids get upset and start yelling, 'You're driving past the house!' from the backseat. I turn, look right at them, and say, 'Who the hell are you, and what are you doing in my car?'"

Even some of the people who appeared to be sleeping joined in the laughter. Margaret laughed herself into a coughing fit.

I found another trivia question in the notebook. "Name three people who make you laugh."

This time, Margaret looked at me and, drawing back her head with an almost Bette Davis–type delivery, answered, "You."

QUALITATIVE OBSERVATION #8

Fuck Emanuel Swedenborg. I'm hooked.

FIELD NOTES

I left, telling the group that I wouldn't be back the following day because I had an appointment with an eye doctor and that I thought I'd probably be getting glasses and therefore looked forward to actually seeing them soon.

I never go to the eye doctor, but I was starting to have trouble with small print, and I was hoping there was something magical that could be done to reverse that loss.

The following day at my appointment, the ophthalmologist was extremely thorough and did a bunch of tests. She even gave me a "field test," which usually means checking the field of vision with one of those huge machines that you lean forward and look into, but this doctor actually hid in a field and had me come find her. She was very good.

When she was finished with the examination, she looked at me seriously and asked if I'd ever heard of glaucoma. I said, "Yes, isn't it that place in *Finian's Rainbow* that everyone was concerned about?"

"No," she said, and explained that the condition was caused by pressure on the eyes, which narrows peripheral vision, causing tunnel vision and, if left unchecked, ended in blindness.

She showed me my test results, including a little illustration of my eyes with the areas of vision loss shaded. Fortunately, there wasn't much impairment and it was mostly confined to the bottom of my eyes, which could explain why I trip over things so often. She told me that further loss could be arrested by using drops each night.

It didn't sound like that big of a deal, but she continued to look quite serious and also slightly blurry. She said, "Now I'm going to tell you what you can't do anymore."

Uh-oh. Now she had my attention. She said, "You can't play the oboe." At first I thought she was kidding, but she wasn't. So, naturally, I'm still mourning that loss. Then she said, "You can't lift weights." How will I fill all of those hours? She continued, "When you do yoga—"

"Let me stop you right there. I can save you some time. I don't know how good your own eyes are, but do I look like I do yoga?"

She had more. "You can't get constipated." Well, there goes that hobby. Do people "get constipated" by design? Has anyone ever answered "Say, let's go to the beach this weekend" with "Nah, I was thinking this weekend I'd take some time to get constipated?"

CONSTANT

I'm not proud of this, but with no one to talk to at home, or even on the road, where I would normally call my son, I find myself watching *Boardwalk Empire* on DVD a lot. It's one of those serialized shows. Originally I saw it on HBO in a hotel room. I don't generally watch television, for this very reason. Which is, once I start watching something, I have a hard time stopping. And *Boardwalk Empire* is so well done. I couldn't take my eyes off of it when I first saw it. I knew I'd never be able to find it on TV again, so I talked myself into buying it on DVD. First I told myself I would only watch it while I was working out, and I did. When I was on the road I would take my goofy little DVD player down to the hotel fitness room and use the treadmill while watching. Then I gradually lowered the bar, telling myself I would only watch while eating Butterfingers. Then it was only while driving. Now I just watch it with abandon.

I have great sympathy for my son's addiction.

I miss him.

FIELD NOTES

I gave platelets a couple of more times and I discovered even more countries where I hadn't had sex.

I got a call from the platelet donation center telling me that there was a patient who had not been doing well but who had responded positively when given my platelets.

ANALYSIS

This was one of the greatest things I'd ever heard! I'm practically stealing recompense! Wow!

FIELD NOTES

I quickly called to schedule another platelet donation time, then I made a quick stop at the copy store to make copies of the lyrics to "Home on the Range," "Lida Rose," and "You Are My Sunshine," so we could have a sing-along in the activity room at the nursing home.

When I got there, I greeted everyone and asked if they wanted to sing. Those who could respond said they were happy to do so. I distributed the lyrics and we belted out a few songs.

QUALITATIVE OBSERVATION #9
Even people who suffer from dementia can remember songs.

FIELD NOTES
As I collected the sheets of music from around the table, Phyllis, who barely speaks and when she does speaks in a tiny whisper, said, "I'm from the range." It turns out she grew up in South Dakota and she talked to me about her childhood.

QUANTITATIVE OBSERVATION #2
A small exchange with Phyllis = three heps of happiness, minimally.

VARIABLE
Gwendolyn does word search puzzles every day. At first, I thought she was just pretending to do them. She can't hear very well so I idiotically assumed she wasn't high functioning. In fact, she does lots of word searches, "jumbles," and crossword puzzles, and she is actually doing them. She has a tremor, so her head wiggles over the table while her fingers, which are so crooked they look like geranium stems, work the pencil across the page.

She has a dusty voice, a twinkle in her eye, and a wonderful laugh. Once a day a physical therapist supports her with a belt while she leans on a walker and walks around the building before she plops herself back down in her wheelchair and fans herself. I am humbled in her presence.

PROCEDURE

I Googled "activities for geriatrics" and found a website with suggestions from professionals. The general consensus is that the best thing you can do to engage and stimulate an elderly patient is to get them talking about themselves. Ask them what they remember, then listen.

Here's where I have a problem. As I've mentioned, perhaps more than once, one of the ways my obsessive-compulsive disorder manifests itself is that I can't stop talking. It's not that I'm not interested in what other people have to say, it's that I can't hear them over the sound of my own voice. I often say that I fly-fish in the stream of consciousness. Unfortunately, I usually say it while a friend is telling me about her biopsy results. Everything that gets said reminds me of something that I absolutely feel I must say. I hijack every conversation, regardless of how little I may know on the subject. There is always some way in which I can relate, and I cannot help telling you about it. It is a deeply humiliating trait. I just can't stop.

The worst part of it is that, especially there at the nursing home, there is a great wealth of oral history to be mined. There is so much I could learn and would enjoy learning about the years before my time and about other people's experiences. But I just can't shut up.

For example, as Victor was telling me about escaping from Russia in the 1950s, I heard myself say something about my fond memories of Siegfried in *Get Smart*.

VARIABLES

Annette is new and will probably live out the rest of her life here, which is understandably a large bitter pill for her to swallow.

Sometimes she's feisty and funny, but other times she just sits and stares, even when you address her directly.

I told her that I once found a hundred-dollar bill on the sidewalk in San Francisco. "I picked it up, ran up to a guy walking ahead of me, and asked if he had dropped it."

Annette was outraged. "He said he did, didn't he?"

"Yeah," I said, laughing. "So I gave it to him. The only thing I knew about that hundred-dollar bill was that it wasn't mine."

Her mouth hung open. "Why would you do that?"

I said, "It was a long time ago. I was a baby."

She shot back, "You were a stupid baby."

I exploded with laughter. She smiled.

FIELD NOTES

I brought my dog Ramona to the nursing home. She's a big brown-and-black dog, lanky, with a long skinny snout, which she insists on sticking directly into the crotch of anyone she meets. A trainer told me that that's a dog's way of gathering information. Surely Ramona is compiling a detailed dossier on all whom she encounters. Therefore, "Ramona, go away!" is the command she hears more than any other, but the people at the nursing home were thrilled to see her. I warned everyone of her passion and tried to hold the leash tight enough to limit her investigations.

People loved talking to Ramona! The activity room was alive with activity! Some patients came by, ones who weren't even regulars in the activity room, just to ask if they could pet the dog. Some of the patients who normally look lifeless until they nod off in front of an open copy of the *Santa Monica Mirror* were awakened by Ramona's kiss, like Snow White by the prince.

It is my habit, when she slobbers on someone, to pull Ramona back, but most people say, "That's okay, I love dogs" and do seem to relish Ramona's dog drooly attention.

As she broke her stony, depressed stare to pet Ramona, Annette told me with a smile that she used to own German shepherds.

Helga and Ursula were scared of the dog. They're both from Germany. Ursula speaks some English, but I've never heard Helga speak any. I tried to assure them that I had Ramona on a leash and that though she is a friendly dog, I would protect them from her.

Katherine had a dog at home. Many of the residents had to leave their pets when they came to live in the nursing home. So the conversation turned easily and joyfully to dog stories. Lots of people joined in.

QUALITATIVE OBSERVATION #10

My dog Ramona is a rock star!

QUANTITATIVE OBSERVATION #3

I am filled with a balou of happiness.

FIELD NOTES

Sometimes Ursula just sits and speaks German, making lively, funny, facial expressions to no one. Like a bad extra trying to distinguish herself in a movie restaurant scene. So when she looked right at me and spoke, I leaned in close to hear. She said, "Stop talking about dogs."

CONSTANT

As I was back at home pouring cat food from an industrial-sized bag of Meow Mix with a "Your chance to win!" sweepstakes ad on the front, a plastic sheath of coupons toppled out. The one on top read, "You are not a winner!" Thank you, Meow Mix. I knew that. If I were a winner, I wouldn't be spending half of my pay on Meow Mix in servitude to sixteen cats.

I found an old picture of Alley and Thomas E smiling with their arms around each other in an inner tube in a pool. It made me cry. Although we're close, my new family, the Vitamixes, really isn't filling the void.

FIELD NOTES

The last time I went to give platelets, my blood didn't have enough iron. There was enough for me, but not enough for someone else.

Oh no! I thought. *What about the patient who responded so well to my platelets? Now I might have killed him!* I felt awful.

QUALITATIVE OBSERVATION #11

Giving giveth and giving taketh away.

FIELD NOTES

Without anyone to talk to at home, my talking backs up like a toilet. It's making my OCD-riddled social skills even worse.

Today when Olga said, "I fall down," I said, "You fall down? I tripped over a cement wall yesterday." I pulled up my pant legs and showed her my bruises. It seemed to take her by surprise.

When Annette told me she was angry because she couldn't drive anymore, I responded, "I'm not allowed to do yoga."

Helga was looking sad and distant, so I squatted down beside her wheelchair and said, "Boy, you never really miss the oboe until you're told you can't play it, huh?" Fortunately she doesn't understand much English.

VARIABLE

I can't imagine how stunning Lorraine must have been in her youth because she's beautiful now, despite being very wrinkled and having no teeth. She sits in her chair and sleeps a lot. She'll talk if I speak directly to her, but she often looks confused. I've been visiting two mornings a week for months now, but pretty much every time she encounters me, I can see her rummaging through her memory bank, like I might formerly have hunted for an inkling on my desk (before the first Get Organized experiment). She asks, "Are you Abigail?" I put my hand on her shoulder, crouch down so she can see me better, and say, "No, I'm Paula." It baffles her every time. "I thought you were Abigail," she replies, right on cue. Then she'll see Ramona and say, "Is that your dog?" as if this is part of the script.

FIELD NOTES

When my kids were growing up, we sometimes had balloons left over from a party or an event. We loved playing the keep-the-balloon-up game in the living room—you know, where you just hit the balloon back and forth through the air, with just a finger usually. There were no rules other than to keep the balloon up. There were no points or scoring system but for long and delightful stretches of time, we'd throw ourselves around the living room like it was the World Cup. It was never planned and no one ever suggested we play. It wasn't Family Game Night. It just kind of happened, wordlessly, and it was always fun.

So I brought a balloon to the nursing home. I blew it up and I tossed it to Margaret, who was sitting at one of the big round tables. All I said was, "Let's keep the balloon up." I pumped up the volume on a classic oldies rock CD in the boom box and we played the most spectacular game of keep the balloon up in sports history.

Margaret hit it to Olga. Olga hit it to Michael. Michael hit it to Elaine. Elaine hit it to Gwendolyn. Gwendolyn missed it. I ran around behind her, grabbed it, and shouted, "Saved! Miraculously, it's still in play!" before shooting it back to Gwendolyn. They made dramatic saves. It bounced off Frank's head, off Elaine's elbow, off Ursula's elevated foot. We laughed and cheered. They played like athletes. I would love to have collectible cards with pictures of them in their ready positions, or reaching for the save with their gnarly fingers, and on the back would be their stats. It was pure good old-fashioned fun.

QUALITATIVE OBSERVATION #12

There is joy to be found in this world, even without the possibility of playing the oboe.

UNCONTROLLED VARIABLES

When Thomas E's stint at the wilderness program had almost expired, we needed a program and a school that neither used nor allowed computers and electronics. These machines had stolen into our homes and schools under the deceptive cloak of the word *educational*. Despite glaring evidence of decreasing test scores and educational outcomes as a result of wholesale reliance on computers in the classroom, even with the help of professionals I could find only two programs in the entire country that eschewed their use. One was in Texas and one was in Virginia.

I flew to Utah, where my son was living in a tent in the wilderness, to pick him up and deliver him to the school in Virginia, where he now lives in another tent in the woods.

On the off chance that I am wrong, and there is an afterlife, I hope Steve Jobs's is not pleasant.

QUALITATIVE OBSERVATION #13

It is not always easy to be charitable.

FIELD NOTES

I brought my dog Sirius with me when I returned to the activity room at the nursing home. He alternates with Ramona. Lorraine was awake and alert. I put my hand on her shoulder, smiled, and asked how she had been. Katherine, the activities director, had suggested that it might be less confusing to Lorraine if I just go along with what she thinks. So when she asked, "Are you Abigail?" I said, "Yes." And when she said, "Is that your dog?" I said, "It sure is" with a big, happy, love-is-all-around smile.

Lorraine's eyebrows descended low over her eyes. Her mouth curled with disgust. The lack of teeth seemed to give her lips more room to do so. "Drop dead!" she said, long and drawn out, like Play-Doh oozing out of the Play-Doh Fun Factory. "Cut that fucking dog's tail off!"

My hair stood up! I was shocked. It never occurred to me or Katherine that Lorraine didn't have a good relationship with Abigail, but apparently she had been looking to settle a score with Abigail and her poor dog for years.

CONCLUSION

For the sake of science, I'm going to move onto another experiment, but I'm going to continue to volunteer at the nursing home. I love the old people. Besides, my dogs practically drag me there.

Lorraine has no memory of having sought her revenge on Abigail and now, no matter who she thinks I am, I say, "No, we've never met before, but it's lovely to see you."

We've played the keep-the-balloon-up game many times and it's always great. I wish I could film it for you, but it's a medical facility so there are privacy issues. You'll have to find your own nursing home and balloon. I highly recommend that you do. The Get Over Here and Help experiment has given me oodles of heps and several balous of happiness.

THE
GET QUIET
EXPERIMENT

I'VE BEEN READING a lot about the brain in the last couple of years. Meditation has come up frequently. It is said to work wonders. The practice is credited with lowering anxiety, re-wiring the brain, and even producing bliss. Those are wonder works. Still, I have always felt that sitting quietly in a room full of people who were hoping to do the same would be, if not an impossibility, then a living hell for me.

HYPOTHESIS
Bliss could be good.

CONDITIONS
Toshia seems to be enjoying her adult life. She's active, social, and gets herself around. I'm thrilled for her. Thomas E and I write letters to each other and I fly out to see him in Virginia

once a month. Alley is a senior in college. She took an abnormal psychology class last semester. I offered to be the visual aid for her oral presentation. She is home for winter break and we have relentlessly rung in the season with a Christmas movie almost every night.

I get all riled up every year by Betty and Bob in *White Christmas*. They are so indirect with one another. It's no surprise at all that they break up just days before Christmas. And they do it every year. They have a misunderstanding, Betty runs away, she comes back, and they get together again—all without ever talking about what went wrong. I'll give you odds they won't make it to New Year's.

PROCEDURE

Last summer Alley took meditation classes at a place called Unplug. You have to sign up for the classes online. Surely they'll take at least first-runner-up at the Ironies next awards season. Alley signed us up for a class together.

ENVIRONMENT

Unplug Meditation has a storefront on Wilshire Boulevard, which is a busy street in Los Angeles. There was no street parking out front and no parking lot nearby. I got the sense that most of their patrons floated in as a vapor and materialized into a solid in the fruity-scented bamboo garden, which you pass through to enter the lobby.

I give Unplug credit for creating a calm and serene ambience in the midst of Wilshire Boulevard. This is a neighborhood full of heavy traffic, office buildings, banks, medical supply stores, imaging facilities, and mattress stores, but we walked into Unplug and into another world. The lights were low. The walls were white. The sign-in sheet at the front desk was surrounded by short, glowing candles. There was a tall, white shelf of books for sale and a case of shiny, polished stones and crystals of many hues.

While Alley signed us in, some sort of wooden flute music played interminable notes and a very sweet fragrance steamed out of a glowing container in the lobby. My allergic reaction to anything with an artificial scent causes frequent coughing fits. I was about to go into a quiet room. The forty or so people in the lobby whispered while waiting for the prior class to let out. Whispering makes me cough, too.

Alley, being familiar with the place, helped herself to a cup of tea from the white shelf, which also held a glass jug of kale-infused water. I sipped my Diet Pepsi on a white bench and surreptitiously tweeted, "I'm stressed out about my meditation class" before turning off my phone as required. Alley sat beside me on the white bench and pointed out the white cubbies below, where we placed our shoes.

When I looked up from tucking in the papers I keep in my shoes to keep my socks from going through the holes in the soles, I saw a large white sign hanging on the wall with raised white letters that read: STILLNESS. That's when I knew for sure I wouldn't be very good at this.

At 6:00 p.m. we heard the pure tone of a small bell, which signaled it was time to enter the meditation room. It was dark in there. The floor was covered in rows of small black futons with internal metal frames. They looked like poolside chaise lounges at a fancy resort, but without the legs. Alley found us two of these chairs together on the far side of the room and kindly began adjusting the back of mine for me. They're tricky and they make that clicky chaise lounge noise when you position them. The teacher sat on a raised platform in the front of the room.

FIELD NOTES: CLASS #1

I think the teacher said her name was Emily, but I wasn't focused yet. It might have been Ficus Nitida. She gave us a few minutes to settle in. "How far back do you want it to go?" Alley asked me softly as she tried to set the pitch of the back of my chair. "If you fall asleep and snore, she comes and taps your foot."

"Put it straight up," I said louder than I would have liked, but if I whispered I would cough. "You should have told me that before we came. I would have brought a nail to sit on. Can you make it at a forty-five-degree angle, so I'm leaning forward? I really don't want some lady tapping me awake because I'm snoring in front of forty people."

A guy wearing a cloth thrown over one shoulder and drawn up between his legs and back into a headband gave me a look that seemed to say I was talking too loudly. "I have allergies," I said. "Whispering makes me cough." I started to cough. "Talking about coughing makes me cough." I laughed. He never changed his facial expression and I sheepishly went back to trying to figure out the chair. I glanced over at him later and saw him tugging on his headband, probably because it was too tight in the crotch.

Alley assured me that if I fell asleep and started to snore, she would wake me before the teacher came over.

From her perch, Ficus spoke in a measured tone—very smooth and composed. She explained that we should all get comfortable. She said this would be a guided meditation. She asked if anyone had any questions. I knew Alley wouldn't like it if I raised my hand to ask, "Is this wooden flute player going to change to another note anytime soon?" So I didn't.

I know there's a special way you're supposed to breathe for meditation, but I can never remember it. It's in through your nose and out through your mouth or out though your nose and in through your mouth or suck your eyes in really hard or something. Ficus didn't say anything about it. She said to feel your body on the chair. She said to acknowledge if something hurt. I came this close to moaning, "Fuck, my neck hurts at this forty-five-degree angle," but on second thought, I figured she meant to acknowledge it to yourself.

Ficus said that if your worries and thoughts about the outside world came into your head to acknowledge them, then let them go and return to the sound of her voice. She said, "You are walking through a forest."

Lions and tigers and bears, oh my, I thought right away. I couldn't stop wondering, now that I was thinking about it, *Why would lions and tigers and bears all be in a forest? Bears might be in a forest, but not lions and tigers. Shit. This is not what I'm supposed to be thinking. Acknowledge and let it go. Fuck, now the others are all up ahead of me in the forest. I have a guide on this meditation and I'm still going to get lost.*

I heard Ficus say to imagine you are standing in front of a big, beautiful, wise old oak tree. I took a shot at the breathing technique. I inhaled through my mouth and exhaled through my nose. *Fuck, that's not right*, I thought. *Now I need a Kleenex.* It was the rare occasion in which I didn't have one wadded up in my pocket. I glanced over at Alley. She looked so peaceful. I think she really was in front of the oak tree.

Then, of course, it started—my nagging, hacking cough. And it's a loud cough, too. I coughed three times. "Sorry, it's the tree pollen," I said. Ficus glared at me. Alley's eyes rolled under her closed lids.

Lots of stuff I do embarrasses Alley. I remember when I went to her middle school's open house. Open house is sort of a strange event. They specifically ask the parents not to talk to the teachers about their kids. They say that that is best done at a parent-teacher conference. I agree that a parent-teacher conference is a good time to talk to a teacher about my child, but then I don't know what to talk about at the open house. My child is really the main thing I have in common with the teacher. They say you're supposed to look at the bulletin boards and talk about the class in general. So, what do you say to the math teacher? "Hi, I'm Paula Poundstone. I am the mother of one of the students in your class. Of course, I'll not mention which one. So this is the room you teach him or her the math in, huh? I like all of the numbers on the bulletin board."

I stood with Alley in her history classroom at the middle-school open house, looking at a collage of pictures of the kids' heroes hung on the classroom wall. The students had written short essays on their heroes. Alley had chosen me. My picture hung alongside Martin Luther King Jr., Gandhi, and Michael Jordan.

Meeting the teachers at this event was grueling. I had a mother myself once, so I'm certainly aware that when you are fourteen your mother can be embarrassing, particularly at your school. I tried to be careful. After we walked through the classrooms, we stepped out onto a patio area with snacks, where the teachers milled about meeting the parents. That alone would have been stressful. These teachers were half my age, and although thankfully my drinking days were almost a decade past, some of my failures were quite public and the shame of it never drags very far behind me at a local school event. So I was fairly self-conscious without any help at all, but add to it the constant hiss of Alley's whispered directions about what I had to do and not do, and say and not say, and it put me on edge. Bob Fosse wasn't as demanding a choreographer.

"Mom, don't stand like that."

"How am I standing?"

"I don't know. Just turn around. Look over there, so she can't see you."

"Alley, she's a biology teacher. She has seen the inside of fetal pigs. How bad could I look?"

And I was supposedly her hero! What if I weren't? What if I were Gandhi? She'd make him crazy. "Oh my God, she's looking. Pull up your loincloth." What if I were Michael Jordan? "Crouch!"

"The leaves are falling gently all around you," Ficus intoned.

Acknowledge and let go, I reminded myself. *Get back to the leaves. Damn it, I really need a Kleenex. I look like a fussy three-year-old on a cold day. Acknowledge and let go. The leaves, get back to the fucking leaves . . ."*

". . . you turn the leaf over and there is a message to you, from the tree, written on the back," said Ficus. "What message would the tree have for you?"

Really? I thought. *I could maybe picture a tree, but I can't possibly imagine that a tree has written me a message. I'd wipe my nose with that leaf if I had it.*

The roots of the big tree in our front yard have been growing through our sewer pipes. Maybe that's the message. "Sorry about your pipes. Oh, yeah, they're not your pipes anyway. You rent. Ha ha! Signed, the Tree."

"Slowly open your eyes and return to the room," I could hear Ficus saying. "Become aware of your surroundings."

A fellow student in a crepey, flowing blouse and drawstring pants walked past, kicked over my soda, and didn't say a word. So much for awareness. Maybe she was upset because her tree broke up with her.

QUALITATIVE OBSERVATION #1

Now, in addition to obsessively checking my home answering machine, cell phone voice mail, Facebook, email, and Twitter every day, I have to check my oak leaves. That doesn't reduce anxiety.

ANALYSIS

I flew off to work in Salt Lake City. I have the greatest job in the world. The audience is my best friend. There is just nothing like being in a roomful of people laughing. The fact that they are laughing at stuff that I say is the icing on the cake. I was teasing the audience in Utah about polygamy when it dawned on me that marrying a polygamist might work well for me, since I don't like sex. I could get someone else to take my shift. "No, no, you two go on ahead. I'll just do the dishes again."

Perhaps my mind was more open to possibilities because of meditation.

VARIABLE

Alley started school up in Portland again. So now I was on my own going to meditation class.

FIELD NOTES: CLASS #2

The parking is awful around Unplug Meditation. I barely made it on time for that evening's class. I finally found a space at a parking meter, but all I had in my pocket was a nickel. I put the nickel in and quickly reached back into the car for some change in the glove compartment. When I popped back out again, the meter had expired.

While I signed in, I overheard the sales clerk at the front desk explaining the uses of the crystals to a barefooted customer: "This one is good for balancing stress, this one is for the heart's chakra, this one is good for Chaka Khan, and this one is for prosperity." I made a note to ask what the return rate was on the prosperity crystals. I'm still paying off a day's Lamborghini rental.

I heard the bell and assumed that I was for whom it tolled. Tonight's teacher was a guy. I didn't get the name. I don't think it had any consonants, though. It was Ooey or something. I was the last person through the door and I couldn't find a chair. Ooey had to get one for me. You're supposed to push the back of the chair all of the way forward, then back to where you want it, and it should catch and stay in place. I kept clicking it forward, but it would just go flat. Everyone else was already aware of their bodies and I couldn't make the back of the chair stay folded. I tried to do it quietly. Click, click.

"Let all of the stress of the day just melt away."

Click, click, click, click. Click, click, click.

I tried making it sound like I was accompanying Ooey on some sort of African instrument.

"Relax your toes."

Click, click.

"Relax your ankles."

Click, click. I couldn't make the thing work. I finally leaned the two parts up against one another on their sides and made a little A-frame. Ooey's voice was muffled now. "There's nothing that needs doing," I heard him say from beyond the walls of my fort. *He doesn't know about my littler boxes*, I thought.

Ooey suggested that we silently repeat our mantras. So I began, "I'm an idiot. I'm an idiot. I'm an idiot . . ."

ANALYSIS

After I'd done a few meditation classes, and don't hold me to this, I thought I felt uplifted. It wasn't like heps of happiness were raining down on me, but I felt lighter and more alert. Normally, I would have been thrashed by my last two weeks of flying, driving, working, and little sleep, which culminated in a trip to Virginia for a visit with Thomas E, yet I felt remarkably good and able.

Thomas E and I went to historic Williamsburg. It's sort of a reenactment of a colonial village. We stayed at an inn and visited a silversmith, a pewtersmith, a blacksmith, a cobbler, a milliner, an apothecary, a wig maker, a printer, and a cabinetmaker. The tradespeople there are the real deal. They apprentice for several years and most of them we met had worked as Williamsburg artisans for decades. They assume the roles of colonists as well. So the experience is a mix of theater and history. We attended a speech by George Washington at the courthouse and heard an argument between two captured slaves in the jailhouse.

Thomas E and I talked a lot about his future and the uncharted path he faces. They were difficult conversations, because despite having abstained from screen use for almost a year, his cravings for video games, in particular, remain strong and burdensome. This is not a coincidence. In fact, video game companies actually hire behavioral psychologists to make the games addictive. Electronics addiction is considered the number-one threat to public health in China and South Korea. Here in the United States though, concerns about it have been painfully slow to receive recognition.

At a restaurant one night, while we waited for our dinner to arrive and after Ye Olde Magician had left our table to circulate to other tables with his sleight-of-hand card tricks, Thomas E said, "Mom, maybe you should write a book about electronics addiction."

"Maybe I will," I answered.

"Tell them what happened to me."

After three nights in Williamsburg, I drove Thomas E back to school, then ate waffle creme cookies and cried the entire two-hour drive to the airport. I flew back to Los Angeles, cleaned, slept for two hours, and headed back to the airport to fly to

Lansing, Michigan. The Lansing crowd was great, as always. However, I did talk from the stage to a woman in the audience who taught a college-level interpersonal communications class *online*.

CONSTANT

We are in big fucking trouble.

ENVIRONMENT: CLASS #8

Among the variety of meditation classes on the Unplug schedule is a Sound Bath Experience. A sound bath sounded good to me. It took place in the darkened meditation room and lasted an hour and a quarter. When I entered the bamboo garden on my way into the building, I saw the class teacher unloading his equipment. I saw large thick brass bowls, bells, chimes, rains sticks, mallets, and gongs.

FIELD NOTES: CLASS #8

I entered the meditation room at the ding of the bell in the lobby, found a futon chair, adjusted it as best I could, and followed the teacher's directions to get comfortable. We were instructed to focus on just the sounds. He explained that the sound bath was designed to redirect the listener's focus away from intrusive thoughts and back to the sounds, and that if it got too intense we should feel free to leave quietly. I couldn't imagine running in horror from the sound of a rain stick, but maybe he had darker tools that I hadn't seen. Maybe he played Wolf Blitzer audio at unbearable decibels. "UH, HERE, UH, IN THE SITUATION, UH, ROOM TODAY WE ARE FOLLOWING A STORY THAT WE, UH, KNOW

NOTHING ABOUT, UH, BUT THAT WE HOPE WILL, UH, TURN INTO A, UH, TRAGEDY, UH, OR AT LEAST SOMETHING WE CAN, UH, SPECULATE ABOUT AND, UH, BLOW OUT OF PROPORTION AND, UH, MILK FOR, UH, WEEKS." I made note of the location of the closest exit.

Sinking into the chair with my eyes closed, I felt my shoulders lower almost instantly at the first simple, cool peal of a small bell. There followed waves of deep, sonorous tones. I recognized the bell sounds, the bowl sounds, the chimes, and the rain sticks. It was amazing. He also played recorded sounds. I was so relaxed that when I next heard what sounded like a truck driving over me, I didn't even try to get up. The entire room shook.

It lasted about fifteen seconds. Then I felt my restless leg syndrome go crazy. My eyes popped open, and down somewhere near the end of my legs, I could see my feet spinning around on my ankles like uncut carrots in a blender. I tried restraining my left foot with my right and stepping on my right foot with my left. Nothing worked. Fortunately, the sound bath came to an end soon after. I sat up, reached forward and grabbed my feet. It was like trying to stop a fan with my hands. Once I was standing, my miscreant appendages fell into place beneath the rest of my body and carried me hurriedly from the room.

QUALITATIVE OBSERVATION #2
So much for stillness.

ANALYSIS
Again, to my surprise, I felt energetic and optimistic when I returned home from Unplug. It had to be a few heps of happiness.

I still felt good even after I fielded my first radio interview of the day at 5:00 a.m. the next morning.

"Good morning, Paula Poundstone, you're on with Crazy Steve and his Side Chick!"

"Well, thanks for having me Crazy Steve . . . and um, Chick. I was in Portland, Oregon, last weekend. They have emotion-activated paper towel dispensers in their airport restrooms. You have to break down and cry in front of them to get a towel to come out.

"I fell asleep with my hands in the Dyson Airblade hand dryer at the Detroit airport and when I woke up my mittens were too big."

"So, what kind of comedy do you do?" the Side Chick asked.

ENVIRONMENT: CLASS #10

I used the bathroom at Unplug Meditation for the first time the other night. As I sat there realizing I was so constipated I might go blind, I looked around at the lovely interior. It's the only room in the place that isn't painted white. The trim is white but the bathroom walls are a shade of black, somewhere between lead and licorice, I believe. As in the lobby and the meditation room, many framed platitudes hang on the bathroom walls. I tried to internalize them all: "Be happy, be bright, be you"; "It's up to you"; and my personal favorite, "Keep going."

I had finally arrived early enough that once out of the bathroom, I had time to peruse the books for sale on the shelves. It was upsetting. Many of the books were of a similar theme to mine. There were rows and rows of them: *How to be Happy*; *Breathe in Happy*; *Color Me Happy*; *Happy Is My Middle*

Name; and the sequel *Happy Is My First Name, Too, and I Married a Guy Named Happy, Now I'm Happy Happy Happy.*

FIELD NOTES: CLASS #10

The bell rang. I went in and lay flat on a chair. Giant Sea Slug told us to concentrate on our breath. She said anytime you found yourself drifting you should "come back to your breath."

I sucked in an angry breath, aware that that's probably not what Giant Sea Slug meant.

It's sickening, I thought. *That's what it is. It pisses me off because I know I thought of it first. It has taken me years to write my book on happiness. It probably took a week to write* Color Me Happy. *I didn't look inside any of the books. They might be coloring books.* How To Be Happy *is probably the first Pulitzer Prize–winning coloring book. There's probably no science at all in* Breathe in Happy. *It's not even good fucking English. Shit, I could have written that in about a minute.*

I startled at the sound of my teeth grinding.

Oh, yeah, my breath. In and out, in and out, in and out. When Dorothy Parker died they found her on her living-room rug surrounded by cats and cat feces. Fortunately, I'm not that good a writer . . . In and out, in and out, in and out . . . At least I've enjoyed writing my book. I have. I've been doing these experiments for seven years. My book will have chronicled seven years of raising my children. Breathe in Happiness *probably doesn't even have children. You don't have time to breathe when you have children. Fuck, I wish mine were little again. I feel like Jimmy Stewart in* It's a Wonderful Life; *Help me, Clarence! Get me back!" I want to do it all over again.*

"Follow your breath . . ." Giant Sea Slug cooed.

Right, my breath, goddammit . . . in and out, in and out, in and out . . . Boy, you don't nail this meditation thing right away . . . The blacksmith actually made the nails the artisans built with in Williamsburg. Thomas E enjoyed it there. He's coming along. Who knew I'd even be able to get him to go into the craftsmen shops? I figured he'd stand outside the Ye Olde Print Shoppe and yell in, "Hey, Silas, email me!" or that he would have heckled George Washington. "So, you cannot tell a lie, huh? How many kid's lives do you think you've ruined with that dumb ass story? What do you mean you cannot tell a lie? I can tell fifty lies in the time it takes you to pollute the Potomac with coins."

"Returning again and again to your breath."

Oh, for Christ's sake, not again. I'm lucky I remember to breathe, let alone focus on it . . . in and out, in and out . . . I have to remember to call the hair guy to dye my hair. I have a two-inch-thick gray streak at my part. My head looks like a rural highway.

"I want to thank you for sharing this experience with me," I heard Giant Sea Slug say. "And thank yourselves for me."

"I will if I see me," I mumbled to myself, getting up to make my way through the lobby filled with people wearing shapeless shirts and cloth that hasn't been tailored into anything yet.

QUALITATIVE OBSERVATION #3
After taking a few minutes to shake off the dim lighting, I felt energetic. Wow.

CONCLUSION

My ability to focus is so sorely lacking that I'm an unfair judge of the effects of meditation. I think, like swing dance, the real benefits come with mastery. I'm going to go out on a limb, though, maybe even the limb of a wise old oak tree and say that I noticed during The Get Quiet experiment that I have felt more optimistic. I used to need music or a *Perry Mason* or *Columbo* video playing while I did chores—if my kids weren't around to talk to, that is. Now I have found that I like the silence. I am entertained by just thinking.

That's not like me.

Although my science may be screwed up here and I can't prove that there is a causal relationship, since the inception of the Get Quiet experiment I have felt more creative. This in turn has made my work even richer for me. These days, I pour myself onto the stage. I'm so excited to get to be with an audience that marshaling my thoughts is like Sea Biscuit's racehorse rival War Admiral at the starting gate. He was so anxious to run, he would spin, shirk, and bang into the side of the enclosure. If there is a possibility that meditation strengthens my ability to do my silly, stupid stand-up comedy job, then you can count me in.

FINAL REPORT ON THE TOTALLY UNSCIENTIFIC STUDY OF THE SEARCH FOR HUMAN HAPPINESS

HAPPINESS IS MORE complex than I had realized. Maybe the true answer to the secret of happiness is that it is a combination of things and they don't always happen all at once. If you're happy without interruption for days on end, you're likely daft. Happiness, I think, falls in among a wide array of other emotions during the daily struggles that make up a real life. For me, I'll feel successful if happiness can be the backbeat to the emotional score of my biography.

In the past, I have confused happiness with fun. Driving the Lamborghini was fun, and although I cherish the memory of driving it with the top down through the streets of Santa Monica late at night with my son at my side, it did not give me any kind of lasting happiness. Deep-rooted happiness may require a sense of purpose. If I don't feel that I am in some small way contributing to the greater good, holding on to happiness is like carrying water in my hands.

I have continued to volunteer at the nursing home. I know for sure that makes me happy. Although even knowing it's going to make me happy, it's not always easy to drag myself there. Isn't that weird? It's the same with exercise, good nutrition, and a healthful sleep schedule. I think most people know that these are the low-hanging fruits of good mental and physical health. They grease the chute from which happiness may slide. So you'd think it would be easy as pie to get yourself to do these things, but it's not. Achieving real happiness takes work. You have to set the table for it.

I want to tell you about one more meditation class. Unplug's website lists the type of class and its time slot but, because I didn't know what any of the names meant, when I signed up for Breath Work, I had no idea what I was in for.

It started at 8:00 p.m. So I wouldn't be so stressed about parking, I arrived early, found a space on the street, and sat in my car listening to public radio until it was time to go in. A local reporter was interviewing a Cal State San Bernardino professor, who studies hate crimes and extremism. Over the weekend, he had gone to a Ku Klux Klan rally in Anaheim to further his research. I was shocked to hear that such an event had taken place at all but also so near to where I live and in the shadow of Disneyland. Counterprotesters had also shown up. Fights broke out covering a square block, and the professor, who was Jewish, had thrown himself over the body of a Klansman who was being stomped and beaten with a metal pole.

Now it was 7:50 p.m., so still thinking about the whole thing, I snapped off the radio and went into Unplug. The bell rang. I found a chair on the far side of the room. The teacher began to explain the breathing technique we would be using. It was a deep, quick breath into the lower belly and continuing with a sharp pull of air into the upper chest. Then she, Salad Bar, I think her name was, said words that struck fear into my heart. She said that the purpose of this breathing was to "let go" and that if we started to cry to please be respectful of the people near us. This was not my idea of a good time. If I had an emotional reaction, I would have had to wade through a room full of forty people to get to the door. But with trepidation, I began breathing with the others.

As music with a steady pulse played, Salad Bar walked around the room making rhythmic noises like a breathing drill instructor. Sometimes I breathed into my chest and then my stomach. Sometimes I stopped after I breathed into my stomach and skipped my chest because I was behind. I was pretty sure that I was doing it entirely wrong and I was just thinking, *Salad Bar's going to make an example of me. She'll say, "You're the one who didn't get a note from the wise old oak tree"* when suddenly my chest seemed to wrap itself around my heart and tears streamed down the side of my face.

I sobbed and sobbed. I thought of the KKK rally. Why? Who are these people? I thought of the constant drumbeat of the terrorist threat and the cynical, ignorant way that politicians and others have stirred our fears of one another. I thought of how large the crowds are that buy into this. I believe that human beings have far more in common than we have differences. How did we get to this place? My chest heaved. I tried to stay still and quiet so I wouldn't disturb the others, but I thought of my black son and my black daughter and how ashamed I was to be an adult in a world I can't make safe, or even reasonable for them, and I could feel my breath catch. I worried that I might hyperventilate.

Then I heard Salad Bar say to take a moment to think of what you feel grateful for. Of course, I thought of Toshia, Alley, and Thomas E, but then an image of a face I didn't know flashed before me. It was someone I passed on the sidewalk that morning while walking my dog Sirius to visit the old people at the nursing home. Then another face and another face appeared in my head. They were all of the people I passed that morning on the street and to whom I had said, "Good morning." Some were pleasantly surprised and seemed to wake up from some dark place and answer back with a "Good morning." Some ignored me. Some had headphones in and didn't hear me. That's it. That's who I am grateful for: the people who I don't know. The people I see every day. I am grateful for them. I love them. People need each other. Our well-being is tightly tethered to the well-being of people we do not know, most of whom look nothing like ourselves. Happiness, I realized right there in that breathing class, requires engagement.

The nuts and bolts of it are this: Get some exercise. Go dancing. Avoid letting stuff pile up. Remember, you likely only wear 20 percent of what's in your closet. Don't hold on to what you don't need. Be kind to one another. Go for a walk in the woods. Don't bring your food in your tent. Once or twice in your life, watching an *I Love Lucy* episode is even better than sleep. Never use an email when you could give a hug or a handshake. Put your stupid smartphone down, and keep your cat census in the single digits.

I will miss recording my data in the interest of science. I will miss you. Please come see me in a theater near you.

—Paula "Sugar Push" Poundstone

ACKNOWLEDGMENTS

I DON'T KNOW how anyone writes for a living. Every writing session is a deep dive into a sea of self-doubt. Once I get going it can feel exciting and rewarding, but I often have to lure myself with the promise of Butterfingers or raisin toast as a reward for writing progress. It's a really hard job and can cause weight gain. That's why writers write acknowledgments. It's also why they always begin, "This book wouldn't have been possible without the help of . . ." Without support and guidance while writing a book one would go mad.

There is no better manager than Bonnie Burns. The lion's share of the support and guidance I have relied upon to write this book has come from her. She makes me feel creative and funny, even when I am at my worst. She is an invaluable resource. She is Timothy Mouse and I am Dumbo.

Bonnie and I both have limited experience in the world of publishing, so we often turn to Colleen Mohyde from the Doe Coover Agency for her wise counsel. She shovels the path. Even though Colleen usually works with real writers, she has been a wonderful advocate for my writing and has spent countless hours giving me the illusion that I could actually do this.

Shaye Areheart, who published my first book at Random House got me started on this one, for which I am grateful. Plus, she hooked me up with Kim Meisner, who edited the early drafts of the first half, with humor, patience, and kindness and seemingly no judgment about my overuse of the comma.

Amy Gash at Algonquin Books made draconian cuts to *The Totally Unscientific Study of the Search for Human Happiness*, every one of which practically made me bleed, but were the only thing that will keep it from being used as a door stop or a flat thing heavy enough to kill bugs in the bedroom in Florida. She spared nothing to make it a book, and then to make it a better book, and I appreciate it, as I think you will.

I thank my eighth-grade English teacher, Mrs. Forbes, who at ninety-eight years old still remembered where I sat in her classroom forty-three years earlier. She taught with passion and belief in her students. She also turned me on to Charles Dickens, which led to my overuse of the comma.

It'll come as no surprise to you that I thank Toshia, Alley, and Thomas E for putting up with all of me all of these years. Obviously, I couldn't have written this book without them. You may not expect, however, that there is a Dick Van Dyke episode that I am especially grateful for. It's the one when Rob goes to the cabin to work on his novel for a week and writes only the dedication. It made me feel less alone. Thank you, Carl Reiner.

OH, AND ONE MORE THING

A PROGRESS REPORT, WITH PING-PONG

THE TOTALLY UNSCIENTIFIC Study of the Search for Human Happiness has been out in hardcover for a year. I am proud to tell you, it shot to the top of the "*New York Times* Sold Some List." I wish the president would hate my book.

Many readers have contacted me to let me know how much they enjoyed reading my book. This has provided a steady stream of heps of happiness for me to splash around in. They almost all ask for a current census of my home, so I'll tell you: I am at fourteen cats (Matilda and Rutherford died), one dog (Ramona died), and no kids at home (Toshia, Alley, and Thomas E are alive and well, and currently living elsewhere). Many people gasp when they learn that my kids are out of the house. They say, "Don't you miss them?"

"Yes, I miss them," I assure my concerned readers, "but if I want them back, all I have to do is take out my checkbook and make a tapping sound with my pen."

They are all three young adults, and they are all three finding their way. Sometimes one or two live at home, and sometimes they don't.

When I no longer needed to isolate the variables for science, I chose to return to many of the activities that provided balous of happiness in the course of my research for *The Totally Unscientific Study of the Search for Human Happiness*. I take swing dance lessons with Rusty Frank, and we expanded to tap, as well. One day we even put on a little show, featuring the classic "Take Me Out to the Ballgame" tap dance routine, at the nursing home where I still receive heps of happiness from volunteering two mornings a week. It continues to be crushingly depressing, and really fun, at the same time. It's an emotional salted caramel.

Beatrice is a tall, stately, angry patient at the nursing home. Maybe she's not really angry, but her hearing is so poor that she shouts, even to hear herself, I think. Anyway, I was kind of scared of her. I decided that was a good reason to try to engage her in conversation. I sat down at the table where her wheelchair was parked, looked her in the eye, and asked how she was. And then, of course, it happened—human connection. It's just like in *Beauty and the Beast*:

Barely even friends
Then somebody bends
Unexpectedly.

Eventually she warmed, and even smiled. She asked me something about my husband, to which I responded (loudly, because you have to), "Oh, I'm not married. I'm single."

"Then you're a prostitute!" she shouted, so loudly that every head in the activities room snapped around and looked shocked.

"Not yet," I said. "I'm not above it, but so far I'm able to pay the bills."

I returned to Mr. King's taekwondo studio. I work out three or four times each week. Unfortunately, as I learned in "The Get Fit Experiment," grueling physical exercise is uplifting. It's even harder now than when I first did the experiment. I don't remember having this feeling, like the muscles are pulling away from my rib cage, before, but now I have it all the time.

I recently decided that, as I may be moving into my declining years, maybe I should have a regular doctor. I usually just go to an urgent care center if I need medical attention. Or sometimes when I have a cat at the veterinarian, I sneak in a question about myself, as if it's about an animal at home. "My dog moans a lot after he does push-ups. Do you think his muscles could be pulling away from his rib cage?"

Fearing that this was not a comprehensive approach, I got a recommendation for a general practitioner and made an appointment. I arrived promptly for my physical. Among the stack of new patient forms I filled out, I found a questionnaire. It had only two questions. Number one was, "Do you feel hopeless, depressed, and tired?" I stared at the question and then looked up to see if anyone was watching. Was this a joke? Had this doctor not seen the news for a while? It felt like one of the handful of times I studied for a test in school, when I didn't even need to look nervously at anyone else's paper to see if I was right. The answer was so obvious that I don't even know why they needed to ask it. YES! Of course! Question number two was, "How often?" There were choices: "rarely," "occasionally," "once a week," or "every day." EVERY DAY! *Am I being punked*, I wondered, as I evened the stack of papers on the clipboard and returned them to the desk.

"Easiest questions I ever answered," I said to the office clerks, assuming they were in on the joke.

I was very pleased to be called soon thereafter by a nurse standing at the entrance to the examining rooms. She walked me to a room, took my blood pressure and temperature. She weighed and measured me, and delivered the bad news about my not being tall enough to weigh that much. She then handed me a gown, told me to strip down to my bra and put the gown on, and left. I don't wear a bra. I sat in the plastic chair and began to sweat. I didn't want the doctor to come in and think I couldn't follow directions.

I hate the gown. They only used to give you the gown if they wanted access to a particular body part. Now doctors don't even ask how you are feeling before they give you the gown. It has nothing to do with the practice of medicine. The sole purpose of the gown is to take away the patient's ability to self-advocate. In the past if you were at the doctor's, fully dressed, and they kept you waiting a really long time, as they always do, you would walk down the hall to the reception desk and say, "Excuse me, is the doctor coming or not?" But once you put the gown on, you are theirs. Maybe, after an hour or so, you might try to reach behind yourself, gather both sides of the back of the gown in one hand, quickly poke your head out the door, and attempt a weak, "Hello?"

This nurse gave me a gown with only one string. Was it some kind of intelligence test? I twisted it around my waist and tried to turn in the opposite direction. I tried tying the string to a cabinet handle and winding myself toward it. Eventually, I just sat in a chair, the string hanging, the gown flapping in the air-conditioning, my breasts gently brushing against my knees. I looked up when the nurse opened the door again and tossed something onto the crinkly paper that covered the padded examining table. She said, "Here's a drape, in case you need it," and she ducked out.

I had no idea what the drape was for. Where it sat on the table, it looked like a folded-up, paper birthday party tablecloth. I stared at it from my chair and began to panic. Finally, I decided that it was in case I leaked. So I got up from my chair and sat on the drape. Then, I began to vaguely suspect that that was not what the drape was for. I panicked more. Apparently, everyone but me knows what the drape is. I was sure the doctor was going to come in, take one look at me, and ask, "Where's the drape?"

"I'm sitting on it," I would say, before she disgustedly chastised me with, "That's not what the drape is for, for Chrissake!" Then she'd lean back into the hallway and yell, "We need another drape for Poundstone in room four. She sat on it!" Behind the closed door I'd hear howls of derisive laughter and volleys of, "Sat on the drape?"

"Sat on the drape?"

"Oh, man, this I gotta see."

"Who the hell sits on the drape?"

"Sat on the drape? Stop your lyin'."

Instead, the nurse opened the door yet again, to deliver an additional questionnaire, which was apparently triggered by my answers on the first questionnaire. Now they wanted to know if I was suicidal, unable to leave the house, or unable to work due to depression.

I am not suicidal. I love to work, and if I couldn't leave the house, I wouldn't have been at the doctor's office.

The doctor didn't show up for an hour, so I left.

These are dark times, I thought as I walked to my car. *Feeling hopeless and depressed and having a podcast are the only things that all humans have in common right now.* Therefore, I decided, I would do one more happiness experiment—for my readers, for mankind, for science.

HYPOTHESIS

We had a Ping-Pong table in the basement when I was growing up. Once I got tall enough that the corner of the table wasn't right at the level of my temple, I began to enjoy the game. I've played ever since. Life is no good at all without a Ping-Pong table. It's not that I play well. I just love the game.

When I was eighteen, I lived in a room in a Boston rooming house, five floors up, with no elevator, and I had a Ping-Pong table. I slept under it.

Now we have a table outside in our backyard. I taught my kids to play when they were little. We have probably hosted more than seventy Ping-Pong parties over the years. We put our guests' names into a hat and randomly pull out teams for a doubles tournament. We hang a vintage electric scoreboard, set up some table-side chairs for viewing, provide pizza, junk food,

Louie Prima music, and plenty of trash talk, and it is a hoot. I'm always so busy with my hosting duties and running the tournament, however, I barely hold a paddle the whole night.

If there was a Ping-Pong table in the doctor's waiting room, I suspect they'd never have to hand out the second questionnaire. I decided to spend a whole day playing Ping-Pong.

PROCEDURE

I have cultivated a number of regular players at my Ping-Pong parties over the years. For many of my guests, the playing time at the parties is only enough to make them want more. This event would be for those guys—the unquenchables. I made a schedule with a start time of 11.00 A.M., and I invited a different player for each hour. They could stay beyond their hour, if they wanted, but I needed to make sure that I had at least one opponent per hour, until 8:00 P.M. It wasn't a *They Shoot Horses, Don't They?* kind of thing—not a marathon. I wasn't planning on playing every minute, just playing plenty.

It was more bare bones than our parties. There were no colorful lights, no alcohol, no fruit plates, no crudités. I ordered a couple of pizzas and shared my stash of "fun size" 3 Musketeers bars.

11:00 A.M.

My agent, Josh, arrived promptly, and had his friends Chris and Kevin with him. Perfect.

QUALITATIVE OBSERVATION #1

I usually have lots of anxiety when the first guests arrive at a party. Partly because I gave a party once in high school and only one person showed up. It wasn't 'Nam, but I still have flash-backs. And partly because I know no one likes to be the first person to arrive. It's just so much pressure. Usually the hostess isn't ready yet, so she answers the door in high heels and a robe. The guest is left in the living room, awkwardly petting a little dog on the couch, while the hostess steps into another room to finish getting dressed and shouts conversation from behind a door. "That's René. He's a Sharpoodle. Don't pet him—he has an oozing wound on his penis, from the wrinkles."

When three people are the first to arrive at even a pared-down Ping-Pong party, there is no awkward conversation. There's doubles.

11:01 A.M.
We played Ping-Pong.

VARIABLES

In doubles Ping-Pong, you and your teammate alternate hitting the ball. It is not like tennis. It doesn't matter where the ball lands; when it is your turn to hit the ball, you have to hit the ball. The key to the whole thing is that when it is not your turn, you have to get out of the way. Your opponent will try to hit the ball to where your teammate is standing when it is your turn to hit the ball. Hit and move. Hit and move. Hit and move.

11:02 A.M.
Josh was my opponent, which is hopefully not the case in real life, as he is my agent, but surely there are some issues that we have with each other that fueled our rivalry at the table. "Where's

my starring role in a Marvel movie?" I said, while burning one low across the net. "Why do you have to have Kleenex in your dressing room?" Josh grunted on his return, clearly sick of negotiating my tough personal appearance contracts.

"I'm one of the only people in Hollywood who hasn't played Spider-Man. Don't I look like I could crawl up the side of a building?" I snapped, while I tossed the ball from my open palm and spun the shit out of my serve from my quadrant of the table, diagonal to Josh's. "You don't sleep in a bed at home. Why do you have to have a hotel when you play Poughkeepsie?" he asked, sweeping the backside of his paddle over the ball.

11:15 A.M.
My daughter Alley came to watch, play, and criticize my music playlist.

11:16 A.M.
My assistant, Wendell, came to watch, play, and criticize my music playlist.

QUALITATIVE OBSERVATION #2
I have a fantastic music playlist.

11:20 A.M.
I ran into the house to put on a sports bra.

QUALITATIVE OBSERVATION #3
If you can put on a sports bra when you are already clammy, you don't need to work out.

12:00 P.M.
Our friend Judy showed up right on time. Judy was a preschool teacher who taught all three of my kids. She makes a great Ping-Pong opponent because all you have to do is hum "The Itsy-Bitsy Spider" and she drops her paddle and starts to crawl her fingers up the water spout. It's muscle memory. It's also an easy point for me, and I'm not a good enough player not to exploit a weakness like that.

QUANTITATIVE OBSERVATION #1
Now we had seven players. We played singles. We played doubles. We had already crushed a couple of balls, stranded one in the alley, and lost one deep in the bougainvillea.

QUALITATIVE OBSERVATION #4
To play Ping-Pong well, one must bend one's knees and engage one's core. I get most of my exercise when I play, however, from bending over to pick up the balls.

1:19 P.M.
I hoisted up the waistband of my underwear, exposing the thick, cottony, high-waisted pink-and-orange tie-dyed briefs that an audience member recently presented me with, in a gift bag of four, at a meet-and-greet after a show I did in Columbus, Ohio. I demonstrated to the other players how, if I tucked them under my sports bra, it was like a onesie.

1:20 P.M.
My daughter Alley went into the house.

QUALITATIVE OBSERVATION #5

Ping-Pong is a mental game.

1:21 P.M.

More Ping-Pong, more Ping-Pong, more Ping-Pong.

2:00 P.M.

Josh and his friends had to leave. Their participation brought me heps of happiness. They were terrific guests, and just the tonic that the beginning of my Ping-Pong happiness experiment needed. Plus, I had the feeling that, now that Josh knew me better as a person, I'd get more rom-com auditions.

3:00 P.M.

My neighbor Andrea came at her appointed time and we played, and laughed, and played some more.

4:00 P.M.

My friend Jynn showed up. We played in every combination of the now six of us. My beat-up sneakers filled with the dust and bark mulch of our backyard. We high-fived, hugged, or clapped paddles when we won a hard-earned point, and I yelled "motherfucker" really loud when, seconds later, I threw away all of that effort by serving one right into the net.

5:00 P.M.

Tim came. The trash talk, always an important element of Ping-Pong, got even funnier.

6:00 P.M.

My friends Tom, Cathy, and Milan joined us. We had a gallery of folding chairs a few feet from the side of the table so that when someone wasn't playing, they could sit and watch.

I love to win, but I care more about the individual volleys. Tom and I have played singles together for many years. He is tall and he has a huge wingspan. I knew if I kept hitting it deep, he'd casually run me back and forth on my end of the table, like a cat with a string toy. I had to alternate enough backspin and chop shots to keep him, at least, having to take one step forward while I did wind sprints on my end. Our friends cheered, without caring who won. They cheered the point, the exchange, the dance.

QUALITATIVE OBSERVATION #6

There is nothing like the feeling of stress and elation from a long and impossible volley.

6:15 P.M.

I played a singles match with Wendell. A Frank Sinatra song came on, maybe "I Did It My Way." Wendell grumbled that you can't play Ping-Pong to Frank Sinatra. That's when I knew I had him. You *can* play Ping-Pong to Frank Sinatra. That's why I love Ping-Pong. It's like harmonizing. You listen to the note of the melody and you figure out what to do about it, and when it's great, it's intuitive. Frank Sinatra and I beat the crap out of Wendell.

6:32 P.M.

I took a break to grab a soda off a nearby snack table, and when I looked up from sucking down some caffeine, I saw at least five people on their smart phones.

QUALITATIVE OBSERVATION #7
Smart phones are the turd in the pool.

6:33 P.M.

We played some more. My back hurt, but I didn't care. I didn't think about nuclear war. I didn't think about money. I didn't think about the subversion of our democracy. I didn't think about pipelines, or cyberwarfare, or Ruth Bader Ginsburg's age. The saddest thing I thought about was that I don't have a backhand.

7:00 P.M.

I was tired by the time Marc, my seven o'clock guest, arrived, but I was still smiling and eager to play him. Marc's a good player. He's a drummer, so he has fast hands. We had a bunch of really competitive matches. Some points fell to him and some to me, but the volleys were long and satisfying. I tried to stay low and keep my paddle in front of me.

Marc hit the ball. I returned the ball. Marc hit the ball. I returned the ball. I love the sound of the ball on the table. He hit the ball to my left. I felt my feet shift quickly, to place me right where I needed to be before the ball even arrived, and there it was—flow! Flow is a psychological term. It means you're in the zone. It's exhilarating. I felt fantastic.

QUALITATIVE OBSERVATION #8

You can achieve flow doing almost anything. I've had it from doing the dishes. This was better, though.

8:00 P.M.

I hugged and thanked all of the players. My legs were wobbly, but I was headed to the airport on an emergency trip to help my son.

CONCLUSION

Aficionados call it "table tennis." I don't think that's what I play. I play Ping-Pong. It doesn't require expensive lessons. Good Ping-Pong is full of laughter. Even the sound of the ball is filled with humor. It's the rhythm. It's that weird feeling of knowing exactly where the ball is going to land. The chorus of voices cheering or oohing and aahing over the surprise get of a ball that just barely ticked the corner of the table.

As I hypothesized, Ping-Pong provided balous of happiness. You don't have to win. You don't even have to have a backhand.

MICHAEL SCHWARTZ

PAULA POUNDSTONE is a popular panelist on NPR's weekly comedy quiz *Wait Wait . . . Don't Tell Me!* She tours regularly, performing stand-up comedy throughout the country. The first woman ever to host the White House Correspondents' Dinner, she has had numerous HBO specials, starred in her own series on HBO and ABC, is included on Comedy Central's list of the Top 100 Comics of All Time, and has won an American Comedy Award for Best Female Stand-Up. Her website is www.paulapoundstone.com.